Their Name
Liveth for Evermore

Dedication

For Charlie and Evelyn

Dedicated to all the men and women from Carshalton
who served during the First World War

And did you leave a wife or sweetheart behind
In some loyal heart is your memory enshrined?
And, though you died back in 1916,
To that loyal heart are you always 19?
Or are you a stranger without even a name,
Forever enshrined behind some glass pane,
In an old photograph, torn and tattered and stained,
And fading to yellow in a brown leather frame?

Eric Bogle, *No Man's Land*
(Copyright Larrikin Publishers, Sydney)

Their Name Liveth for Evermore

CARSHALTON'S FIRST WORLD WAR ROLL OF HONOUR

Andrew Arnold

The History Press

First published 2014

The History Press
The Mill, Brimscombe Port
Stroud, Gloucestershire, GL5 2QG
www.thehistorypress.co.uk

British Library Cataloguing in Publication Data.
A catalogue record for this book is available from the British Library.

ISBN 978 0 7524 8991 9

Typesetting and origination by The History Press
Printed in Great Britain

Contents

Acknowledgements

In the course of my research I have been fortunate to have made contact with relatives and descendants of many of the men named on the memorial, and this book would not have been possible without the information they have provided and their permission to reproduce photographs and letters. In particular I am indebted to Mario Fuller, who is connected to no fewer than ten of the men on the memorial, and Rowena Preston, granddaughter of Frederick Parsons, for their continued support for my research and for encouraging me to develop it into a book. My thanks also go to Des Adams, Jackie Askew, Nick Cannon, June Davies, Ann Dowsing, Sue Ealing and family, Peter Etter, Paul Evans, Nick Fairbrother, Keith Fazzani, Stephen Glanville, Michael Hayball, Barbara Holmes, Sue Hutton, Hazel Kirby, Jean Lambert, Jane Morey, Liz Moss, Roger Pickering, Wendy Pogmore, Derek and Shirley Prothero, Glenys Rands, Cheryl Rogers, Barbara Russell, Lindsay Seagrim-Trinder, Nick Shepherd, Jim Shirley, Mike Stepney, Anne Stevens, Bryan Stokes, Jim Stracey and Susan Wicks.

Many other people have also provided me with information, records and photos of the men. Some have visited their graves in France and Belgium on my behalf. Much of the information in the book has been gleaned from sources held by Sutton Local Studies and Archives Centre, and I am very grateful to Kath Shawcross and the staff there for their help and assistance with my research, along with Margaret Thomas and Bev Walker from the Circle library in Carshalton. Special thanks also go to Steve Garnett, with whom I travelled to the battle-fields on a bitterly cold February weekend in 2013, and who accommodated my many requests to stop at cemeteries where the Carshalton men lie. My thanks also go to All Saints church, Stuart Baxter, Eric Bogle and Larrikin Publishers, Gill Clarke (Churchers College), Humphrey Clarke (St Barnabas church), Peter Collins (archivist at Sutton Grammar School), Dick Flory, Mark Gardiner, Clive Gilbert, John Murray publishers for permission to quote from Martin Gilbert's Somme: The Heroism and Horror of War, Russell Gore, Andrew Holmes, David Humberton, Simon Jervis, Peter Leonard and St Olave's School, Pam and Ken Linge, Andrew Lock, Bill MacCormick, Mick McCann (British War Graves), Neil Mackenzie, Penguin for permission to quote from Lyn MacDonald's 1914–1918: Voices and Images of the Great War, John Porter (Prudential), Susannah Schofield (Alleyn's School), Frederik Sohier, Dave Stuckey, Michael Taylor, David Underdown, Neil Uwins, and William Wood for pictures of the old Whitgiftians, reproduced with the kind permission of the Headmaster of Whitgift School. To The History Press I am grateful for the opportunity to share the stories of the men and the belief that they are worth telling. My sincere apologies to anyone I may have missed from this list.

Finally, I would like to thank my family and friends, who have encouraged and supported me, not least my wife, who has tolerated my interest (some might say obsession!) despite a number of competing priorities over the last few years including wedding preparations, a house move and the birth of our daughter. For her support and understanding I am especially grateful.

Every reasonable effort has been made to trace copyright holders and the author welcomes correspondence on this matter from any sources where it has not been possible to obtain permission to quote.

All information presented has been researched and is evidenced where possible; however, due to the length of time that has passed since the war and the nature of some of the sources used, it is possible that some errors have been introduced. Any errors are mine alone, and any clarifications or additional information about these men will be gratefully received.

Note on the text: Any mention of 'the local paper' in the text refers to the *Wallington and Carshalton Advertiser.*

Introduction

Carshalton war memorial sits in an idyllic spot on the edge of the Carshalton ponds and was officially unveiled on 13 March 1921. A further dedication ceremony and opening of the Garden of Remembrance took place after the Second World War, in 1951.

The names of 249 men are inscribed on the memorial's plaques. Although it is now dedicated to the men who fought and died in both world wars, almost all of the names on the memorial are from the First World War.[1] At the time of writing a further memorial displaying the names of those who died in the Second World War has recently been unveiled in the Garden of Remembrance.

The motivation for compiling this record about the men named on the memorial came from my own experiences researching my family tree. In 2008 I found out that my great-great-uncle had been killed in the war. I started researching his military service and gradually pieced together the story of his life and death. Until then the sacrifices of those who had fought in the war, although always respected, had meant little to me personally. I started thinking about all those who died but have been forgotten, or who have no descendants to remember them. Around this time I paid my first visit to the Carshalton memorial, and looking at the names wondered about the stories behind them. My first trip to the Somme in April 2008 really reinforced the scale of the losses suffered during the war and the effect this must have had on communities across the country. Visiting memorials such as Thiepval on the Somme, one cannot help but be overwhelmed by the sheer number of names inscribed upon them.[2] The countless cemeteries in the region feature row upon row of headstones, some named and some indicating only the final resting place of 'A Soldier of the Great War, Known Unto God'. On my return from the Somme, I started researching the men recorded on Carshalton war memorial in earnest.

War memorials exist in almost every town and village yet most of the year are often passed by without a second glance. However, with the centenary of the First World War now upon us, it is clear that the war remains a subject that evokes passionate feelings and fierce debate. Those who fought in the conflict and survived are gone; it is therefore now more important than ever to keep alive the memories of those who laid down their lives. As Martin Gilbert expresses in his book about the Somme campaign, 'Every headstone in each cemetery, each name on the long lists of those whose bodies were never found, hides a human being, a man, a story, a cry of pain and a grieving family.'[3] The aim of this book is to tell some of these stories.

1. Carshalton before the War

The original settlement of Carshalton had sprung up along the road between Sutton and Croydon, later on spreading to the north and south. By the early 1800s it was developing faster than other villages in the area, including Sutton, a trend that continued until the turn of the century. During the Edwardian period it was still relatively small, but expanding rapidly, covering 2,926 acres in 1914. In 1901 the population stood at 6,746; by the time of the 1911 census it had nearly doubled to 11,634.[4] When war broke out it is likely to have been approximately 13,000. There were 2,247 inhabited buildings, with an average of 5.18 people living in each and, whilst overcrowding was present, it was not rife. The main residential areas were situated south of the railway line. The most built-up area was Mill Lane and the roads around it, with their rows of terraced houses. The area north of the railway line was mainly taken up by larger houses with big plots of land. Alongside palatial mansions such as The Oaks and Carshalton House (now St Philomena's Catholic High School for Girls), Carshalton had a number of other fine family houses such as Honeywood, Bramblehaw, Strawberry Lodge, Shepley House and Barrow Hedges.

The presence of the River Wandle meant that water power could be harnessed for industry. Several watermills were developed (ten by 1842) for processing commodities such as snuff and corn, providing some industrial work for local residents. The 1911 census recorded 3,055 men and 1,735 women engaged in work, the predominant employment being building work and agriculture for men (including lavender and watercress growing) and domestic service for women.

The High Street formed the hub of the community with a diverse array of shops serving the needs of the local population. They included Woodman's butchers, a general store, Comyn's chemist shop, Wardill's cycle shop and garage, the London and Provincial Bank, a timber and builder's merchant, a saddler, a corn merchant, a hairdresser and tobacconist, a grocer's, a watchmaker and optician, a draper, 'Holts library, stationery and fancy warehouse', a children's outfitter, the post office and a dairy. At the eastern end of the High Street, Carshalton Public Hall[5] had been built in the 1870s and was later converted to a skating rink before being requisitioned by the military during the First World War. Those in need of liquid refreshment could visit one of the local pubs, many of which still exist today, including The Greyhound, The Sun, The Windsor Castle, The Fox and Hounds and The Coach and Horses. At least two of the local landlords would lose sons in the war.

A leisurely stroll could be taken in the 19 acres of Carshalton Park, or, for those of a more active disposition, Carshalton Lawn Tennis Club had been formed in 1912.

Carshalton St Andrews football club had been founded in 1897 and they played at Wrythe Green. Mill Lane Mission had been founded in 1903 for boys to play football at Carshalton Park, and later changed its name to Carshalton Athletic Football Club. The St Andrews team merged with the club in 1908.

The structure of the historic All Saints church dominated the skyline of the area. A programme of enlargement commenced in 1890 overseen by architect Sir Arthur Blomfield, whose nephew Reginald Blomfield would go on to design war memorials such as the Menin Gate in Ypres. The rector of the church, Revd G.B. Vaux, acted as referee for many of the Carshalton men who applied for an officer's commission during the war. In addition, the village was served by Emmanuel church, Park Lane; a United Methodist chapel in North Street; the Church of the Good Shepherd in Stanley Park Road; the United Methodist Free Church in Ruskin Road; and a non-denominational chapel, West Street Hall, in West Street. The education of local children fell to a number of schools including Carshalton College, Barrow Hedges School, St Philomena's and a national infant school in Mill Lane. Law and order was maintained by the presence of a police station at the junction of West Street and Pound Street.

Carshalton was connected to Croydon by the tramway which ran down Park Lane, along Ruskin Road and onto Carshalton Road, before terminating on Westmead Road. Carshalton's first railway station opened in 1847, at the site of what is now Wallington station; the current Carshalton station opened in 1868. Carshalton Beeches station was built in 1907 to cater for those living in the new houses to the south of the village. Sewers had been installed in 1899, and gas street lighting lit the area at night. Medical needs were met by Queen Mary's Hospital for Children (opened in 1909), a large facility with over 1,000 staff and patients, and Carshalton and District Hospital on Rochester Road (also known as Cottage Hospital), which had opened in 1899. Village matters were governed by the Urban District Council which operated from the building in The Square, built in 1908, that until recently housed Carshalton library. This building also served as the fire station.

On the northern periphery of Carshalton, the area known as 'the Wrythe' formed a distinct entity geographically and socially. It formed the backbone of working-class Carshalton, and the people who lived there were fiercely proud. It was made up of just four main roads – St Andrew's Road, St John's Road, St James Road and William Street – yet men from these four roads were to contribute over 10 per cent of the men from Carshalton who enlisted during the war, and would account for 15 per cent of the casualties. Many of the families were closely related and the effects of the war on them was typical of many communities up and down the country. After the war the *Wallington and Carshalton Advertiser* wrote about the area:

> There is something very distinctive about the people there. They are very clannish, very proud of their record in the war, and very sensitive as to the way in which the Wrythe is spoken of by Carshaltonians who happen to reside in other parts of the parish. In this respect the Wrythe and Beddington Corner

are very much alike. They are both outposts of their respective parishes, little communities which resent any attempt on the part of neighbours to patronise, criticise, or advise.

From 1887 the spiritual needs of the Wrythe community were served by St Andrew's Mission church, situated on the corner of Wrythe Lane and Brookfield Avenue. However, the church was never consecrated and it closed in 1962, later to be demolished. The Cricketers public house was a focal point for the local community and its landlord a prominent figure both within the Wrythe and the wider community of Carshalton. The pub also acted as the headquarters for Carshalton Athletic Football Club, which was to be deeply affected by the war. Play stopped during the war due to the shortage of players and Wrythe Green recreation ground where they played was put to agricultural use.

2. Carshalton War Memorial

As in towns and villages across the country, after the war ended the civic leaders of Carshalton turned their thoughts to how to commemorate the area's fallen. As early as April 1916 the Urban District Council had discussed what form a memorial should take, one suggestion being a memorial fountain in Carshalton Park. In January 1919 the local newspaper reported that a committee had been appointed and a proposal put forward for the erection of a permanent memorial, as well as the provision of an enlarged hospital. As prominent local figure Hugh Peirs emphasised, they wanted 'something which would look well a hundred years hence'.

Unfortunately, the records of the war memorial committee do not appear to have survived, though the updates in the newspaper suggest that several schemes were considered prior to the current memorial. The memorial was paid for by public subscription, and there was enough money left over to contribute to the construction of the war memorial hospital as well – an indication perhaps of how deeply the local community had been affected by the war.

The design of the memorial has more than an echo of Edwin Lutyens' Cenotaph that dominates Whitehall in London. The Cenotaph (literally 'empty tomb') was first unveiled as a temporary structure in 1919, and made permanent in 1920. It was deliberately non-denominational, and it would be interesting to know if the Carshalton committee also took a conscious decision to erect a non-religious structure. Many memorials are located in the grounds of the local church, but the location by Carshalton Ponds was probably chosen as it was more prominent, and at the time quite a tranquil location given the relative absence of traffic. The design contrasts with other war memorials in the area which are religious, such as Sutton's, which features a cross and angels mounted at each corner of its plinth, and Wallington's, which has a cross cut into the obelisk. The inscription on the memorial – 'Their Name Liveth Forevermore' – does, however, have religious origins.[6]

The memorial was unveiled on Sunday 13 March 1921 bearing an inscription of 237 names. An account of the unveiling appeared in the two local newspapers; both are worth quoting at length as they help to paint a picture of the feelings and emotions of the time. The *Wallington and Carshalton Advertiser* reported:

> The memorial takes the form of a tomb, the design of which is based on a fine 18th century example. This surmounts a simple base and platform, the whole composition forming a dignified monument free from any ornate features and depending for its effect entirely on its proportions and simple lines. It is of

Portland stone, and has on each side panels containing the names of upwards of 200 men of Carshalton to whose sacrifice the memorial stands as a permanent record, and which is expressed in the quotation over each panel: 'Their name liveth for evermore'.

With appropriate symbolism, the memorial has been placed on the banks of the pond in the constantly moving waters of which it is reflected. A margin of stone flagged paving affords the public every opportunity of reading the names, and a raised platform is provided for flowers.

The memorial has been executed by Messrs. Burslem and Son,[7] Tunbridge Wells, from the designs and under the supervision of Messrs. Bouchier, Tatchell and Galsworthy, architects, of London.

The unveiling was performed by Major-General Longley, officer commanding the Woolwich district, of which Carshalton forms a part, who was received by Major Lovelock (honorary secretary of the War Memorial Committee). His approach was signalled by a fanfare of trumpets by the buglers of the local Boy Scouts, whose colours were draped in black.

At each corner of the Cenotaph was a soldier standing with arms reversed, on the right was drawn up a contingent of the East Surrey Regiment from Kingston, and on the left was a party of Territorials from Sutton.

The memorial after the stolen panels had been replaced in February 2012. (Author's collection)

Dr Pealing (Chairman of the Cenotaph Sub-Committee) said:

'Major-General Longley – on behalf of the Carshalton people I have to ask you to unveil our memorial to those men from the parish who died in the Great War. We are proud of the fact that the men of our village did not hesitate when they knew their country to be in danger, but proudly gathered together, rank on rank, to the number of nearly 1,000 volunteers, in answer to the bugle call of war. In all Carshalton sent more than 2,000 men to fight their country's battles, and of all of those valiant hearts who hopefully marched away 237 never returned. Upon that rising ground across the water where now stands our Parish Church the first inhabitants of this village, barbarous in customs, pagan in their religion, raised a mound above the body of their dead chief. It was the first Carshalton memorial to a dead hero, and throughout the changes of time and the difference of faith that spot has always been and always will be hallowed ground.

'Today in a brighter and happier belief in the future state we have raised another memorial to the dead heroes of this village. We cannot inter them here with the honour that is due to them. Peacefully their bodies lie upon the battle-fields of three Continents, and we have here an empty tomb. But this spot will ever be sacred and always associated with grateful memories of those men who left their homes and loved ones, who laid aside their hopes and ambitions and cheerfully marched out into the great unknown.

'The memorial is erected upon ground given by the Urban District Council for the purpose, and will be taken over by them and carefully tended.

'I will now ask you, sir, to unveil this memorial and to reveal for all time the names of those Carshalton men who fought and died for their King and country.'

Major General Longley: 'I unveil this memorial in the honoured memory of the men of this place who gave their lives for their King and country in the Great War. Let us consider for a moment all that this implies. Let us think also of those whom it commemorates – what they did for us and our children, of how they died in the performance of duty to preserve the liberty and freedom of the world. When we reflect on the truth of the words inscribed on this memorial we shall lose some of our sadness and be tinged instead with a glow of pride and satisfaction that those who have been taken from us have added to the glory and power of the country and the freedom of the world.

They do not die who fall in freedom's name
Their souls live on, a pure and holy flame.

This memorial will remind us who are living and those who come after us of the splendid sacrifices made by our brothers, fathers, and sons for the glory of the place they held so dear, and may we all be inspired by their noble example.'

Dedicatory prayers were then read by the Rector of Carshalton (the Revd W.R. Corbould), after which Major Lovelock read a list of the names of the fallen. Three volleys were discharged by the firing party, and *The Last Post* and *Reveille* sounded by the buglers brought an impressive ceremony to a conclusion.

Representatives of the local branch of the National Federation of Discharged and Demobilised Sailors and Soldiers were present under Major Miller, DCM, and headed by two children, Allan and Ernest,[8] the sons of the late Private Baker (East Surreys), who carried a wreath, which was placed on the Cenotaph on behalf of the federation. Mr F.W. Bird headed a procession of war widows from the Wrythe carrying a large Union Jack surmounted with a laurel wreath, and a floral wreath, which was also placed at the foot of the memorial, while among others who placed their tributes were the Rev. J.E. Jasper[9] and Couns. R. Brownsmith, J.P., and W.E. Davis.

Before and after the ceremony peals were rung on the bells of the Parish Church.

The *Wallington and Carshalton Times*' report was more emotionally charged:

Carshalton never lags behind. At Duty's call her sons were amongst the first citizens who became soldiers and the first soldiers who became heroes. Those heroes were the foremost in the thickest of the fight, bore the brunt of the early days of the war, but unyielding, wrote in letters of precious blood, 'Victory'. They did not wait to ask themselves what would be the fruits of that victory; they did the one great thing which lay before them – duty in, above and through, and left all thoughts of right adjustments abroad and at home, and even in little Carshalton, to the politicians. The world knows how well they did their duty, how bravely they fell for their country. On Sunday was unveiled

The only known photograph of the war memorial being unveiled on 13 March 1921. Note the crowds lining the far side of the ponds. (Sutton Local Studies)

on an ever sacred spot a memorial token of thankfulness to God and in grati-
tude, in honour, in love, to those who made the supreme sacrifice of their lives.
Engraved on that cenotaph, as reverently as on a tomb, are the names which
will never be forgotten so that posterity shall lay laurel wreaths upon it to the
memory of the best, the bravest, the flower of Britain's sons. Many in the future
will die unknown: these names will ever be great ones to think of or speak
upon. If it be that their victory in the war prove to be the victory over war,
there will have been real glory attained. In the old days were beacons round
the coasts to guide the ships: these monuments throughout Britain today are
the beacons that must guide men to everlasting peace. While our eyes read with
mingled sorrow and pride the wording of the cenotaph, our hearts read into it
a decade of broken spirits, but with stout resolution and determination may our
minds see in and by it only two final words, 'never again!' Then though in the
homes none stood to gain, yet in the end of wars the district, the nation, the
world will be the better.

It continued:

Sunday was indeed a day of mourning for the bravest and the best of Carshalton's
honoured sons. The great and silent messenger to posterity, which will grace the
quietude and seclusion of the green lawn on the side of the lake, was unveiled
in the afternoon in the presence of two thousand bereaved and sympathisers.
Each name was read aloud and each struck home a sorrowing note to wounded
hearts. On every hand could be seen tears running down the cheeks alike of
those whose loved ones were among the fallen heroes and those whose hearts
were melted with another's sorrow. One could see the tide of generous sorrow
working a passage from men's big hearts to the eye and stealing in silent without their leave, the mark of nature by which sincerity is shown; others shedding
tears by the tenderness of feeling at the warm round drops of softness from the
mother's or widow's heart.

The scene of the tomb and the gathering in black, the firing of the volleys,
and the sound of the bugles in The Last Post, was such as to affect any human
being whose heart was not of stone. It would have been easier for a man to have
tried to stop the flow of the Wandle[10] at its source than to restrain the tear of the
true and tender hearts.

Why this mournful scene in a small Surrey village? Here stood in silent
sorrow and bowed heads noble mothers of noble sons, dutiful fathers of dutiful
and courageous sons; heroic widows of heroic husbands, who gave all for their
country. Just six and a half years ago the war cry rang out through Britain, and
Carshalton, hearing the call of King and country, never waited a moment. Her
sons were among the first to join the Colours. A thousand men volunteered and
went, and a thousand mothers, wives, and sweethearts never said 'nay'. These
men were the first in the trenches, and 237 were the first to fall; those women
were the first to sacrifice, and 237 the first to wear the widows' weed.

Carshalton provided altogether as its quota of the great victory two thousand men, or half of its adult males. Men indeed, women indeed. There they stood with broken spirits unhealed by time; with the loss in this world's treasures of all that counted for happiness; their fields of life barren of the fruits of victory. They came from the scenes of the vacant chairs to see the names of the occupants written boldly, that all forever shall honour and revere those who went gallantly forth, forgetting self, forgetting all they held so dear.

It is the widows' one sacred tomb, to which they go in loving and tender thoughts and lay down floral tributes, which the majority owing to their poor estate in life could never afford to do in those sacred spots which hold the remains of the fallen in the fields of Flanders and France.

Evidence of that desire was shown on this occasion, when the large base of the cenotaph was a mass of wreaths, including one of laurels from the War Memorial Committee, the People of the Wrythe, and from the Carshalton branch of the National Federation of Discharged and Demobilised Soldiers and Sailors.

The roads all round the lakes were absolutely packed, but places were reserved for the relatives near the cenotaph, which was completely covered with a Union Jack. On each side stood a squad of the East Surrey Regiment, in front were the Carshalton Fire Brigade in uniform and at the approach were the Carshalton Troop of Scouts forming a guard of honour.

The details of the ceremony and memorial are then reported in a similar vein to the *Advertiser*.

Early photographs of the memorial show that the names were originally inscribed in stone, but at some point the original panels were replaced with metal ones. The history of the memorial in more recent years has been chequered. In 2007, thieves stole several of the flagstones around the base of the memorial, and in September 2011 struck again, the target this time being the metal plaques themselves. The theft caused public outcry, nationally as well as locally, particularly as it occurred so close to Remembrance Sunday. Sutton Council thankfully arranged for temporary plaques to be installed in time for the commemorations. Permanent replacement plaques carved in Portland stone were unveiled on 7 February 2012, the cost of the replacement funded by a local scrap metal dealer who had been outraged by the theft.

3. Other Memorials

Carshalton's war dead are not just remembered on the civic war memorial; there are several other memorials in the locality. Probably the best-known is the 'Willie Bird' or Wrythe memorial cross located in the graveyard at All Saints church. The cross was donated by Frederick Bird, the landlord of The Cricketers, a prominent figure in the local community and often referred to as the 'Father of the Wrythe'.[11] The cross is named after his son, who died in 1915 from appendicitis.[12]

As already noted, the Wrythe was a community in itself and obviously wished to commemorate its own fallen on a separate memorial. An overtly religious memorial, it consists of a cross which originally had a crucifix figure as its centrepiece (now missing). The inscription reads 'To the heroes of the Wrythe who have died in God for the King and for you. May they rest in peace.' Below this are the names of forty-five men from the Wrythe area who were killed in the war. Of these thirty-three also appear on the civic memorial. The cross was originally sited outside St Andrew's Mission church in the Wrythe, but was moved after the

Above: The Willie Bird cross in the graveyard of All Saints church. (Author's collection)
Right: The Willie Bird cross in its original location outside St Andrews Mission church. (Jean Lambert)

The War Memorial Hospital. (Mario Fuller)

church closed in 1962. However, from photos that exist of the cross in its original location, it seems to have been much bigger and the inscription slightly different.

All Saints church contains a number of other memorials. Most obvious are the Commonwealth War Graves Commission headstones in the churchyard; nine of the men on the memorial are buried here, as are a further three who are not on the memorial. Inside the church there is a roll of honour, painstakingly written in calligraphy. This shows 213 names, 208 of which are on the memorial and five that are not. The reason for the disparity is unclear.

The church contains several other private commemorations to local men, mostly those with close ties to the church or those of a higher social standing and whose families therefore had the money to pay for a private memorial. Interestingly, not all of these men's names appear on the war memorial itself.

In addition to the civic memorial, enough funds were raised to build the war memorial hospital that was situated on The Park until its recent sale and demolition to make way for a new housing development.

At the time of the war about one-third of the parish of St Barnabas lay within the civil parish of Carshalton. After the war, funds were raised for a dedicated war memorial chapel, and this memorial in the church in St Barnabas Road bears the names of at least thirty-six of those who are on Carshalton war memorial. St Barnabas had a Band of Hope[13] Cadet Force, founded in 1890. Many of these cadets went on to serve during the war, and at least five would lose their lives. Further memorials include one at Sutton County School (now Sutton Grammar School), which eight of the men on the memorial attended, and Sutton Post Office.

Local men are commemorated on other memorials as far afield as Lincolnshire, York, Gloucester, and Perthshire, and it is not unusual for a man to be commemorated on several memorials. Sutton war memorial was unveiled in June 1921, and

A list of St Barnabas Band of Hope cadets who served in the war. (St Barnabas church)

Some of the St Barnabas Band of Hope cadets who had enlisted to fight. (St Barnabas church)

thirty-six of the men whose names are inscribed on Carshalton memorial are amongst Sutton's 527. Wallington war memorial followed in March 1922 with 278 names; four men on Carshalton memorial are also commemorated here.

After the war the Carshalton Athletic Football Club purchased the war memorial sports ground on Colston Avenue and planted thirteen poplar trees in memory of the thirteen players the club had lost.[14] Unfortunately, the trees are no longer there; until recently a more lasting legacy was the poppy incorporated into the club logo. The Surrey County FA Junior League was also played in memory of local casualty David Kirby.

4. The Second World War

After the Second World War there was not as much local interest in creating a war memorial as there had been after the Great War. A war memorial sub-committee was set up once more but as well as sources of funding the committee had to contend with the matter of obtaining an accurate list of all those who were killed. Its minutes from 1947 record that 'It will be appreciated that it may be difficult to ensure that the information thus obtained will be complete, particularly having regard to the fact that, since the war period, a number of near relatives of the fallen have left the district.'

The decision was taken to commemorate the soldiers and civilian casualties collectively rather than having a memorial displaying all of their names. This led to the dedication of the Garden of Remembrance in 1951 and the creation of a Book of Remembrance, which was held at Carshalton library until its closure in 2012 and is now on display in the library at Westcroft Leisure Centre.

The four names from the Second World War that are currently on the memorial appear to have been added over the years at the request of the men's families. In total, 270 local casualties are named in the Book of Remembrance, although research has shown that there are many more with a connection to the area. A long-running campaign to commemorate these casualties culminated in the construction of a new separate memorial in the Garden of Remembrance. This was completed in summer 2014 and dedicated at a commemoration service on 3 August 2014.

5. The Men

In total, more than 5.5 million British men were mobilised during the First World War, and over 700,000 (12 per cent) were killed in action or died of wounds or illness. From surviving records it is known that at least 1,900 men with connections to Carshalton served,[15] over 1,000 of whom volunteered prior to the introduction of conscription in 1916. The 243 names on the memorial therefore represent approximately 13 per cent of those from Carshalton who served, largely commensurate with British casualty figures as a whole.

The names range from those who were born in Carshalton to those who lived in the locality or had family members in the area. All branches of the Armed Forces are represented, although the majority of the casualties served with the infantry on the Western Front. Unsurprisingly, many men joined the local regiments, the Queen's (Royal West Surrey Regiment) and the East Surrey Regiment. However, soldiers were often sent to regiments that were short of men, and over sixty different regiments are represented on the memorial. Most of the major campaigns of the war can be traced through the dates of death of the men, from the first battles of 1914 to the final German campaign in spring 1918 and the closing battles of the 'Hundred Days Offensive' in the summer and autumn of that year. Unsurprisingly, the first day of the Somme campaign (1 July 1916), a date indel-

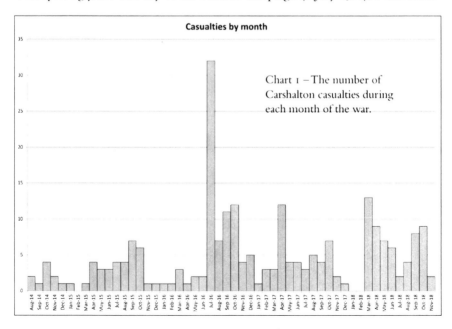

Chart 1 – The number of Carshalton casualties during each month of the war.

ibly ingrained into this country's national consciousness, accounts for many of those killed from Carshalton – nineteen in total, eight from the 7th Battalion The Queen's alone. Altogether, thirty men lost their lives that month, and fifty-nine in the whole Somme campaign in the period July–November 1916, accounting for a quarter of all the names on the memorial.

Some men died as a result of illness or accident, but the vast majority were killed in action or died from their wounds. At least five were shot by snipers, an ever-present threat in trench warfare. Machine guns were also increasingly used, their high rate of fire coupled with their ability to rain down bullets from over a mile away making them a particularly effective weapon. The biggest killer, though, was artillery, which was used to devastating effect during the war. Preparatory bombardment was seen as the key to a successful attack, and as the war progressed more sophisticated ways to utilise artillery power were developed.

The men of Carshalton are buried in or commemorated at over 100 cemeteries and memorials. The Thiepval memorial to the missing of the Somme alone displays the names of thirty-nine local men amongst its 72,203; 111, almost 50 per cent, are commemorated on memorials – in other words, they have no known grave – whilst 125 have a final resting place. In a war characterised by the development of more brutal, industrial and effective ways of taking men's lives en masse, it is not surprising that many have no known grave, their remains lost in the ravaged landscape or destroyed by further fighting and shelling.

The age of those who died on active service ranges from 15 (Reginald Brooks) to 46 (Ernest Dale), although the oldest man commemorated is Harry Tyler, aged 74, who did not serve overseas. At the beginning of the war the lower age limit for recruits was 18 (17 in the Territorial Force), although they initially had to be 19 to serve overseas. This was subsequently reduced to 18 and a half in 1918.

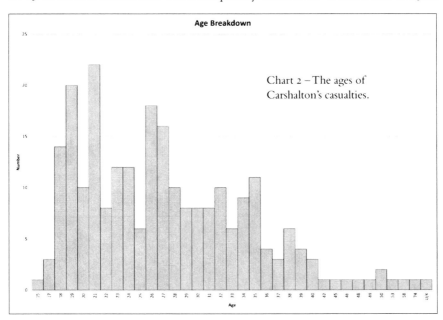

Chart 2 – The ages of Carshalton's casualties.

At least five of those named on the memorial are believed to have enlisted under-age. The upper age limit was 38 in 1914, later increased to 41. A lesser-known fact is that many older men also gave a false age in order to serve: Albert Rogers is one such example.

There are fourteen sets of brothers on the memorial, accounting for thirty of the names (12 per cent). Included in this figure are two families, the Rogers and the Brooks, who both lost three sons. In the Brooks' case all three were killed within little over a month in 1918. The impact this must have had on the family is unimaginable. Carshalton was a close-knit community and many of the men were connected through marriage. Neighbours and work colleagues often signed up together, and the impact of the news of every death must have been a devastating blow.

Focusing as it does on the local casualties, this book is naturally about the role of men during the war, but of course women played key roles too. In January 1916 the St Barnabas parish magazine reported that Millicent Hawkins, a former Sunday school teacher at the church, had been nursing in France for a year and was being sent to the Mediterranean theatre. Muriel Peatling, the wife of local GP Dr Peatling, worked for the Red Cross, and Mary Vaux, daughter of the Revd G.B. Vaux, was a VAD (Voluntary Aid Detachments) nurse. It is likely that many more local women were also engaged in similar work, as well as fulfilling roles left vacant by men who had gone to war. Some women worked at Brocks firework factory in Sutton, which during the war shifted its focus to the production of munitions. Sutton even fielded a women's football team.

The effects of the war would have been apparent even to those who were not directly engaged in war work. Manor Park House in Manor Park,[16] close to the top of Sutton High Street, was used to house Belgian refugees. Later, as wounded soldiers began to return from the battlefields, they needed places to recuperate, and many large houses were converted into hospitals. Benfleet Hall in Benfleet Wood Road was one such building. The hospital was funded by public donations and opened in June 1915.

Mary Vaux, VAD nurse. (Simon Jervis)

Staff and patients outside Benfleet War Hospital. The soldiers are wearing 'hospital blues' - uniforms issued to convalescing troops. (Sutton Local Studies)

In the course of my research, I have come across almost 130 men who had local connections but are not commemorated on the memorial. They include Lionel Morris, the first pilot to be shot down by the infamous Red Baron,[17] whose parents lived at 'Merlebank' in Rotherfield Road. The reasons for these non-commemorations are hard to establish after so much time has passed. One reason for their omission could be the method in which the names were collected, particularly as this was probably not undertaken until about 1920. In some towns and villages forms were delivered to local households for completion, in others notices were put up asking families to submit the details of their loved ones. This, of course, could lead to omissions if the soldier had no family or if the family did not see the requests for names. Relatives may have pre-deceased the soldier or moved to another area, in which case he may be commemorated on another memorial. It also has to be considered that some families may not have wanted the name of their loved one on the memorial, serving as a constant and visible reminder of their loss.

Many families who bade farewell to a husband or son setting off to the war were lucky and were able to welcome them back home after it was over. The Priest family of Beeches Avenue, for example, sent seven members to war and all came back. Revd Vaux had six family members serving in the army and navy, who all made it through the war. Whilst we tend to focus on the loss of life caused by the war, it should be remembered that some 88 per cent of those who served returned home.

6. The Roll of Honour

Compiling a book such as this is a difficult task, not least because of the varying amount of information available about each man. Decisions also had to be made about the best way to present the information. In telling the stories behind the names, a broadly chronological approach has been adopted, broken down by geographical theatre of war. In this way it is hoped to provide some context to the war and what the men went through. But this approach is not without its drawbacks. The book should not be read as a comprehensive history of the course and conduct of the war: not every battle and campaign is included. It does not go into the causes of the war, or evaluations of tactics and battles. There are a plethora of books available written by accomplished historians that deal with these aspects of the war in great depth.

Basic information about individual soldiers is taken from the Commonwealth War Graves Commission (CWGC) database. Sometimes this conflicts with information from other sources, including the memorial itself, particularly regarding the spelling of names and the ages of the men. In these cases, the most likely details based on all available sources have been presented. Where addresses are given these are in Carshalton unless otherwise stated. Where present, the CWGC notes have been included; this additional information was given by the soldiers' next of kin at the time of confirming their details, but not all entries on the database have information in this field, either because it was not provided, the information was not returned to the Imperial War Graves Commission (precursor of the CWGC), or there were no next of kin to complete the information. Many soldiers who have a known grave have an epitaph included on their headstone, a personal inscription that could be added by the family.[18] Where known, this epitaph has been included in the individual's biography. For some of the men, their CWGC record may be the only source that can be confirmed. For others, a more in-depth biography is provided from a variety of sources. Being able to put a face to a name somehow helps bring the men on the memorial to life. Pictures of around sixty of the men have been tracked down; where they exist, they may be of variable quality, but I make no apology for including them, as they may be the only photographic record of the man that survives.

War diaries provide the bulk of information about a soldier's unit, its movements and actions it was involved in. However, these diaries vary widely in content, length, and the standard of information provided. Where verbatim extracts from war diaries are used, these are shown in quote marks or displayed apart from the main text, but some liberties have been taken in editing these extracts to standardise the terminology or make them more readable if necessary.

Place names referred to in war diaries do not always refer to towns or villages but can also be references to trench names or strongpoints.

Ascertaining which action or battle a man was wounded in, or even where, can prove difficult. Not all casualties fit into the neatly defined timeframes for battles and campaigns that was set out after the war by the 'Battles Nomenclature Committee'.[19] Even when not engaged in battles or campaigns, units would still be holding the line, conducting trench raids and patrols, and subject to indiscriminate artillery fire. The nature of the casualty evacuation process can also make it difficult to ascertain where and when a soldier was wounded. If a soldier was wounded, he would be taken to the Regimental Aid Post (RAP) close to the front line, where he would receive immediate assessment and treatment. If further treatment was required, he would then be sent to an Advanced Dressing Station (ADS), where he could be prepared for evacuation to a Casualty Clearing Station (CCS) away from the front line. It was here that most surgery was carried out. Finally, soldiers could be transferred to a base hospital prior to heading back to England on a hospital ship. Of course men might succumb to their injuries at any stage of the process and most ADS, CCS and base hospitals had associated cemeteries where those men were buried; the further down the evacuation process a man was when he died, the further away from his battalion's location he is likely to be buried.

Readers without any knowledge of the organisation of the British Army in the First World War may at this point benefit from a brief introduction to the army hierarchy employed during the war, as this will help in understanding many of the terms used, particularly in the unit war diaries. The war was fought on an unprecedented scale and naturally the British Army evolved and developed as the war progressed. This should therefore not be read as the definitive structure employed throughout the course of the war, but rather as the framework that was broadly in operation. The numbers and fighting strength quoted would vary as men were moved around to fill gaps left by casualties and were moved in and out of the front lines.

The units most commonly referred to in this book are regiments and battalions. Regiments provided a common identity for the men who served in them, but battalions of the same regiment did not necessarily fight alongside each other. The battalion was the main tactical unit of the British Army. Commanded by a lieutenant colonel, it consisted of about 1,000 men, split into four companies. Companies were commanded by a major or captain, and were split into four platoons. These were commanded by a second lieutenant or lieutenant. Second lieutenants were the junior officers in the army but held a crucial role in motivating and commanding their men. Platoons themselves were split into sections, under the responsibility of a non-commissioned officer (NCO). Alongside the fighting troops, battalions also had a headquarters and a number of support troops.

Four battalions made up a brigade, commanded by a brigadier general. A division, commanded by a major general, consisted of three brigades and numbered approximately 20,000 men; four divisions made up a corps (commanded by a lieutenant general); and roughly four corps were in an army, commanded by a general who was accountable to the General Headquarters (GHQ) and the Commander-in-Chief (John French at the beginning of the war, and later Douglas Haig).

A glossary of some of the commonly used abbreviations and acronyms of the war is included at the end of the book.

Despite my best efforts, there are a few men for whom I have not established a link to Carshalton. This does not mean a link does not exist, of course, but that no evidence of it has been found during my research.

7. The Western Front

1914

In the weeks leading up to the war there is little sign that Carshalton was aware of the enormity of the conflict that lay ahead. The local newspaper ran stories about flower shows, near misses with motor vehicles and local weddings. Recreation ground bye-laws were debated, there was a local parade and the disappearance of a local bank clerk was the hot topic of conversation. Shortly before war broke out the new nave and baptistery at All Saints church were dedicated.

Following the assassination of Archduke Franz Ferdinand and the ultimatums and political manoeuvrings that followed, war broke out on 28 July 1914. Britain declared war on Germany on 4 August, and Britain's Regular Army was quickly mobilised. As the Germans swept through neutral Belgium as part of the 'Schlieffen Plan' thousands of British men flocked to sign up, in many cases overwhelming the recruitment offices. These volunteers would form Lord Kitchener's 'New Army'.

The tone of the local newspaper quickly changed. On 7 August the editorial reported with some solemnity:

> With startling suddenness war has been declared, and this country finds itself face to face with the life or death struggle which has been so glibly talked of and so confidently expected for the last 20 years … Even the quietness and peacefulness which usually pervades our district has been affected by the war scare, and the atmosphere has been charged with excitement and wonder.

It continued:

> On Wednesday the war fever seemed to be at its highest so far as our district is concerned and it is surprising how everything else was put aside. Little groups at the street corners and elsewhere discussed the latest news and the early editions of the papers were bought up eagerly, indeed the newsagents seem to be the busiest people amongst the tradesmen. Even in the shops war news was discussed over the sale of the goods and, instead of the usual pleasantries about the weather, salesmen and customers exchanged opinions on the latest phase of the European trouble, the active intervention of England, and there was only one opinion really heard.

The men of the borough stepped up to do their bit: 'Always patriotic, Wallington, Beddington and Carshalton have risen to the occasion admirably and quite a large number of Reservists and Territorials have left the district to serve the country in different parts.'

Reports soon turned to talk of spies, the victimisation of a Sutton baker with a German surname people believed to be poisoning the bread, and guarding bridges, railways and utilities against the threat of German invasion. There were also reports of panic buying of food, which was discouraged. The local council was quickly convened to consider how the war would affect the local area, and there was talk of how to assist the dependents of reservists who had been called up. Recruitment drives were held in the area, urging local men to do their bit.

The British Expeditionary Force (BEF) of 80,000 men landed in France on 12 August, and was quickly thrown into battle at Mons on 23 August. Here the British fought well against the numerically superior Germans, but ultimately the Germans gained the upper hand and the British were forced to carry out a series of fighting retreats. At the battle of Le Cateau on 26 August the Germans attacked along the whole British front, forcing the BEF to make a stand on open ground until they could retire from the battlefield when French reinforcements arrived. Carshalton's first casualties occurred that day.

HAYBALL, George Henry

Age:	31
Rank:	Private
Regiment/Service:	Somerset Light Infantry
Unit:	1st Battalion
Service Number:	7542
Died:	26 August 1914
Cemetery/Memorial:	La Ferté-Sous-Jouarre Memorial

CWGC Notes: Husband of Annie Hayball, of 39 North St, Carshalton.

Although George was born in Nottingham, the Hayball family were originally from Chard in Somerset, an area known for its lace production. George became a lacemaker, but it was a poorly paid profession and it seems that he decided to join the army. In 1911 he was serving in Malta with the 2nd Battalion Prince Albert's Somerset Light Infantry. Between then and the war breaking out he had left the army and was working as an attendant at the Wallington Picture Theatre. However, he was still a reservist attached to the Somerset Light Infantry, and shortly after the outbreak of war the local paper reported that he had left for Taunton to rejoin his old regiment.

During the fighting on 26 August the Somerset Light Infantry suffered nineteen dead, 159 wounded and 100 missing; overall, the BEF suffered 7,800 casualties. George's wife received a postcard from him dated that day saying he was alright, but heard nothing further until 28 September, when she received an official document stating that he was missing.

KNIGHT, Frank

Age:	19
Rank:	Driver
Regiment/Service:	Royal Field Artillery
Unit:	122nd Battery
Service Number:	74224
Died:	26 August 1914
Cemetery/Memorial:	La Ferté-Sous-Jouarre Memorial

Born in Epsom, Frank was the nephew of Mrs Knight of 38 Mill Lane, Carshalton. He worked as a carman,[20] but in September 1913, aged 18, he signed up for six years in the army and became a driver in the Royal Field Artillery. The First World War developed into an artillery war, with each side raining down millions of shells upon the other. An adequate artillery bombardment came to be seen as key to a successful attack, and artillery caused almost 60 per cent of British casualties during the war. British artillery was split into three units: the Royal Horse Artillery (RHA), consisting of light, mobile guns; the Royal Field Artillery (RFA), providing close support to the front line troops; and the Royal Garrison Artillery (RGA), whose long-range heavy guns were sited way behind the lines. Frank had arrived in France only a week before he died. During the battle his battery engaged the enemy at a distance of 2,400 to 1,300 yards. The German artillery was unsuccessful in their counter-battery fire, but Frank's battery came under rifle fire from a wooded spur about 800 yards away. In the afternoon machine guns opened fire on them as they tried to retreat. Within a minute nine men had been killed and fifteen wounded, along with many horses. Only three out of six guns managed to limber up and escape from the advancing German infantry. Frank died that day, after being captured. He was related to two other Carshalton casualties: he was the cousin of Ernest Knight and nephew of William Knight.

With the British and French armies in retreat, the German Army threatened Paris itself. At the beginning of September the British and French forces confronted their pursuers at the River Marne. The attack came as a surprise to the Germans and they retreated to the River Aisne. The Allies reached these positions on 13 September and renewed their attack. Fighting continued in the area until the end of the month, but it soon became clear that frontal infantry attacks against entrenched positions were not succeeding.

Back on British shores it seems Carshalton's reputation had spread far and wide. The Newcastle Journal *reported on 16 September:*

Of 55 playing members in two football clubs at Carshalton, Surrey, 40 have enlisted. From one road in the village 30 men have joined the forces, 14 going from three houses – six brothers in one case, five in another, and three in another. Three sons of the rector, the Rev G. Bowyer Vaux, are in the Army, and a fourth in the Navy.

Local men continued to enlist, and the people of the Wrythe in particular were proud of the contribution the area was making to the war effort. At the end of September the Wallington and Carshalton Advertiser *wrote that:*

> Host Bird, of The Cricketers, has a notice painted on the wall of his house call-ing attention to the fact that the Wrythe district is represented by over 80 men in the forces of the Crown at present. Painted in black letters is the inscription 'Heroes of the Wrythe Gone to Fight for England 1914'. Then follows a list of the names. The residents of the district have every reason to be proud of such a splendid record, and Carshalton as a whole is proud of them too. The 'ther-mometer' giving the number of men from the district is now fixed outside the Windsor Castle, and the mercury stands at 325, but it is rising so fast that now it should be at 350. Bravo, Carshalton!

Right: The 'Heroes of the Wrythe' sign posted outside The Cricketers pub. (Sutton Local Studies)
Far right: The names on the 'Heroes of the Wrythe' sign. (Mario Fuller)

St Barnabas church also displayed in its porch the names of parishioners who had enlisted. In the editorial to September's parish magazine, the Revd Bartlett wrote:

> Little did we think a month ago what August would bring us. Suddenly we have been plunged into a war to which there has certainly been no parallel in our own lifetime, and which seems indeed to be the greatest and most dreadful war the world has ever seen. Well, neither we ourselves, as individuals have sought it, nor our Government; and we can only leave the final issues in the hands of God ... Of prayer for the brave men who have gone out to defend our homes and our coun-

try, and to help the Belgians in the great wrong done to them, I need scarcely speak: for everyone feels moved already to such intercession. We are proud to think that our own parish has contributed more than a hundred.

The parishioners also played their part, from fundraising and dispatching garments to the Red Cross Society, to making splints for wounded soldiers.

Following the German invasion, the Belgian Army had carried out a fighting retreat to the fortified town of Antwerp. From late August to mid-September they carried out a series of raids from the town in an effort to divert German resources. The Germans launched a retaliatory offensive and from late September the town and surrounding forts were under siege. The British government, concerned that the German capture of the town would leave the channel ports exposed, sent troops to assist the Belgians in the form of the Royal Naval Division. But it was not enough, and the town finally surrendered on 9 October.

NASH, James Alfred

Age:	18
Rank:	Private
Regiment/Service:	Royal Marine Light Infantry
Unit:	Chatham Battalion, Royal Naval Division
Service Number:	CH/18527
Died:	6 October 1914
Cemetery/Memorial:	Schoonselhof Cemetery
Reference:	II.A.83

CWGC Notes: Son of Mary and Charles Nash, of 47 St James Rd, Carshalton.

James Nash was a florist's porter and footballer for Carshalton Athletic; he enlisted in June 1914, two weeks after his 18th birthday. The Chatham Battalion had been sent into Antwerp on 4 October. Two days later:

Hostile shelling increased in intensity … later pm verbal orders received that the battalion is to retire to an intermediate line about Boschoek–Eggerseel–Vremde where Royal Engineers are digging a defensive line. The retirement is conducted in good order … The troops were heavily shelled during the retirement.

On 30 October the *Wallington and Carshalton Advertiser* reported:

Another of Carshalton's soldiers has fallen on the field of battle, and he is Pte J.A. Nash, of the Royal Marine Light Infantry, whose home is at 47 St James Road. Nash, who is only 18, enlisted last June and was at first stationed at Deal. Afterwards he was at Chatham, and although such a short time in the forces he was sent to the front some few weeks ago. Apparently he took part in the defence of Antwerp and it was there he received his wound. No information is at hand as to the nature of the wound or Nash's present whereabouts, inquiries from headquarters bringing a reply to the effect that it is not known yet where he was. He is believed to be in France. His name was published in the list of casualties of Antwerp on Wednesday. Nash has a brother, Pte W.G. Nash, in the 1st Battalion The Queen's, now in training in Purfleet, while he has several relatives in the forces, including two cousins named Nash and five members of the Wyatt family, well known on the Wrythe, who are distant relatives.

British casualties were small but many troops were captured by the Germans or fled to neutral Holland, where they were interned for the remainder of the war. The Royal Naval Division casualties records confirms that James fought at Dunkirk from 20 September to 2 October, and in the defence of Antwerp from 3 to 6 October, where he was reported missing, assumed dead. His name is also on the Willie Bird cross.

On the Western Front both sides now tried to outflank each other all the way to the North Sea, in what became known as the 'race to the sea'. The Battle of La Bassée began on 10 October; the intention was to try and outflank the Germans who were attacking the French to the south. The initial attacks were not very successful and on 20 October the Germans launched their own offensive. This period of battles until mid-November is known as the First Battle of Ypres. Back home, the reality of the war was sinking in. In his editorial to the parish magazine, Revd Bartlett wrote sombrely 'We read sensational descriptions of battles, but we hardly dare to think what a battle really is.'

PACKHAM, William

Age:	29
Rank:	Private
Regiment/Service:	Worcestershire Regiment
Unit:	3rd Battalion
Service Number:	8906
Died:	20 October 1914
Cemetery/Memorial:	Le Touret Memorial
Reference:	Panels 17 and 18

Born in Croydon and lived at 'Preston', Westmead Road. William served in the army for several years prior to the outbreak of war and in 1911 was with the 4th Battalion Worcestershire Regiment in India. He was killed in action. On 20 October the 3rd Battalion Worcestershire Regiment, part of the 7th Infantry Brigade, were situated at Bois de Biez near Neuve Chapelle. During the early hours they left their billets and occupied an old line of trenches at Le Hue, strengthening the position as night fell. Casualties that day were one officer and twelve other ranks. William's name is also on Sutton war memorial and St Barnabas church memorial.

The German attacks were repelled although they captured the village of Neuve Chapelle on 27 October. South of Ypres the British were engaged in the Battle of Armentières from 19 October to 2 November.

WELCHMAN, Edward Theodore

Age:	33
Rank:	Captain
Regiment/Service:	West Yorkshire Regiment (Prince of Wales's Own)
Unit:	1st Battalion
Died:	26 October 1914
Cemetery/Memorial:	Boulogne Eastern Cemetery
Reference:	I.A.7

(The Sphere)

CWGC Notes: Son of Edward and Alice Welchman, of 63 North St, Carshalton. A member of the Royal Staff College, Camberley. Served in the South African Campaign and on the North-West Frontier of India (1908).

Edward joined the army in 1900 and served in the South African War. He received the Distinguished Service Order (DSO) in 1902 'In recognition of services during the operations in South Africa' and was mentioned in despatches. He went on to serve in India in 1908 and was promoted to captain in 1910. He joined his battalion in France in early October 1914 and was wounded in action during the Battle of Armentières. On 19–20 October his battalion was holding Ennetières, near Lille:

> 3am- Night attack on left of line. Stood to arms. 7am- General attack on whole line began. Enemy advanced to wood and farms within 600 yards of position. 8am- Own machine guns and artillery doing excellent work. Whole line was heavily shelled all day. Battalion occupied frontage of 700 yards. 3.30pm- Reinforced by one company Durham Light Infantry which was utilised to strengthen right company. Enemy retired in front of my left and attacked in force in front of my right company. The regiment on the right retired to meet a flank attack. 5pm- Enemy occupied Ennetieres. The regiment on right of 17th Brigade also retired. Position very precarious. Enemy worked around right flank compelling withdrawal of men from left to protect right flank and the latter to be thrown back. The battalion held the line and was congratulated by General Officer Commanding 6th Division and 18th Infantry Brigade. 12pm- Whole brigade fell back two miles.

The battalion's casualties were three officers, including Edward, and thirty-four other ranks. Edward was evacuated and died in the Base Hospital in Boulogne a few days later. He is also commemorated on the war memorial in Heckington, Lincolnshire, and on a plaque in the parish church there that reads 'In loving and honoured memory of Captain Edward Theodore Welchman DSO West Yorkshire Regiment, who died of wounds received in battle in France October 26 1914 aged 33. He spent his boyhood in this parish. RIP.'

The Germans intended to attack the British line between Gheluvelt and Ploegsteert Wood,[21] *and on 29 October launched an assault to try and capture the village of Gheluvelt itself.*

BRISTOW, John

Age:	21
Rank:	Private
Regiment/Service:	The Queen's (Royal West Surrey Regiment)
Unit:	2nd Battalion
Service Number:	L/10278
Died:	29 October 1914
Cemetery/Memorial:	Ypres (Menin Gate) Memorial
Reference:	Panels 11-13 & 14

John lived at 27 St James Road and had already served for two years prior to the war breaking out, having previously worked as a carter. His battalion rendez-voused at Veldhoek in the early morning of 29 October, coming under enemy shell fire as they sought shelter in dugouts in the woods. At 8 a.m. they moved up the Gheluvelt road and were ordered to reinforce the Guards in Gheluvelt itself. The battalion's A Company was brought up but driven back by 'hot fire' coming from the Gheluvelt–Menin road. The remainder of the day was spent manoeuvring the battalion to help form the British defensive line and occupy strongholds such as farms. In some places the troops were just 70 yards from the German trenches. Casualties in the battalion that day amounted to twelve killed, sixty wounded and twenty missing. John was injured during the battle and died of his wounds; his name is also on the Willie Bird cross.

The main attack occurred the next day, the Germans breaking through the British lines in some places by 31 October. This put the Germans in an excellent position to launch an attack on Ypres itself, which would have left the way to the channel ports open, potentially forcing the British Expeditionary Force back across the channel. This attack was only halted through a daring counter-attack by the 2nd Battalion Worcestershire Regiment, who charged across open ground to retake Gheluvelt Chateau in vicious hand-to-hand fighting.

Back in Carshalton, at the end of October the Wallington and Carshalton Advertiser *reported:*

Not at home: Carshalton's fame is spreading. A short time ago Mr H.V. Peirs, who has a son in the forces, and who has taken great interest in the compila-tion of the list of local soldiers, thought it would be a good idea to let all and sundry know where soldiers lived, and so he designed a unique card, to be placed in the window or other conspicuous place. The card is round in shape, and red with white type. Right across the middle appear the words 'Not at home' and all around it is printed 'A Carshalton man from this house is now serving in His Majesty's Forces' while on the back is space for the name of the soldier and his regiment. The idea has been taken up with enthusiasm, and Mr Peirs has received numerous letters about it. This week an illustration of the card appeared in a daily paper, and already inquiries have been received as a result. Of course the card has another value, for great is the force of example, and when able-bodied men see the cards they may realise that it is their duty to join the Army, too. Perhaps the one corner of Carshalton where the cards are most abundant is the Wrythe. In St James' Road there is one house with no less than five cards in the windows, and in the same road is another with four, while there are several with two.

The St Barnabas parish magazine also proudly reported that that over 240 of the men from its congregation and parish had joined the colours.

This card appears to be of a similar design to the one mentioned in the local paper. The soldier pictured is Sidney Glanville, killed in 1917. (Stephen Glanville)

Following the attacks at Gheluvelt, fierce fighting continued in the Ypres salient. William Kilty lost his life in an attack launched to try and force the Germans from their trenches near Zillebeke, south-east of Ypres.

KILTY, William Henry

Age:	25
Rank:	Corporal
Regiment/Service:	The Queen's (Royal West Surrey Regiment)
Unit:	2nd Battalion
Service Number:	L/8931
Died:	7 November 1914
Cemetery/Memorial:	Ypres (Menin Gate) Memorial
Reference:	Panel 11-13 & 14

(Bryan Stokes)

William was born in Carshalton and had already served in the army for eight years prior to the outbreak of war. The battalion history records:

It was a very misty morning, and at this hour it was only just becoming light enough to see objectives. The first two lines of The Queen's advanced over the rise when heavy machine gun fire at once opened upon them; the two lines then charged the German trenches, the Germans leaving them in all haste and bolting to the rear. The advance was continued, and a further German trench was taken with three machine guns, but the position could not be held by reason of the enfilade fire[22] now experienced, while no further advance could be made owing to the fire from the houses and trenches held by the enemy. The line gained was maintained all day under continuous fire of all kinds, which caused much damage, and in the evening the brigade was relieved.[23]

Ninety-seven men of the battalion became casualties during this attack. After his death the local paper reported that another local man, Private Donovan, had seen William shot during the attack. William's brother Leonard was also killed during the war and another brother, Patrick, served with the Australian Imperial Force (AIF). William is also commemorated on the Willie Bird cross.

After a final unsuccessful attempt to break through the British lines on 10–11 November, the Germans ceased their efforts and the First Battle of Ypres was over. The war of movement had stagnated; both sides dug in and the stalemate of trench warfare began.

RAPLEY, Edwin Alfred

Age:	31
Rank:	Private
Regiment/Service:	Leicester Regiment
Unit:	2nd Battalion
Service Number:	8550
Died:	19 December 1914
Cemetery/Memorial:	Le Touret Memorial
Reference:	Panel 11

CWGC Notes: Son of William Henry and Mary Ann Rapley.

Edwin was born in Middlesex and lived at 53 Mill Lane. He had served in the military for six years, five of which had been spent in India. His division had moved to France from India in October 1914. In the trenches from the end of October it suffered a steady trickle of casualties from artillery and minor engagements with the enemy. On 19 December Edwin was part of a bombing party that conducted a raid on the German lines. The advance commenced at 3.30 a.m., when the bombing party cut the German wire and started bombing their barricade. The left company had barely gone 20 yards when two Maxim guns[24] opened fire on them, but they managed to capture the trench and the two guns. The right company was also subject to machine gun and small arms fire. The bombing party advanced in front of the rest of the men, and all but one became casualties. Due to British artillery fire the troops remained where they were; with dawn approaching they put the trench into a state of defence in readiness for a counterattack. However, the trench was very narrow and had no traverses,[25] offering little protection. As the Germans counter-attacked with machine guns and mortars the British were pushed back along the trench until they held just 30 yards of it. With the situation untenable, they were forced to retreat, taking with them the two machine guns and four prisoners. Edwin was amongst those killed. Another account of this operation recounted that 'The enemy, not caring to face this class of men, had bolted as we neared the objective, but the Leicesters once started are hard to stop, and into the hail of another gun which had opened on them went the men from the Midland County.'[26]

As the first Christmas of the war approached, Revd Bartlett of St Barnabas church wrote gloomily:

> Many must be wondering what sort of Christmas we shall be able to keep this year. The war has already brought a dark cloud of sorrow or, where not actual sorrow as yet, a weight of anxiety on thousands of homes. There will be sad gaps in many family parties. Christmas will make us think more than ever of those whom the war has taken from us for a prolonged period, perhaps forever.

1915

1915 opened as 1914 had closed, with both sides looking at how they could break the dead-lock. As Revd Bartlett now wrote:

> How we should all like to know what the year 1915 will bring to us and to our country! Victory such as we hope for, followed by a righteous and lasting peace? Or partial success for us and our allies, great issues left undecided, and utter exhaustion of all the combatants? Or even something worse?

BRADBURY, Thomas Ernest

Age:	27
Rank:	Lance Sergeant
Regiment/Service:	Scots Guards
Unit:	1st Battalion
Service Number:	4916
Died:	25 January 1915
Cemetery/Memorial:	Le Touret Memorial
Reference:	Panels 3 & 4

CWGC Notes: Son of Thomas Henry and Mary Ann Emily Bradbury, of Carshalton.

Thomas was another career soldier and had enlisted in the Scots Guards in 1902 on boy service as a drummer.

Tom is first mentioned in the *Wallington and Carshalton Advertiser* in November 1914:

> On Wednesday night Mr Bradbury, of the Coach and Horses, High Street, received an intimation that his son, Sergt-Drummer Tom Bradbury, of the 1st Scots Guards, was wounded on the 2nd of November. So far as can be gathered the sergeant is not seriously injured. A piece of shrapnel struck him in the face below the eye and he is in hospital at Versailles. In a letter home he said he did not expect to be sent back to England, but expected to rejoin his regiment before long. Bradbury has 12 years' service to his credit, two of which he spent in Egypt.

Tom Bradbury is believed to be one of the sergeants pictured on this postcard, which he sent to his parents on 10 August 1914 from Aldershot Barracks. (Simon Jervis)

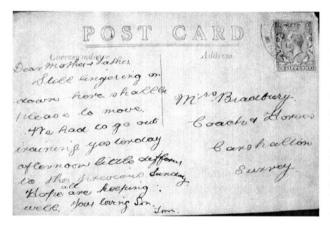

The postcard reads 'Dear Mother and Father. Still lingering on down here. Shall be pleased to move. We had to go out training yesterday afternoon little difference to the previous Sunday. Hope all are keeping well. Your loving son, Tom.' (Simon Jervis)

However, in February 1915 the paper then reported that 'Much anxiety is felt as to the whereabouts of Sergeant Thomas Bradbury … a letter from his friend who is at the front states he has not been seen since 25 January. Mr Bradbury has since received official intimation from the War Office that his son is missing.'

On 23 January Tom's battalion had gone into the front line trenches at Cuinchy, east of the town of Béthune. In some places they were only 25 yards from the Germans. On 25 January they were subject to an attack, and although they had been warned by a German deserter half an hour previously that the attack was going to take place, they suffered heavy casualties. An initial bombardment had been followed by the detonation of several mines along the sector, causing much chaos.[27] The advance was checked and a counter-attack delivered, but little ground was retaken. The casualties for that period in the trenches were thirty-one killed, 123 wounded, and 242 missing. Only forty-five men from the battalion returned unscathed.

In February, in an effort to break the stalemate on the Western Front, a naval bombardment of the Dardanelles Straits (Gallipoli) had commenced. The failure of this bombardment led to British, French and ANZAC[28] troops landing at Gallipoli in April. On 10 March the British launched their first major attack of the war on the Western Front, with the aim of capturing the village of Neuve Chapelle and the high ground of the Aubers Ridge and pushing the Germans back from the salient they had made south of Ypres.

CANNON, Harry Royal

Age:	27
Rank:	Private
Regiment/Service:	Cameronians (Scottish Rifles)
Unit:	2nd Battalion
Service Number:	9204
Died:	10 March 1915
Cemetery/Memorial:	Le Touret Memorial
Reference:	Panel 15 & 16

Born in Canterbury and previously a resident of Stratford, Harry later moved with his family to 5 Caledon Road, Carshalton. Harry had already served for nine years when war broke out, and had seen service in India and South Africa before being posted to Malta. Known as 'Toby' to his comrades, he was noted as a fine shot and a good boxer. In December 1914 he wrote to his parents:

> Just a few lines to let you know that I have felt the weight of a German bullet on the top of my head; it has parted my hair in centre and has grooved my skull a bit, and then run thin off. I got this lot on the 30th November at 7.30, I had been up on the parapet of the trench giving them socks for two days.[29] I have to my credit one officer and four men for certain, and a few wounded, and when we go back I am going to have some more for my wound. I may as well, as I have a souvenir from the Germans for life, for I will always have my scar. It is alright at present, only it aches at night. Don't get alarmed about me as I am just going into the trenches as if nothing had happened as everybody says I am a lucky man, for another quarter of an inch and I would have had my brains out, but never mind, God was good to me and spared my life. I suppose you will be surprised to hear that His Majesty the King was out here. He was only a quarter of a mile out of one firing line. I suppose it will be in the papers by now. What would the Germans say if only they knew it; their gunners would have tried for a dozen iron crosses.

Harry's battalion played a leading role in the battle of Neuve Chapelle, and the German defences were largely overrun. The Cameronians' war diary for that day simply states that:

> B Company reached the first German trench with very little opposition – not so A Company who met with a heavy rifle and MG fire – the German wire too

was not well cut in front of this company by the guns. A Company experienced a heavy enfilade fire as the battalion on its left – the 2nd Middlesex – could not get forward.

Harry was awarded the Distinguished Conduct Medal (DCM)[30] for his actions that day. The *London Gazette* of 1 June 1915 reports that he was 'Brought to notice for gallant conduct at Neuve Chapelle on 10 March 1915, when he was the first man to enter the German trenches in the attack.' As well as the DCM, Harry was awarded the Russian Order of the Cross of St George, Third Class. Harry is mentioned in *The War Illustrated*'s account of the battle, which recorded that:

> They rushed forward as gaily as the rest, but a dreadful experience met them before they reached the German trenches. The barbed wire entanglements, the trenches, the machine guns, everything was there just as if there had been no bombardment. As they tore with their naked hands at the wire, the Germans shot them down in scores.[31]

The British failed to exploit their initial successes and, although the village was captured, further gains were not made. British casualties during the period 10–12 March were just under 12,000. The offensive had shown the importance of the preliminary artillery barrage and good communication.

After Neuve Chapelle the remainder of March and April saw the stalemate continue, punctuated by ongoing raids and patrols.

PACKWOOD, Charles John Coventry

Age:	35
Rank:	Sergeant
Regiment/Service:	East Surrey Regiment
Unit:	2nd Battalion
Service Number:	SR/6992
Died:	3 April 1915
Cemetery/Memorial:	Dickebusch New Military Cemetery
Reference:	C.33

(*Wallington & Carshalton Advertiser*)

Born in Dunedin, New Zealand, Charles had joined the Rifle Brigade when he was 15 and had served in the South African War. He married the daughter of a reverend in 1909 and had five children, one of whom was born after he left for the front. In 1911 the family was living in Tooting, having previously lived at Inglemere Road, Mitcham. Charles re-enlisted in March 1914, prior to which he was an 'asylum attendant' at Chelsham mental hospital. He landed in France on 24 March, just ten days before his death, and joined his battalion on 28 March, when they moved into the front line.

Relieved on 30 March, they returned to the front line on 1 April. On 3 April at St Eloi Voormezeele, the battalion war diary records: 'Battalion in trenches. Moved trenches at St Eloi worried by trench mortar. Our trenches not touched. Those of 2nd Buffs hit. Battalion relieved by 1st Lincolns and returned to billets at Dickebusch. Casualties two killed seven wounded.' Although details of his death appeared in the local paper, it is not clear if Charles was living in or was connected to Carshalton prior to his death; by 1919, however, his widow Mary was living at 1 South Avenue.

On 22 April the Germans launched a new offensive and the Second Battle of Ypres began. They attacked the French lines north of Ypres using a new weapon – gas. The French line broke but the gap was not exploited by the Germans, and the following day the British counter-attacked. The 2nd Battalion of the East Surrey Regiment was part of the 28th Division holding the eastern edge of the line outside Zonnebeke, 5 miles north-east of Ypres. Due to the German attacks they were now defending a salient, under fire from three sides.

COX, William Thomas

Age:	22
Rank:	Private
Regiment/Service:	East Surrey Regiment
Unit:	2nd Battalion
Service Number:	6153
Died:	24 April 1915
Cemetery/Memorial:	Ypres (Menin Gate) Memorial
Reference:	Panel 34

Carshalton born, William lived at 93 Westmead Road. His jobs had included labouring and working for the tramway company before he joined the army in July 1909 aged 17. However, by the time war broke out he had left the army and was working as a miner in South Wales. On the Special Reserve,[32] he was called up in August 1914. He was due to be married at Christmas 1914 but the wedding was postponed, and he went overseas in February 1915. The local paper reported that he was 'a member of an old and respected Carshalton family'. William was killed in action near Zonnebeke during the Battle of St Julien when the Germans attacked the salient being held by the East Surreys:

> 23rd- At midnight the enemy made an attack on centre of battalion line but were repulsed. Second Lieutenant Fardell killed. A quiet day. Casualties seven killed 31 wounded. 24th- At 4am several trench mortars opened on trenches of battalion and continued all day, doing much damage to trenches. Enemy reported to be vacating their front trenches and to be placing boards across them. Trenches were again heavily shelled … Casualties Second Lieutenant Rottman and ten other ranks killed 39 wounded. Very quiet night.

William's name is also on Sutton war memorial and the St Barnabas church memorial.

CHANDLER, Arthur Charles

Age:	24
Rank:	Lance Corporal
Regiment/Service:	East Surrey Regiment
Unit:	B Company, 2nd Battalion
Service Number:	10003
Died:	25 April 1915
Cemetery/Memorial:	Ypres (Menin Gate) Memorial
Reference:	Panel 34

CWGC Notes: Son of Mrs R.J. Dale, of 17 St James Rd, Carshalton.

Arthur was born in Carshalton. His father died in 1909 when he was knocked from his bicycle by a horse and cart. Arthur's two brothers were put into the care of The Waifs and Strays Society (now The Children's Society). Arthur, possibly to escape the hardship experienced by

(*Wallington and Carshalton Advertiser*)

the family, joined the army in January 1910 aged 18. He had previously been employed as a potman by Mr Bird of The Cricketers pub in the Wrythe, who provided a reference for him when he enlisted. According to the local paper 'there are few better known families in the district than the Chandlers, some of whom have lived on the Wrythe for years'. Arthur went overseas in January 1915, and was killed in action during the Battle of St Julien when the Germans attacked again on 25 January:

> At 5am enemy opened fire with shrapnel which continued until 9am when trenches were heavily bombarded. The fumes from the shells … affected men and in some cases rendered them unconscious. Casualties to noon four killed and 18 wounded. At about 1pm the enemy attacked the whole line held by the battalion. They broke through … and some occupied a small trench in rear but were dislodged and eight captured. The remainder made for the railway but the company in dugouts attacked them and captured one officer and 28 men … The enemy succeed in occupying a portion of trench … but were speedily driven out by the 9th Middlesex at point of bayonet … the enemy in attacking were careful not to mask the loopholes of their own trenches and the fire from these loopholes caused heavy casualties amongst the men who were obliged to fire over the parapet.

Casualties for the day were eighty-seven killed, 113 wounded and forty-three missing. Arthur's death was not the family's only loss during the war. After the death of her first husband, Arthur's mother had married another local man, Ernest Dale, who was killed in the last stages of the war in 1918. This appears to be the only case in Carshalton of a woman losing both her husband and her son in the war. Arthur's name also appears on the Willie Bird cross.

SLAYMAKER, David

Age:	37
Rank:	Private
Regiment/Service:	Royal Warwickshire Regiment
Unit:	1st Battalion
Service Number:	10420
Died:	25 April 1915
Cemetery/Memorial:	Ypres (Menin Gate) Memorial
Reference:	Panel 8

(Hazel Kirby)

Born in Carshalton, David was the seventh child of William and Martha Slaymaker of St John's Road, and brother of George, who had died in September 1914. Better known as 'Taffy', David had previously served with the Royal Warwickshires in the Sudan and the South African War, where he had been wounded. Married with three children, after his army service he worked as a builder's labourer and also played football for Carshalton Athletic. He had arrived on the continent in late March 1915; at the end of May the family were informed that David was wounded and missing, believed killed. During the Battle of St Julien, on 25 April the battalion had attacked German lines near Wieltje at 4.30 a.m. The attack faltered at 7 a.m. due to an insufficient artillery bombardment and lack of support. The battalion's losses were heavy, with over 500 men killed, wounded, or missing. David's name also appears on Mitcham war memorial.

Whilst the Second Battle of Ypres raged on to the north, on 9 May the first joint French and British attack was carried out south of Ypres. The French attacked Vimy Ridge whilst the British attacked Aubers Ridge, the objective of their previous attack back in March. A lack of artillery and shells due to the fighting in the north meant that the German lines were largely unaffected by the woeful artillery bombardment. As the British went 'over the top' they were cut down by German machine gun and rifle fire. In one day they suffered over 11,000 casualties.

MOREY, Joseph

Age:	35
Rank:	Private
Regiment/Service:	London Regiment
Unit:	1/13th Kensington Battalion
Service Number:	3103
Died:	9 May 1915
Cemetery/Memorial:	Ploegsteert Memorial
Reference:	Panel 10

CWGC Notes: Son of Thomas and Amelia Morey.

(Jane Morey)

Born in Walworth, in 1911 Joseph was living with his parents and brother in Dulwich, working as a clerk. By 1914 the family was living at 28 The Crescent, Westmead Road. Joseph landed in France on 3 November 1914. He was killed in action at the northern flank of the battle of Aubers Ridge:

2am Wire cut and battalion ready for action. 5am Bombardment began. It appeared to lack the intensity of the Neuve Chapelle bombardment. A battery of 4.7" howitzers were understood to be bombarding Delangre Farm, our chief objective, apparently a strongly fortified position. No shell had struck it as yet. 5.40am Artillery lifted and two mines exploded. The brigade assaulted. The Kensington Battalion assaulted the enemy's trenches on a frontage 50 yards on either side of the right hand mine. Two companies in front line advanced in lines of platoons, remaining two companies followed in lines of platoons. Footing was obtained in the German trenches with heavy losses … Casualties were very heavy. 6.45am … Line was extended to the south of Delangre farm by the remains of two companies who had suffered heavily in getting up. Delangre farm had been hardly touched by our guns and was held by the enemy with at least two machine guns and rifles. The machine guns of the West Riding Division were firing into us. There was no sign of any British troops on our right or behind us. Our right flank was completely in the air and the whole line was suffering from fire from Delangre farm. Our machine gun on the right of the line was disabled. 7am The supply of bombs was running short and a message was sent to Brigade HQ for reinforcements and bombs … 8.25am Message to Brigade HQ 'Have exhausted every available reinforcement' … 9.05am Message from Brigade HQ '2nd Scottish Rifles moving to support you. You have done splendidly.' 9.10am One officer and two bombers of the 2nd Scottish Rifles with a small supply of bombs reached the left of the line … Casualties confirmed to be heavy. 9.20am … Ammunition was running short. The machine gun belts were stripped and the ammunition passed down the line … 11.30am Last grenade used. Ammunition very short. 11.45am Enemy broke through blocked trench and bombed us out of next traverse. Severe enfilade fire brought on our line. Casualties very heavy … Enemy brought up a small trench mortar and drove us further down trench. Enemy also bombed our line. 12.30pm Enemy still checked but position desperate. 12.45pm Five men of Royal Berkshire Regiment reached left of line with bandoliers. 1.15pm Our line … driven slowly back. Enemy worked further up the trenches and poured in a murderous enfilade fire. A large concentration of the enemy was observed … Enemy had worked round to south of Delangre farm. Our line suffering heavily was forced to draw back the right flank. Enemy worked further round the right of our line. Our line was now enfiladed from both flanks and we were forced to retire.

This war diary entry shows the problems of communication and supply once a position had been captured. Approximately 70 per cent of the battalion's initial strength of 623 – 436 men – became casualties. Joseph is also commemorated on the memorial in St Barnabas church.

Back north in the Ypres sector, the Germans continued to use gas in their attacks. Due to the exposed position of the British east of Ypres, at the beginning of May it was decided to pull back to shorten the line of defence.

SMITH, Harry William

Age:	36
Rank:	Private
Regiment/Service:	Essex Regiment
Unit:	2nd Battalion
Service Number:	7839
Died:	14 May 1915
Cemetery/Memorial:	Étaples Military Cemetery
Reference:	II.B.1A

CWGC Notes: Son of Rose Smith; husband of Nelly E. Smith, of 1 Overton Cottages, Downs Rd, Belmont, Sutton.

Born in Halstead, Essex, Harry was a fireman in the Carshalton Fire Brigade for two years and had previously worked for the council at the sewage farm and on the dust carts. He was a keen long-distance runner and had served eight years with the Essex Regiment, mainly in India, and was a Reservist. He had married five months prior to being called up and was living on West Street Lane at the outbreak of the war. He went to France on 22 August 1914, and at the end of May 1915 the local paper reported he had been badly wounded in the head, stating 'He has been at the front some months and his letters to his old comrades have always been of a cheerful character, for Smith was nothing if not an optimist.'

On 13 May at 4 a.m. the Germans started a heavy bombardment all along the front from Shell Trap Farm (100 yards north of Wieltje) southwards. At 6.55 a.m. a body of about 100 men were seen retiring back from the ridge about 100 yards from the farm. At 7 a.m. C Company was ordered to advance on the farm and retake it if it was found to be in enemy hands. At 7.35 a.m. the leading section of C Company reached the ridge and the farm was found to be in possession of the enemy. The attack was held up by the moat around the farm into which several men fell, but the enemy were eventually driven out. At 8.20 a.m. the battalion was ordered to retake further areas of the front line. A and B Companies moved off and:

> The attack by these two companies was splendid and carried out with great dash and determination. They were subjected to a very heavy artillery fire both high explosive and shrapnel, and on reaching the ridge to heavy machine gun fire. They never faltered in spite of fairly heavy casualties.

Later in the morning the battalion was relieved and withdrew to reorganise, sections and companies having been mixed up during the attack. Casualties were thirty-seven killed, ninety-four wounded, and forty-nine missing.

The Second Battle of Ypres drew to a close towards the end of May after the Battle of Bellewaarde. The Germans had made some territorial gains but the British still occupied a small salient around Ypres. In a little over a month British casualties amounted to around 60,000 against the Germans' 35,000.

To the south the British had again tried to attack in the direction of Aubers Ridge, in what is known as the Battle of Festubert. The plan was similar to the failed attempt a week earlier, a pincer movement designed to squeeze the Germans from the north and south. The bombardment opened on 13 May but again lacked high explosive shells. However, the initial attack on the night of 15–16 May was successful, and in the early hours of the morning the 7th Division advanced.

HENTON, Frank

Age:	18
Rank:	Private
Regiment/Service:	The Queen's (Royal West Surrey Regiment)
Unit:	2nd Battalion
Service Number:	G/3633
Died:	16 May 1915
Cemetery/Memorial:	Le Touret Memorial
Reference:	Panels 4 & 5

The Henton family lived at several addresses in the area, including 103 Westmead Road and 'Glenwood', Ringstead Road. In 1911 Frank was working as a domestic house boy. He went to France exactly two months before his death, and his brother Alfred was killed in 1916.

On 16 May the 2nd Battalion attacked in the direction of Violaines (near La Bassée) as part of the 7th Division. The battalion attacked on a frontage of 200 yards; despite the bombardment lasting thirty minutes, the Germans opened fire as they attacked at 3.15 a.m. The objectives were taken by 6 a.m. despite heavy casualties, but throughout the day the position was exposed to enfilade fire and shelling and at 7.30 p.m. the brigade withdrew to some of the German lines captured that morning. Casualties were high, 454 out of a strength that morning of 795. Frank's name is also on Sutton war memorial and the memorial in St Barnabas church.

The battle for Festubert raged on until 25 May but few tactical gains were made, at a loss of 16,000 men for the British. One consequence of the battle was the so-called 'shell shortage' scandal that broke in the British press, causing the government to fall and a new coalition government to be formed.

June and July were 'quiet' months, with neither side launching offensives on the Western Front; however, casualties were still a regular occurrence in the front lines due to the daily grind of trench warfare.

SANDS, Frederick

Age:	26
Rank:	Private
Regiment/Service:	East Surrey Regiment
Unit:	2nd Battalion
Service Number:	7000
Died:	4 June 1915
Cemetery/Memorial:	Elzenwalle Brasserie Cemetery
Reference:	I.E.3

Born in Hampshire, Frederick was a gardener and lived in the Rosehill area on the Carshalton/Mitcham border. He had enlisted in January 1915 and only arrived in France only three weeks before his death. After the fierce fighting of Second Ypres the battalion was relieved from the trenches at the end of May. They went back to the front line on 3 June. Frederick was killed or died of wounds whilst in trenches east of Vierstraat; on 4 June the regiment suffered two men killed and two wounded.

TURNER, Albert Victor

Age:	27
Rank:	Private
Regiment/Service:	The Queen's (Royal West Surrey Regiment)
Unit:	6th Battalion
Service Number:	G/832
Died:	6 July 1915
Cemetery/Memorial:	Longuenesse (St Omer) Souvenir Cemetery
Reference:	II.A.5

(Neil Uwins)

CWGC Notes: Brother of Miss E.H. Turner, of 23 Woodstock Rd, Croydon.

Known as 'Vic'. Albert had often helped out at his father's veterinary practice in Carshalton before getting a job as a carman. He had gone to the front in May 1915 with D Company of the 6th Battalion, and died of wounds received in early July after he was shot in the head by a German sniper in trenches near Armentières. His name is also on the Willie Bird cross and the memorial in St Barnabas church.

STEPNEY, Alfred Kenneth

'Peace perfect peace'

Age:	19
Rank:	Private
Regiment/Service:	The Queen's (Royal West Surrey Regiment)
Unit:	1st Battalion

Service Number: 10731
Died: 13 July 1915
Cemetery/Memorial: Chocques Military Cemetery
Reference: I.D.30

CWGC Notes: Son of Thomas and Amy Stepney, of Haycroft Farm, Hook Rd, Surbiton. Native of Carshalton.

Alfred was a plumber's apprentice and at the time of the 1911 census lived with his family at Acre Cottage, Park Lane. He enlisted in September 1914 and went overseas just before Christmas that year. He died of wounds received on 12 July – the battalion war diary states that he was 'accidentally wounded in billets by a revolver'. He is also commemorated on Hook war memorial.

Alfred's death plaque. These were issued to bereaved families and are often referred to as the 'dead man's penny'. (Mike Stepney)

On 30 July during the Battle of Hooge the Germans had tried to retake a mine crater blown and occupied by the British several days previously. This battle saw the first use of another fearsome weapon: 'liquid fire', or flamethrowers. The Germans took the British by surprise and the troops fell back. A counter-attack was ordered and the 9th King's Royal Rifle Corps was successful in recovering some of the ground lost, though it was not until 9 August that all the ground was retaken.

GOUGH, Bertie Frederick

Age: 22
Rank: Rifleman
Regiment/Service: King's Royal Rifle Corps
Unit: 9th Battalion, C Company, No. 9 Platoon
Service Number: R/502
Died: 30 July 1915
Cemetery/Memorial: Ypres (Menin Gate) Memorial
Reference: Panels 51 & 53

CWGC Notes: Son of Walter Smith Gough, of 52 Mill Lane, Carshalton, and the late Elizabeth Gough.

Born in Carshalton, Bertie's occupation when he enlisted in September 1914 is given as 'carman'. He had also worked at Stevenson's Stores and was a keen footballer, playing for Carshalton Athletic. He went to France at the end of May 1915, and was slightly gassed at Ypres. He was initially reported as missing following the heavy fighting at Hooge. His platoon had attacked a German trench but had come under heavy machine gun and rifle fire, which killed or wounded most of the men:

5am During night heavy bombardment of front trenches heard and orders received at 5am to be prepared to reinforce either flank. 11am Order received for the battalion to carry out an attack … in conjunction with attack by 43rd Brigade to retake trenches lost under liquid fire attack. The battalion moved out of dugouts … and were in position ready to attack at 1.30pm. B and D Companies in communication trench north of Menin Road, C and A Companies in support … south of Menin Road. Considerable losses were suffered whilst moving into these positions. Preliminary bombardment from 2pm to 2.45pm. At 2.45pm guns lifted and bombers … advanced to the attack immediately followed by B and D Companies. The trench … was taken without much opposition – but a lively bombing encounter took place at the top … and very considerable losses occurred from rifle and machine gun fire. Three platoons of C Company charged to their front … in direction of 'Old Bond Street' but were almost wiped out by machine gun fire. The 43rd Brigade failed to retake the trenches on the right.

The Germans tried to retake the trench that night and the following day, but failed to do so. Battalion losses for 30 July to 1 August were fifty-five killed, 241 wounded and thirty-nine missing; overall the 14th Division had lost close to 2,500 men. In December 1915 one of Bertie's comrades wrote to his parents to confirm that he had seen Bertie lying on the ground having been shot in the heart.

BRIDGE, Frederick Charles

Age:	37
Rank:	Private
Regiment/Service:	Leinster Regiment
Unit:	2nd Battalion
Service Number:	5615
Died:	31 July 1915
Cemetery/Memorial:	Ypres (Menin Gate) Memorial
Reference:	Panel 44

Frederick was born in Carshalton, the Bridge family living at 9 Palmerston Road and later 6 Gordon Cottages, West Street Lane. Frederick was a groom and later became a coachman like his father, William. He initially served with the Royal Field Artillery, no doubt due to his experience with horses. He is likely to have been killed near Wieltje when the Germans fired around twelve rounds from a '*minenwerfer*'[33] at 6.30 a.m., inflicting four casualties. Previous shelling on 28 July had also wounded seven men in C Company.

A relatively quiet period ensued, although thousands of casualties were still incurred during that time. Revd Bartlett of St Barnabas church reflected on the anniversary of the outbreak of war:

Our thoughts will naturally go back to the opening days of last August, when the great war-clouds gathered so suddenly, seeming to sail up from all quarters and darken the sky. There was the terrible suspense when we hoped and prayed that war might yet be avoided, though each day made it clearer that it was inevitable. And when we began to understand for what we were called to stand up and fight, there was a sense of relief, yes, and of thankfulness, that at last England had thrown down her challenge and refused to stand aside and leave the strong to trample on the weak unhindered and unopposed. But whereas, at first, we thought that at any rate it could not last many months, we have now had a whole year of war; slaughter, suffering, cruelty and devastation have proceeded on a scale that the world has never before seen, and the end is not yet.

However, it seems that not even the war could dampen the British sense of humour. An article in the same edition of the parish magazine proclaimed:

We have not yet had an invasion, but a daring raid has been perpetrated in our midst, three ladies' bicycles having been stolen from the west porch of the Church during an early weekday celebration on July 15th. We do not know what the police theory is, but we ourselves are strongly inclined to think it must have been the work of the Germans. Who else would be capable of such conduct? The raid had, no doubt, been carefully planned, and was carried out with the enemy's accustomed thoroughness and entire unscrupulousness. It is supposed that a force of at least three must have been engaged on this occasion – as it would be hardly possible for one person to get away with three bicycles so quickly – and that they must have been dressed as English ladies, so as to pass unnoticed when riding ladies' machines; but the enemy has long been known to be clever at disguises.

In September the Allies renewed their offensive, a move designed to take the pressure off Russia in the east, for if Russia fell Germany would be able to transfer many more troops to the Western Front.

COX, John Benjamin
'In loving memory of our dear Jack who died for his country's sake'

Age:	17
Rank:	Rifleman
Regiment/Service:	King's Royal Rifle Corps
Unit:	12th Battalion
Service Number:	R/1090
Died:	12 September 1915
Cemetery/Memorial:	Rue-De-Bacquerot No. 1 Military Cemetery, Laventie
Reference:	II.C.5

(Lindsay Seagrim-Trinder)

CWGC Notes: Son of Charles and Annie Cox, of Nonsuch Farm, Cheam, Sutton.

Born in Cuddington, in 1911 the family were living at Woodcote Farm, Wallington. When he enlisted on 3 September 1914, John gave his age as 19 and his occupation as clerk. A memorial plaque in St Mary's church, Cuddington, states that he was 20 at the time of his death. However, the 1901 census shows that he was born in 1898, and this is confirmed by birth records which give a birth date of January–March 1898, meaning he was 16 when he enlisted and about 17 and a half when he died. He had been in France less than two months when he was killed in action during a stint in the front line near Aubers Ridge on 8–16 September. The battalion was positioned near 'Winchester Post' in Laventie, a farm building used as battalion headquarters and dressing station. The war diary for the period records that they:

> Relieved 12th Rifle Brigade in front line trenches. Situation quiet all the time. Snipers found few targets. They hit three Germans. Our machine guns dispersed various enemy working parties. Casualties – one officer very slightly wounded, one NCO wounded, three riflemen killed, one rifleman died of wounds, 17 riflemen wounded.

On 21 September a British artillery bombardment opened in preparation for the start of a new offensive on 25 September: the Battle of Loos. Although this name is commonly used to refer to the first day's fighting, the offensive lasted until mid-October and took in almost the whole of the British line from Loos to Ypres further north, where subsidiary attacks were carried out. It was part of a wider offensive carried out in conjunction with the French. Loos is in north-east France, a predominantly industrial area that is particularly flat. The British attacked here despite Douglas Haig's reservations about the nature of the terrain and a shortage of artillery shells. The opening day of the battle was notable for the first British use of chlorine gas; in some areas this was effective but in others, where the wind was less favourable, it caused problems for the attackers, in some cases blowing back towards the advancing troops.

To the north the offensive was supported by a diversionary attack on Bellewaarde Ridge, near Hooge on the outskirts of Ypres.

COOPER, James Thomas

Age:	24
Rank:	Rifleman
Regiment/Service:	King's Royal Rifle Corps
Unit:	9th Battalion
Service Number:	R/527
Died:	25 September 1915
Cemetery/Memorial:	Ypres (Menin Gate) Memorial
Reference:	Panels 51 & 53

Born in Bermondsey, James lived at 35 Station Road, was a printer machine hand and played football for Carshalton Athletic. He enlisted in September 1914 and was a signaller in the KRRC. Signallers were used to transmit key messages back to headquarters, whether by telephone or using visual aids such as lamps or helio-graphs. He was killed in action when the battalion carried out a full frontal assault on a German position where the wire had not been cut. The objective was the Bellewaarde Farm position just off the Menin Road, and the 9th KRRC support-ing the attack were quickly called upon to provide reinforcements. The preliminary bombardment had commenced at 3.50 a.m., provoking a retaliatory bombardment from the Germans, causing some casualties amongst the men. The British bom-bardment ended at 4.19 a.m., followed a minute later by the detonation of a mine under the German position. Although the battalion remained in support, casualties were heavy – thirty-eight killed, 191 wounded and twenty-nine missing.

The following five men from the 8th Battalion, The Queen's (Royal West Surrey Regiment) and the 9th Battalion, East Surrey Regiment, had only landed in France as part of the 24th Division on 31 August 1915. They had been hurriedly rushed to the front for the offensive but did not get there in time for the first day's attack on 25 September. They were held in reserve, being sent in the following day to attack the German lines near Hulluch; it was their first, and for many their last, action.

The war diary for the 8th Battalion The Queen's records that:

The battalion advanced under heavy machine gun and shrapnel fire in lines of platoons in extended order. As the advance continued over the Lens-La Bassee road, the machine gun fire from the flanks was very heavy. On reaching the enemy trenches it was found to be protected by barbed wire, which had not been cut and, it being impossible to get through it, the brigade retired. There appeared to be no panic and the men walked back still under machine gun and shrapnel fire.

This brief description of events belies the chaos and carnage the battalion must have faced – eleven officers and 409 other ranks were casualties. Interestingly, the date of death for Harry Marshall and Leonard Stovell of The Queen's is recorded as 26 September; this is likely to be an error.

MARSHALL, Harry

Age:	19
Rank:	Private
Regiment/Service:	The Queen's (Royal West Surrey Regiment)
Unit:	8th Battalion
Service Number:	G/4992
Died:	25 September 1915
Cemetery/Memorial:	Loos Memorial
Reference:	Panels 13 to 15

CWGC Notes: Son of Henry Edward and Emily Ann Marshall, of 50 Sutton Grove, Sutton.

Harry was born in Bermondsey, and the family were still living in that area at the time of the 1911 census when Harry (whose full name was Henry James) was working as an errand boy in the linen trade. He enlisted in Deptford and was reported missing in action after Loos. He is also commemorated on the St Barnabas church memorial.

STOVELL, Leonard

Age:	21
Rank:	Lance Corporal
Regiment/Service:	The Queen's (Royal West Surrey Regiment)
Unit:	D Company, 8th Battalion
Service Number:	G/2976
Died:	25 September 1915
Cemetery/Memorial:	Loos Memorial
Reference:	Panels 13 to 15

CWGC Notes: Son of Samuel and Elizabeth Jane Stovell, of 79 Gordon Rd, Carshalton.

The youngest of eight children, Leonard enlisted in October 1914. Two brothers also served during the war, both being wounded. The local paper reported that Leonard was missing after the 'big advance'.

BALDWIN, Frederick C.

(Peter Etter)

Age:	24
Rank:	Lance Corporal
Regiment/Service:	The Queen's (Royal West Surrey Regiment)
Unit:	D Company, 8th Battalion
Service Number:	2978
Died:	28 October 1918 (wounded 26 September 1915)
Cemetery/Memorial:	Carshalton (All Saints) Churchyard
Reference:	New.17.5

CWGC Notes: Son of Sydney and Ellen Baldwin, of Firview Villas, 117 Stanley Rd, Carshalton.

In 1911 Frederick was working as a trainee carpenter, and later became an architect's draughtsman. He enlisted on 24 October 1914 with his friend George Harrison. After the attack at Loos, Frederick was reported missing; in fact, he had received a gunshot wound to the chest and was taken prisoner. Initially sent to a prisoner of war camp at Limburg, at the end of May 1916 he was sent to Chateau d'Oex, a small mountain town in Switzerland, under a scheme to repatriate British and German soldiers too seriously wounded to return to fighting. Fred stayed with Samuel and Elise Etter, a couple who operated a *pension* and who took in a number of British soldiers during the war. He formed an attachment to their daughter Mariette, and in August 1917 their engagement was announced. Sadly, the marriage never took place; Fred was repatriated on 11 September 1917 and discharged from the army in November but, weakened by his war experience, died in the influenza pandemic of 1918. His 14-year-old sister had died two days previously from the same cause. Despite this rather sad story there was a happier outcome in that an alliance did result between the Swiss and English families; a son, Jean Etter, married Fred's sister Violet and settled in England, where they had three children. Fred is also commemorated on the memorial in St Barnabas church.

The 9th Battalion East Surrey Regiment was also in action, crossing 1,700 yards of open ground to attack the German trenches:

> Soon after 4am … the battalion was ordered to take cover in some German support trenches which had been captured the day before. Efforts were made to bring some rations up to the men but the enemy's shell fire prevented this being done. The enemy's position extended between Hulluch and Cite St Auguste. The attack was launched at 11am and was carried right up to the enemy's trenches but the wire not being cut it was impossible to get through the enemy's lines although several fruitless attempts were made. The casualties were very heavy at this point chiefly owing to some machine guns which formed a heavy cross fire on our men. The order was then given for the brigade to retire to the line of trenches from which it had advanced in the morning. This retirement was carried out in orderly manner under heavy shell fire of all kinds … The enemy continued to shell very heavily until about 5pm … and many of the slightly wounded were wounded again or killed … The casualties numbered 14 officers and 438 other ranks.

BUCKENHAM, William J.

Age:	19
Rank:	Corporal
Regiment/Service:	East Surrey Regiment
Unit:	9th Battalion
Service Number:	2512
Died:	26 September 1915
Cemetery/Memorial:	Loos Memorial
Reference:	Panels 65 to 67

Born in Carshalton, William was a labourer living in St John's Road before enlisting in September 1914. Known as Billy, he played football for Carshalton Athletic. In early October 1915 the local paper reported that he had been wounded. He is possibly commemorated on the Willie Bird cross as 'Buckingham', and was the cousin of Sidney Barber, another Carshalton casualty.

CHALCRAFT, Frank

Age:	23
Rank:	Private
Regiment/Service:	East Surrey Regiment
Unit:	9th Battalion
Service Number:	2598
Died:	26 September 1915
Cemetery/Memorial:	Loos Memorial
Reference:	Panels 65 to 67

Born in Carshalton, Frank was a brick maker and lived at 19 St James Road. He enlisted in September 1914, and was reported as missing, presumed killed, after Loos. He is also commemorated on the Willie Bird cross, and was the cousin of Robert Cairns, who was killed in 1916.

The 24th Division, of which these Surrey regiment battalions were part, suffered over 4,000 casualties on that one day. Gains in the first two days were limited but, despite the huge losses (including three senior British commanders), the fighting continued as the British tried to renew the offensive along the whole front line and the Germans counter-attacked in an attempt to regain lost ground.

GRAVATT, Hubert Charles Alfred

Age:	24
Rank:	Lance Corporal
Regiment/Service:	Honourable Artillery Company
Unit:	2nd
Service Number:	2717
Died:	30 September 1915
Cemetery/Memorial:	New Irish Farm Cemetery
Reference:	XXVIII.E.5

CWGC Notes: Son of Charles Frederick and Alice Mary Gravatt, of 'Beech Dene', The Beeches Avenue, Carshalton.

(Alleyn's School archive)

Hubert attended Lyndhurst Grove School in Southwark and Alleyn's School in Dulwich. A keen sportsman, he played for Beddington tennis club and Wallington hockey club. He was an insurance clerk for the Prudential Assurance Company, enlisted in December 1914, and went overseas in July 1915. On 29 September the battalion was in reserve near Dickebusch, in the Ypres sector. The following morning they marched into the salient; the Germans had exploded a mine on the front of the 8th Brigade near Sanctuary Wood, and the HAC were part of the counter-attack. Dense undergrowth in Sanctuary Wood caused a lot of problems, but the attack was a success despite considerable casualties.

The Prudential staff magazine *Ibis* reported that:

> We have received with deep regret the news that Private Hubert Charles Alfred Gravatt has been killed on active service. Entering the Office in 1907, he was appointed to the Cashier's Department, and, having passed the first of the Institute of Actuaries Examinations, was transferred to the Actuary's Office in 1912, qualifying as an Associate of the Institute in the same year. In his case a sturdy physique was a true index to a strong character, and during his official career he won not only the respect of his colleagues for the able and conscientious manner in which he discharged whatever duty fell to his lot, but also their affection by his straightforward and sympathetic nature. He joined the Honourable Artillery Company in November 1914 and was quickly made a Corporal, but on proceeding to Flanders in June of this year relinquished that rank, as is usual, in favour of those who had seen more active service. A letter received by his parents from the Captain of his company, bears ample testimony to the fact that the characteristics so evident to his office colleagues were strikingly displayed in the trenches. He was killed by a shrapnel shell bursting directly above him in the trench, and it is some consolation that death was practically immediate and painless. We offer our heartfelt sympathy to his parents, brothers and sisters in the irreparable loss they have sustained by his untimely but honourable death.

After his death, Hubert's employer wrote to his parents, 'I think he took up his duty as a soldier in the very finest spirit. In the last conversation when saying goodbye he made it clear that he hated the whole business of war. He felt that he ought to take part in his country's cause.'

Hubert is also commemorated on the Prudential memorial outside their offices in Holborn. His brother Donald also served with the Honourable Artillery Company and survived the war.

PICKERING, Thomas Henry

Age:	27
Rank:	Private
Regiment/Service:	Cheshire Regiment
Unit:	2nd Battalion
Service Number:	28132
Died:	3 October 1915
Cemetery/Memorial:	Loos Memorial
Reference:	Panels 49 & 50

Born in Thornton Heath and lived at 34 Mill Lane, Carshalton. Thomas was married with two children and worked as a carter. He had joined the RFA in January 1915.

The local paper reported that he died of wounds on 3 October having only been in France for six weeks. On that day, at 7.45 a.m. 'The enemy delivered an unexpected attack on our left with bombs and MGs and eventually turned it. The battalion fought well but were driven back. Enemy occupied west face of the Hohenzollern redoubt.' Casualties from 30 September to 3 October were forty-eight killed, 160 wounded and 168 missing.

WYATT, Thomas

Age:	20
Rank:	Rifleman
Regiment/Service:	King's Royal Rifle Corp
Unit:	11th Battalion
Service Number:	R/2305
Died:	6 October 1915
Cemetery/Memorial:	Rue-De-Bacquerot (13th London) Graveyard, Laventie
Reference:	A.9

CWGC Notes: Son of Mr Thomas Wyatt, of Carshalton.

(Jean Lambert)

Thomas was born in Carshalton and worked as a labourer. He was the cousin of Ernest Wyatt and the brother-in-law of Charles Batchelor. He enlisted on 4 September 1914 with his cousin Ernest – they have consecutive service numbers. He had only been in France since 21 July; the war diary for the day he died simply states 'Enemy were quiet except in the morning when shell fire, rifle and machine gun fire were usually opened with little effect. Casualties Rifleman T. Wyatt, D Company, killed 6.10.15, gunshot wound.' After his death, his cousin Ernest wrote to Tom's mother to inform her that her son had been shot in the trenches, and had died shortly afterwards. Tom's name is also on the Willie Bird cross.

A postcard sent home by Tom Wyatt after he had enlisted. It reads 'Dear Ada, Just a line to let you know that I am alright hoping you are the same. Thank you for the cigarettes which you was a silly to buy all I can say at present with love from Tom. Remember me to Mama.' (Jean Lambert)

The Battle of Loos was drawing to an end. One final attack took place, known as the Action of the Hohenzollern Redoubt. This attempt to restart the offensive was only partially successful and cost the lives of three Carshalton men serving with the 7th Battalion East Surrey Regiment, who had only gone to France at the beginning of June. Their battalion war diary for the day records that:

> The division was ordered to attack in conjunction with a general attack more or less all along the line. 12 noon the artillery bombardment began and continued until 2 o'clock; smoke and gas began at 1 and was continued to 2. The attack was made by the 46th, 12th, and 1st Division its main object was to straighten our line and if possible to take from the enemy one or two very nasty positions he had which enfiladed our line … At 2pm exactly B Company two platoons led by Lieutenant Hewat assaulted the whole of 'gun trench' by a frontal attack; at the same time bombing parties from A and B attacked both flanks. The frontal attack got in at once, the Germans running as soon as we got close. A Company under Captain Tomkins with two platoons followed up … but kept too much to the north and were badly cut up by machine gun fire in the open … There was a great deal of bombing on both sides and our men suffered rather heavily from enfilade fire from the quarries on our left … also the trenches were shelled somewhat heavily with high explosive. However the result was exactly what we had set out to do, we won the trench … The enemy made a counter-attack at 5.30am which we easily repulsed with rifle fire … The men fought splendidly all through and attacked with great dash, this was especially creditable as they had been in the trenches for four months without a rest and the last five days had undergone a continual and heavy bombardment.

Casualties were fifty-eight killed, 160 wounded and thirty-three missing.

BATES, Herbert Charles

Age:	35
Rank:	Lance Corporal
Regiment/Service:	East Surrey Regiment
Unit:	7th Battalion
Service Number:	779
Died:	13 October 1915
Cemetery/Memorial:	Loos Memorial
Reference:	Panels 65 to 67

CWGC Notes: Son of Mr John Joseph Bates, of The Field, Beck Row Rd, Mildenhall, Suffolk.

Born in Mildenhall, at the time of the 1911 census Herbert was boarding with a family at 1 Rochester Road. He worked as a labourer and enlisted in September 1914, being sent to the front on 1 June 1915. He is also commemorated on Mildenhall war memorial.

JOHNSON, Arthur

Age:	30
Rank:	Private
Regiment/Service:	East Surrey Regiment
Unit:	7th Battalion
Service Number:	138
Died:	13 October 1915
Cemetery/Memorial:	Bully-Grenay Communal Cemetery, British Extension
Reference:	IX.B.13

A labourer born in Carshalton, Arthur lived at 38 Milner Place and had joined up on 19 August 1914.

STEVENSON, James

Age:	21
Rank:	Private
Regiment/Service:	East Surrey Regiment
Unit:	7th Battalion
Service Number:	6195
Died:	13 October 1915
Cemetery/Memorial:	Loos Memorial
Reference:	Panels 65 to 67

James was born in Carshalton where the family lived at 30 Wandle Mount. He worked as a farm labourer then a carman before enlisting in November 1914, one month after his 20th birthday. He was reported missing after the action on 13 October.

The 2nd Battalion Royal Sussex Regiment was also part of the attack.

LEE, Herbert John

Age:	36
Rank:	Private
Regiment/Service:	Royal Sussex Regiment
Unit:	2nd Battalion
Service Number:	G/4898
Died:	13 October 1915
Cemetery/Memorial:	Loos Memorial
Reference:	Panels 69 to 73

CWGC Notes: Son of John Lee; husband of Ellen Sarah Lee of 33 Lesly St, Roman Rd, Barnsbury, Holloway.

A labourer, Herbert was born in Croydon, Cambridgeshire, and lived at 113 Avenue Road, Wallington. Married with five children, he joined up in January 1915. He was killed in action during the assault, in which the battalion failed to capture any ground. Battalion casualties were nine killed, seventy-two wounded, and thirty-seven missing.

The Loos offensive had cost the British Army over 60,000 casualties. The pre-war Regular Army units had suffered heavily, losing experienced officers and men, and the New Army battalions had suffered too. Another consequence was the replacement at the end of the year of the Commander-in-Chief of the British Army, Sir John French, by Douglas Haig, commander of the First Army.

Back home, Carshalton had seen an influx of soldiers who had been billeted in the area. This had helped boost the numbers attending the services at St Barnabas church, and many of the men also made use of the facilities at The Handy on Carshalton Road, a former Baptist chapel that had been bought by St Barnabas for use as a Sunday school and recreation room. During the war it was put to use as a soldiers' canteen and reading room.[34] *All profits made here were sent to France for the maintenance of the Church Army huts. Christmas 1915 saw 375 Christmas cards sent to serving parishioners; letters and parcels from home were welcomed by the soldiers in the trenches and helped to boost morale. One soldier wrote back:*

Just a line to thank you for your kind letter and card at Christmas. I tell you it came very unexpected. I never dreamed of getting a pick me up from you and the parish of St Barnabas. I hope all the other boys received theirs, because you know it put new life into me just for the time, and there were three of us singing that little song 'Keep the Home Fires Burning' when I received that letter, and I wondered how long I have got to wait for the day of rejoicing. We are having dreadful weather here at present: it is nothing but mud everywhere.

The Handy, *c.* 1916. (St Barnabas church)

1916

Loos was the last offensive of 1915, after which both sides settled down for the winter. An Allied conference in December proposed a renewed offensive in spring 1916. Until this point, Britain's army of over 2.5 million men had been composed entirely of volunteers. However, the campaigns of 1915 had exacted a terrible toll and more men were needed. In January 1916, therefore, conscription was introduced. For the remainder of the war local military tribunals were held to discuss cases where men had requested exemption from service. This could be due to the nature of their jobs or the responsibility they had to provide or care for their families; of course, some men may not have wanted to fight or were opposed to the war on political or ideological grounds. Each case was reported in the local newspaper, although the identity of the men was in most cases withheld.

Back on the Western Front, barely a week of the new year had passed before Carshalton suffered another casualty.

NEWTON, Albert Arthur

Age:	18
Rank:	Private
Regiment/Service:	The Queen's (Royal West Surrey Regiment)
Unit:	6th Battalion
Service Number:	G/700
Died:	9 January 1916
Cemetery/Memorial:	Béthune Town Cemetery
Reference:	IV.H.16

(Neil Uwins)

CWGC Notes: Son of Mrs C. Newton, of High St, Carshalton.

Before the war Albert had worked for a fishmonger in Wallington. His family also owned The Forge on Carshalton High Street, and he and his brother George (who also served) worked there as farriers. Albert enlisted at the outbreak of the war and had been at the front for eight months, serving with D Company of the 6th Battalion. After his death, one of his fellow soldiers wrote to his parents:

> Being your Albert's chum, I thought it my duty to break this sad news to you. We were relieved from the trenches on the 9th, and on our way home had to walk along a road which was being shelled heavily. Of course, the first thing we thought of doing was to get under cover, which we did, behind a field ambulance[35] wall. We stood talking for quite a long time. I was standing just where Albert was. I said to him, 'I shall not be a minute. I am just going down the other side of the wall.' I had not got ten feet away when a shell pitched just where Albert and some more of our lads were standing. It pains me very much to say Albert was killed, but, thank God, he never suffered: he was killed instantaneously. I must say Albert was a great favourite with all who knew him. He will be greatly missed by all his chums. All our lads send their deepest sympathy.

There is just one more thing I must say – that Albert was a plucky lad and a good soldier. He died fighting for his country, which was a hero's death.

His corporal also wrote:

I was your son's section commander and was in charge of the section when the sad affair happened. I carried your son in, and I can assure you on my word of honour that Jerry, as we used to call him, did not suffer at all. He would do anything he was asked to do. So please accept our deepest sympathy.

GRIFFIN, William Alfred

Age:	20
Rank:	Private
Regiment/Service:	Royal Fusiliers
Unit:	18th Battalion
Service Number:	1556
Died:	7 February 1916
Cemetery/Memorial:	Cambrin Churchyard Extension
Reference:	K.13

Born in Plymouth and lived at 'Harold-dean', Nightingale Road. William attended Cranleigh School in 1910–11, where he was in the 1st XI football team. On the day he was killed the battalion was located at Annequin. Whilst cleaning billets and doing work to dugouts a fatigue party was heavily shelled, killing three and wounding four. He is also commemorated on Cranleigh School war memorial.

BOXALL, Leonard Arthur

'Gone but never forgotten'

Age:	32
Rank:	Private
Regiment/Service:	The Buffs (East Kent Regiment)
Unit:	8th Battalion
Service Number:	G/5542
Died:	28 March 1916 (wounded 19 March 1916)
Cemetery/Memorial:	Lijssenthoek Military Cemetery
Reference:	V.B.25A

CWGC Notes: Son of James and Caroline E. Boxall, of Colworth Cottage, West Dean, Chichester, Sussex.

Leonard was born in West Dean and worked as a farm labourer. He enlisted in Croydon, though his link to Carshalton is unclear; it is possible he had relatives who lived at Little Woodcote Cottage, Woodcote. He was overseas from the end of August 1915. On 19 March, C Company suffered several casualties caused by the Germans shelling border dugouts, south-east of Ypres. Leonard died at No. 17 CCS of gunshot wounds[36] to the chest and leg. His mother wrote to the War Office in July 1916, 'I have received the things that you have sent of my darling boy L.A. Boxall and I return you many thanks he was the best boy a mother ever had he has gone to a higher service. I hope and pray my other dear boys be brought back safely to me.' Leonard is also commemorated on the war memorial in St Andrew's church, West Dean.

The following three casualties were all part of the 12th (Eastern) Division, who in early 1916 were holding the line around the Hulluch quarries, the area so heavily fought over during the Loos campaign of late 1915. Fighting continued in the area for several weeks until the division was relieved in late April.

CATTELL, George Clement Towersey

Age:	21
Rank:	Private
Regiment/Service:	East Surrey Regiment
Unit:	7th Battalion
Service Number:	402
Died:	8 March 1916
Cemetery/Memorial:	Loos Memorial
Reference:	Panels 65 to 67

CWGC Notes: Son of Clement and Emma Cattell, of 4 Gordon Rd, Carshalton.

Born in Hackney, a bookbinder, George enlisted in August 1914 before going to France in June 1915. The battalion had gone into the trenches near the Hohenzollern Redoubt on 5 March; on 7 March the Germans attacked one of the craters held by the battalion, and the following day they came under fire from German artillery whilst repairing the trenches, before being relieved later that day.

SHARP, Arthur Henry

Age:	23
Rank:	Private
Regiment/Service:	The Queen's (Royal West Surrey Regiment)
Unit:	6th Battalion
Service Number:	G/728
Died:	18 March 1916
Cemetery/Memorial:	Loos Memorial
Reference:	Panels 13 to 15

(Neil Uwins)

CWGC Notes: Husband of Edith Sharp, of 448 London Rd, Wycombe Marsh, High Wycombe, Bucks.

Born in Sutton, Arthur's parents lived at The Lodge, Sutton Common Road. He worked as a coachman before enlisting, and went overseas in June 1915 with D Company. During March his battalion was involved in mine warfare in the Hohenzollern sector, where the Germans had blown several mines and were holding the resultant craters. On the day of his death, at about 5.30 p.m.:

> Enemy commenced heavy bombardment of our front line reserve and com-munication trenches ... 6.40pm verbal message arrived via East Surrey orderly that Crater C had been lost two mines were blown therein ... At 9.25pm officer commanding B Company reported Crater C was clear of enemy but outer lip was held by them. 11.10pm Second Lieutenant Passmore reported he had two Lewis guns in Sticky Trench. With these two guns he was able to stop enemy advancing between B and C craters ... At 3.45am B Company under Captain Cannon and in conjunction with A Company of East Surrey Regiment seized the inner lip of Crater C and they met with very slight opposition but owing to daylight coming on they had to retire into the saps as they were in full view of the enemy and there was no time to consolidate the inner lip, as pioneers and sappers did not arrive till nearly dawn. Casualties: six killed, sixteen wounded.

Arthur is also commemorated on the memorial at High Wycombe Hospital.

CLARKE, John

Age:	35
Rank:	Private
Regiment/Service:	East Surrey Regiment
Unit:	7th Battalion
Service Number:	820
Died:	12 April 1916
Cemetery/Memorial:	Longuenesse (St Omer) Souvenir Cemetery
Reference:	III.B.2

CWGC Notes: Husband of Kate Clarke of 9 Wrythe Lane, Carshalton.

Born in Croydon and worked as a plumber's mate. John had previously joined the army in 1897 and served with the Royal Scots Fusiliers. St Omer was a large hospital centre, so it is likely he had been transported there for treatment after being wounded. On 30 March his battalion had moved to the front line trenches (Rifleman's Alley to the south of Swinburn Loop, near Vermelles). Three mines were blown on the evening of 31 March, followed by attempted enemy assault, leading to thirty casualties. John is also commemorated on the Willie Bird cross.

Following the failure of the Gallipoli offensive, Douglas Haig was determined that the main focus of the war should be to defeat the Germans on the Western Front. In February the Germans launched an offensive against the French city of Verdun. A symbol of France's resistance, they hoped that the French would do anything to protect the city, committing all their troops and eventually consuming all of their resources. The Somme offensive was designed in partnership with the French to relieve the pressure on the beleaguered city. A huge preliminary bombardment lasting seven days was supposed to destroy the barbed wire and German trenches, leaving the way open for the British to carry out a sweeping advance. The battle is characterised by the use of 'Kitchener's Army', the new battalions formed from the recruitment drive at the outbreak of the war, many of which were referred to as 'Pals' battalions due to the groups of friends or co-workers who joined together. The British attacked along 14 miles of front line, the French 8 miles. Over 150,000 British soldiers were in the attacking divisions.

British objectives started with a diversionary attack at Gommecourt at the north of the line, in order to occupy the German forces there and stop them from sending troops to the main battle further south. The British line continued through Serre and Beaumont Hamel to the north of the River Ancre; then through Thiepval, La Boisselle and Pozières (astride the Albert–Bapaume road), and the fortified villages of Fricourt, Mametz and Montauban to the south. The French then took over the sector south of the River Somme itself.

ASTILL, Reginald

Age:	21
Rank:	Rifleman
Regiment/Service:	London Regiment (Queen Victoria's Rifles)
Unit:	1/9th Battalion
Service Number:	2010
Died:	1 July 1916
Cemetery/Memorial:	Thiepval
Reference:	9C

Born in Brixton, Reginald worked as a clerk and played cricket for Dulwich Hamlet Cricket Club. As part of the diversionary attack, his battalion was involved in an assault on a series of trenches near Gommecourt. Although many men were wounded or killed by German machine guns and artillery, the assault was initially successful and the battalion advanced to the German third line. However, a shortage of grenades meant it became difficult to hold their position against counter-attacks and by mid-afternoon they had been driven back to the first line of German trenches. A few survivors were holding the line but by 7 p.m. they were driven out. They suffered 352 casualties and 192 missing – over half of the battalion. Reginald is also commemorated on the Dulwich Hamlet Football Club memorial, along with his brother Ernest, who was killed in 1918.

Francis Ingram, John Rumsey and Archibald Warner were all serving with the 1/5th Battalion London Regiment and also took part in the diversionary attack. The troops were formed up in assembly positions near Hébuterne, then:

The bombardment which was most effectual commenced at 7.16am and at 7.37am the first wave moved forward followed by the remaining ones exactly in accordance with orders. The line advanced in excellent order and the movements went like clockwork, so much so that by 7.50am all our objectives were reached. By 8.07am the work of consolidation had commenced. Soon after this the first serious opposition was encountered in the shape of strong enemy bombing parties whose advance was covered by snipers ... Heavy machine gun fire was also opened. Bad casualties began to occur and A Company ... had to be reinforced by a platoon as they were having a hard fight in Gommecourt Park where hostile troops were particularly active. Bombs now began to run short and German ones were freely used. Owing to the very heavy and accurate barrage across no-man's-land the reserve company, although attempting it several times, were unable to get across with reinforcements and extra ammunition and bombs. The situation now became serious as our men were being driven out of the enemy's second and third line trenches by strong bombing parties, and finally men began to withdraw to our own lines ... at 8.45pm we had no unwounded men except those who had [been] taken prisoners in the hostile trenches. It seems probable that although the actual attack was unsuccessful and was very costly, we killed a large number of Germans, but undoubtedly the attack failed on account of the lack of success by the division on our left and also because we were unable to get the reserve company across with the supply of bombs that were so urgently needed. 2nd- During the early hours of the morning a good many wounded were brought in, but hostile machine guns were active which prevented much being done.

One of the officers who took part in the attack reported, 'It was really magnificent the way every man, cool and collected, strolled out through quite a stiff barrage.' The battalion's total casualties on 1–2 July were 588.

INGRAM, Francis Wilton

Age:	33
Rank:	Rifleman
Regiment/Service:	London Regiment (London Rifle Brigade)
Unit:	1/5th Battalion
Service Number:	301715
Died:	1 July 1916
Cemetery/Memorial:	Thiepval
Reference:	9D

Born in Stanwell, Middlesex, son of a congregational minister. An insurance clerk, Francis was living in Enfield in 1911 and had previously lived in Ilford. By 1914 he was living at Hellvellyn, Rotherfield Road, Carshalton.

RUMSEY, John Crook

Age:	21
Rank:	Lance Corporal
Regiment/Service:	London Regiment (London Rifle Brigade)
Unit:	1/5th Battalion

Service Number: 100
Died: 7 July 1916
Cemetery/Memorial: Etretat Churchyard
Reference: II.D.19

CWGC Notes: Son of Annie Rumsey, of 'Broomfield', Queen Mary's Avenue, Carshalton, and the late William Edward Rumsey.

Better known as 'Jack', he had previously been sent home wounded in June 1915. He died of wounds most likely incurred during the battalion's action on 1 July. He was probably evacuated to No. 1 General Hospital in Etretat near Le Havre, but died before he could be transferred back to England.

WARNER, Archibald

'They shall shine as the stars for ever & ever'

Age: 32
Rank: Second Lieutenant
Regiment/Service: London Regiment (London Rifle Brigade)
Unit: 1/5th Battalion
Died: 1 July 1916
Cemetery/Memorial: Hebuterne Military Cemetery
Reference: IV.D.7

(Whitgift School)

CWGC Notes: Son of John Warner, of Waddon House, Croydon; husband of Norah E. Marriage (formerly Warner), of The Parsonage, Broomfield, Essex. Served as Pte. in 3rd Bn. Artists' Rifles.

Born in Waddon and attended Whitgift Grammar School between 1896 and 1898, The Limes in Croydon, and Leighton Park School, Reading. Archibald was secretary of Croydon Borough Swimming Society, a water polo player, captained the boat at Queen's College, Cambridge, and was captain of Reigate Priory Football Club. A solicitor by profession, he married in September 1914 and lived at 'Penarth', Carshalton. He joined the Artists' Rifles in June 1915 and was commissioned to the London Rifle Brigade in October that year. A soldier who was with Archibald during the attack on 1 July recounted that the heavy machine gun fire forced them to take cover in a shell hole. Despite the losses already incurred, Archibald was clear that they had to obey their orders and proceed forward; he stood up and within a few seconds had been riddled with bullets. Archibald's brothers Evan and Bertram were also killed during the war, but are not commemorated on Carshalton war memorial.

Two other local men, both in other battalions of the London Regiment, were also casualties of the attack at Gommecourt.

EVANS, Reginald Ernest Kenneth

Age:	23
Rank:	Rifleman
Regiment/Service:	London Regiment
	(The Rangers)
Unit:	12th Battalion
Service Number:	471554 / 4342
Died:	1 July 1916
Cemetery/Memorial:	Gommecourt British Cemetery
	No. 2, Hébuterne
Reference:	I.B.14

(Paul Evans)

Reginald was born in Carshalton and lived with his
family in Rochester Road. The battalion history records that:

> The hours before the attack were far from pleasant, and heavy shelling gave
> us many casualties. Our intense bombardment, the largest of the kind that had
> been effected up to that date in the war, started at 6.25am. The Boche artillery
> retaliated considerably, though the explosions of their shells, unless very near,
> were drowned by the noise of our own bombardment. This lasted up to 7.30am
> when the artillery lifted on to the final objectives, and the infantry, covered by
> a smoke screen, moved forward to the attack. The battalion had a particularly
> difficult task in front of it. With the exception of the Queen's Victoria Rifles it
> had to cross a wider stretch of no-man's-land than any other battalion in the
> two divisions attacking Gommecourt Wood.[37]

The battalion suffered most of its killed and wounded from the numerous
German machine guns entrenched in and around the wood. Casualties were
forty-nine killed, 347 wounded and 182 missing.

WAIND, Arthur

Age:	31
Rank:	Rifleman
Regiment/Service:	London Regiment (Queen's Westminster Rifles)
Unit:	1/16th Battalion
Service Number:	4225
Died:	1 July 1916
Cemetery/Memorial:	Thiepval
Reference:	13C

CWGC Notes: Son of the late Frederick Waind; husband of Edith M. Waind, of
The Gables, New Earswick, York.

A Yorkshireman, Arthur was born in Heworth in 1885. He was an insurance clerk
by profession and was married in York in 1914; it is not clear why he moved to

Carshalton but by 1916 was living at 'Coniston', 28 Avenue Road. He was presumed killed on 1 July whilst with No. 2 section HQ bombers. The battalion encountered heavier resistance than was expected and found that the artillery barrage had not cut the barbed wire. Communication was poor and many of the officers leading the attack were killed or wounded. Although they managed to advance as far as the German third line, reinforcements could not be brought up due to the enemy artillery bombardment. Also lacking hand grenades, the remaining men were eventually driven out of the German trenches and back to the British lines. Casualties amounted to eighteen killed, 123 wounded and thirty-three missing. Arthur is commemorated in the 'King's Book of York Fallen Heroes' at York Minster. His picture appeared in the *Territorial Services Gazette* on 26 August alongside an appeal for further information from his wife. Two weeks later the publication reported that the photo:

> was recognised by a comrade who is in a military hospital at Blackpool, who wrote to her stating that he spoke to Rifleman Waind and they bound up each other's wounds – Waind's was a flesh wound in the arm. A few minutes before, nearly all in the trench were made prisoners, but the lad at Blackpool managed to escape and reached the British lines at midnight, receiving two more wounds on the journey. In all probability Mrs Waind will get a card from Germany. We hope so for her sake.

On 30 September further details were furnished:

> A letter has been received by Mrs Waind from a comrade who was with him in a shell hole between the second and third German lines on July 1st, when Rifleman Waind was very seriously wounded. He attended to him and made him as comfortable as possible and then had to leave him. He thinks Waind may have been taken prisoner as the wounded had to be left behind.

It seems Arthur died of the wounds he sustained, but in March 1917 his wife was still requesting any further information about her missing husband via the *Territorial Services Gazette*.

Although the diversionary attack had been a success, the two British divisions involved had suffered over 2,500 men killed and many more wounded. Six of those killed were men from Carshalton.

The Battle of Albert is the name given to the opening phase of the main attack on day one of the Somme campaign and operations until 13 July. George Allen, Harty Ayling and Sidney Godfrey were all involved in the Border Regiment's attack on the Beaucourt Redoubt, just south of Beaumont Hamel at the northern edge of the main operations. At 7.20 a.m. a huge mine was blown beneath the Hawthorn Ridge Redoubt, but this alerted the Germans that an attack was imminent. The attack commenced at 7.30 a.m., the battalion war diary stating:

The 1st Battalion … then went over the top from our support line, and over our first line, the bridges over our front trench having been ranged by the German machine gunners the day previously. We met with heavy losses while crossing these bridges and passing through the lanes out in our wire. The men were absolutely magnificent, and formed up as ordered outside our wire, made a right incline, and advanced into 'no-man's-land' at a slow walk, also as ordered. The advance was continued until only little groups of half a dozen men were left here and there and these, finding that no reinforcements were in sight, took cover in shell holes or wherever they could.

By 8 a.m. the advance had ground to a halt. From a total of 822 men, 639 were dead, wounded, or missing – over 77 per cent of their original strength.

ALLEN, George Victor

Age:	19
Rank:	Private
Regiment/Service:	Border Regiment
Unit:	1st Battalion
Service Number:	23044
Died:	1 July 1916
Cemetery/Memorial:	Thiepval
Reference:	6A & 7C

George was an errand boy and lived at 119 Avenue Villas. He enlisted in July 1915, lying about his age which he gave as 19 years 3 months; born in 1898, he was in fact only 18, and had just turned 19 when he was killed a year later. Sent overseas in November 1915, he served in the East Surrey Regiment before being posted to the Border Regiment.

AYLING, Harty

Age:	24
Rank:	Lance Corporal
Regiment/Service:	Border Regiment
Unit:	D Company, 1st Battalion
Service Number:	22764
Died:	1 July 1916
Cemetery/Memorial:	Hawthorn Ridge Cemetery No. 2, Auchonvillers
Reference:	B.65

CWGC Notes: Husband of Margaret Hill Ayling, of 26, C Block, Sutton's Buildings, City Rd, London.

Harty lived in Cowper Avenue then at 20 William Street, the Wrythe. A skin mill labourer and leather dresser, he married in 1912 and had three children, the youngest of whom was born just eleven days before he died. Like George Allen, he had served with the East Surrey Regiment before being transferred to the Border Regiment. He was reported as missing after the first day of the Somme and declared killed in action at the end of July. He is also commemorated on Sutton war memorial, and was the cousin of John Morris who was killed in 1917.

GODFREY, Sidney Horace

Age:	19
Rank:	Private
Regiment/Service:	Border Regiment
Unit:	1st Battalion
Service Number:	22985
Died:	1 July 1916
Cemetery/Memorial:	Hawthorn Ridge Cemetery No. 2, Auchonvillers
Reference:	B.84

Born in Sutton, Sidney was a milkman who lived at 16 Station Road, Carshalton. He joined the East Surrey Regiment in March 1915 and went to France in November of that year. Initially reported missing, at the end of October 1916 he was declared killed in action.

Further south, XV Corps attacked the village of Fricourt in an attempt to encircle it and cut it off. The village had been heavily fortified by the Germans with numerous deep dugouts and machine gun emplacements.

PAYNE, Sydney

Age:	21
Rank:	Corporal
Regiment/Service:	East Yorkshire Regiment
Unit:	1st Battalion
Service Number:	8545
Died:	1 July 1916
Cemetery/Memorial:	Thiepval
Reference:	2C

CWGC Notes: Husband of Frances Grover (formerly Payne), of 10 Ladywell Park, Lewisham, London.

Sydney was born in Sutton. The family were living in Robin Hood Cottages in 1891 but by 1901 had moved to 18 Sutton Grove. In 1911 they were living at 11 Rectory Road but Sydney was not living with them. He was in the Regular Army prior to war breaking out, and went overseas in September 1914. His battalion was on the left flank of the attack on Fricourt, tasked with clearing the Germans from the trenches and woods to the north of the village:

The battalion moved up to the assembly trenches on the night of 30th–31st … On the way up Second Lieutenant Gatrell was killed and three other ranks wounded while in the communication trenches, the battalion getting into place at 3.30am in its position of assembly. A heavy and continuous shelling was maintained throughout the night, which at 6.30am became intense and continued until 7.30am. When the artillery barrage lifted off the German front line the infantry moved forward to the assault … Although our bombardment had been very severe and the German trenches were badly damaged, there were still a few machine guns untouched and these took a heavy toll of the battalion. In spite of heavy losses the brigade pushed on and seized the first objective i.e. the Crucifix Trench and the sunken road, though the Shelter Wood and Birch Tree Wood on the north flank still remained in German hands. This objective was reached at about 8.15am … At about 2pm the Germans counter-attacked in a half-hearted manner from the direction of Shelter Wood, but were repulsed. It was impossible to advance further owing to the heavy casualties the brigade had incurred. All efforts were directed towards consolidating the position and holding the ground already won. Our artillery vigorously bombarded Shelter Wood and its vicinity to which the enemy replied on the sunken road, but his range was not good and although the fire was at times hot few casualties resulted.

The battalion remained in that position until relieved the following morning. Casualties during the period 1–4 July were nineteen officers and 441 other ranks. Sydney's name is also on Sutton war memorial and St Barnabas church memorial.

GILBERT, Claude Herbert Edwin

'The dead in Christ shall rise first. Thessalonians 1st Chp. 4 Verse 16'

Age:	26
Rank:	Private
Regiment/Service:	West Yorkshire Regiment (Prince of Wales's Own)
Unit:	10th Battalion
Service Number:	16042
Died:	1 July 1916
Cemetery/Memorial:	Fricourt New Military Cemetery
Reference:	C.16

CWGC Notes: Son of Mr and Mrs Edwin Gilbert, of Carshalton.

Claude was born in Carshalton and was a painter. He enlisted in September 1914 and went to France in July 1915. The battalion was part of the 50th Brigade, 21st Division, and assaulted Fricourt itself in four lines along a front of 600 yards. Two lines got through to the German fourth line (helped by the detonation of large mines under the German trenches) but were cut off, the attack on the left having failed. Once the Germans had recovered from the shock of the mine explosions, they inflicted heavy casualties with their machine guns. These fired from enfilading positions on the third and fourth lines trying to cross no-man's-land, bringing the attack to a standstill. Casualties were twenty-two officers (including the battalion commanding officer and the second in command) and approximately 688 other ranks – the highest for a single battalion on the first day of the Somme.[38] Claude was killed in action, and Fricourt remained in German hands.

Nine men from Carshalton were part of the 7th Battalion The Queen's (Royal West Surrey Regiment). The battalion was in the 18th Division, formed in September 1914, and most of the men had arrived in France with the division at the end of July 1915. They did not participate in the campaign of late 1915, and, although they had spent time in the front line, the Somme was the battalion's first major engagement. They took part in the attack on the village of Montauban at the eastern edge of the British sector, assaulting the German trenches on a front of about 400 yards. After reaching the German second line they were held up by a machine gun being fired from the third line. Unsupported and without communication, they pushed on and secured their first objective, taking over 160 German prisoners. After twelve hours' fighting, the final objective west of Montauban was reached and consolidated on a front of about 260 yards, one of the few successful results of the day. Casualties amounted to 181 killed, 293 wounded and fifty-eight missing – in all the 18th Division suffered nearly 4,000 casualties.

BAKER, Arthur Sidney

Age:	21
Rank:	Private
Regiment/Service:	The Queen's (Royal West Surrey Regiment)
Unit:	7th Battalion
Service Number:	G/1949
Died:	1 July 1916
Cemetery/Memorial:	Thiepval
Reference:	5D & 6D

CWGC Notes: Son of William and Harriet Baker, of 19 St John's Rd, Carshalton.

Born in the Wrythe, Arthur worked as a shop boy before joining up.

CHURCHER, Gilbert Alfred

'Till we all meet again'

Age:	26
Rank:	Private
Regiment/Service:	The Queen's (Royal West Surrey Regiment)
Unit:	7th Battalion
Service Number:	G/1583
Died:	1 July 1916
Cemetery/Memorial:	Dantzig Alley Cemetery, Mametz
Reference:	VIII.Q.I

CWGC Notes: Son of Mrs E. Weston, of 2 Western Rd, Burgess Hill, Sussex.

Gilbert was born in Hambledon, Hampshire. In 1911 he was a resident of Haywards Heath, living off private means. He later moved to 31 Bernard Road, Wallington.

DUFF, Sidney

Age:	35
Rank:	Private
Regiment/Service:	The Queen's (Royal West Surrey Regiment)
Unit:	7th Battalion
Service Number:	5658
Died:	1 July 1916
Cemetery/Memorial:	Dantzig Alley British Cemetery, Mametz
Reference:	VIII.N.2

CWGC Notes: Husband of Hilda Duff, of 21 Mitre St, Buckingham.

Born in Carshalton, Sidney was the youngest of nine children. The Duff family lived at 78 Mill Place, but by 1911 Sidney was living with his sister and her husband in West Street working as a carman. He married in 1912 and had a son. Visiting his grave on a bitterly cold morning in February 2013, I was touched to find that a small metal cross sits at the base of his grave, placed there by his granddaughter Marilyn in 1991.

The cross at the base of Sidney's grave in Dantzig Alley British Cemetery. (Author's collection)

KING, Frederick Thomas Payne

Age:	26
Rank:	Private
Regiment/Service:	The Queen's (Royal West Surrey Regiment)
Unit:	7th Battalion
Service Number:	G/1468
Died:	1 July 1916
Cemetery/Memorial:	Thiepval
Reference:	5D & 6D

CWGC Notes: Son of James Henry King, of 5 St John's Rd, the Wrythe, Carshalton.

A leather work labourer by trade, Frederick is also commemorated on the Willie Bird cross.

KIRBY, Thomas

Age:	34
Rank:	Private
Regiment/Service:	The Queen's (Royal West Surrey Regiment)
Unit:	7th Battalion
Service Number:	G/1890
Died:	1 July 1916
Cemetery/Memorial:	Thiepval
Reference:	5D & 6D

(Hazel Kirby)

Born in Lincolnshire, a skin mill labourer, and lived in St James Road. Thomas also played football for Carshalton Athletic. He enlisted in early September 1914, and his name is also on the Willie Bird cross. Brother of David Kirby.

NORTH, William John

Age:	29
Rank:	Private
Regiment/Service:	The Queen's (Royal West Surrey Regiment)
Unit:	7th Battalion
Service Number:	G/2107
Died:	1 July 1916
Cemetery/Memorial:	Thiepval
Reference:	5D & 6D

CWGC Notes: Son of the late William North and of Mary E. North (step-mother), late of 50 West St, Carshalton.

Born in Cardiff, William was a labourer and enlisted in September 1914.

SHEARMAN, Francis James

Age:	20
Rank:	Private
Regiment/Service:	The Queen's (Royal West Surrey Regiment)
Unit:	7th Battalion
Service Number:	G/1388
Died:	1 July 1916
Cemetery/Memorial:	Thiepval
Reference:	5D & 6D

(Sutton Grammar School)

Born in Brockley, Francis attended Sutton County School from 1909 to 1911 and lived with his family at 'Tarrys', Hill Road. He enlisted in September 1914 and was promoted to corporal before arriving in France. During the attack he was shot above the leg. A shell exploded near a shell hole in which he was taking cover, killing him. His name is also on the memorial at Sutton Grammar School.

STRACEY, Eustace

Age:	22
Rank:	Lance Sergeant
Regiment/Service:	The Queen's (Royal West Surrey Regiment)
Unit:	7th Battalion
Service Number:	G/1476
Died:	1 July 1916
Cemetery/Memorial:	Thiepval
Reference:	5D & 6D

Born in Carshalton and lived in Mill House, Butter Hill. In 1911 he was working as an iron foundry labourer, living at 3 Devonshire Road.

HERBERT, Jesse
'Gone to the city of God'

Age:	27
Rank:	Private
Regiment/Service:	The Queen's (Royal West Surrey Regiment)
Unit:	7th Battalion
Service Number:	5818
Died:	2 July 1916
Cemetery/Memorial:	La Neuville British Cemetery, Corbie
Reference:	I.A.46

CWGC Notes: Son of Thomas Herbert, of Sunbury, Middx; husband of M.E. Herbert, of 26 St John's Rd, Carshalton.

Born in Whitton, Middlesex. In 1911 Jesse was living at 2 Palmerston Road with his wife and daughter, working as a decorator. He went overseas at the end of August 1915. It is likely that he died of wounds received in action during the battalion's attack on Montauban. La Neuville was the site of No. 21 Casualty Clearing Station, part of the chain of evacuation for wounded soldiers.

The 8th Battalion of the East Surrey Regiment was also part of the 18th Division's attack on Montauban. One of the battalion's officers, Captain Wilfred 'Billie' Nevill, famously gave the men footballs to dribble across no-man's-land. After the battle they became known as the 'football battalion'.[39]

LONG, Frank

Age:	35
Rank:	Private
Regiment/Service:	East Surrey Regiment

Unit:	8th Battalion
Service Number:	11777
Died:	1 July 1916
Cemetery/Memorial:	Thiepval
Reference:	6B & 6C

Frank was born in Carshalton and lived at 25 Harold Road. He was married with five children and worked as a brick maker before joining the army in September 1915. He died during the attack on Montauban Ridge:

From midnight on, the enemy shelled our front line and the assembly trenches mostly with 10.5cm and 15cm shells knocking in the trenches in several places and several small dugouts, causing a total of 13 casualties, three killed and ten being wounded. Enemy artillery was less active from about 5am until 6.30am when he started an intense but distributed bombardment ... At 7.27am B Company started to move out to their wire, Captain Nevill strolling quietly ahead of them, giving an occasional order to keep the dressing square on to the line of advance. This company took four footballs out with them which they were seen to dribble forward into the smoke of our intense bombardment on the Hun front line. The first part of B Company's advance was made with very few casualties, but when the barrage lifted to the second Hun trench, a very heavy rifle and machine gun fire started from our front and left, the latter coming apparently from the craters and the high ground immediately behind them. At 7.50am the Adjutant reported that the battalion was in the German trenches. Hand to hand fighting went on for a long time in the German trenches ... At 8.40am the Adjutant again reported heavy fire from the left causing us a large number of casualties ... At 9.49am a message was intercepted from the craters that the enemy was still holding out in the craters and the high ground ... At 10.30am a message was received ... that the enemy were leaving Mill Trench and Mine Alley and converging on the mill and the orchard, also that they were seen to have machine guns with them. We ordered an immediate intense bombardment on these two points, and this was done practically at once ... The bombardment of the mill and the orchard continued most satisfactorily, and when the line went forward from Breslau Alley and Mill Trench at 12.10pm not a shot was fired from our immediate front, and it was decided to carry on from Mill Trench to Mine Alley, and after a short halt there and finding that the artillery evidently having seen our men go forward had lifted, the whole of the East Surreys advanced to the road west of Montauban, which they reached at 12.22pm with their right resting on the two westerly houses of Montauban, their left about 100 yards east of the orchard ... the whole brigade objective was reached by 1.30pm. Captain Gimson had arrived close behind Major Irwin, and later L/C Brame turned up with a bottle of champagne to be drunk in Montauban 'on der tag'. This bottle was sent round from officer to officer ... At the junction of Mine Alley and Mill Trench where the brigade had ordered a strongpoint to be made we suffered several regrettable casualties ... It was hard to know where to put the men for safety, but as the top of Mine Alley seemed to be suffering somewhat less all men were moved forward. At 9pm a party of Suffolks reported with 25 canvas buckets of water, which were extremely welcome … 2nd July. From midnight on the enemy steadily shelled Mill Trench and the Montauban Road and Mine Alley, 5.9" howitzer shells bursting regularly at the rate of about two per minute. The men were dog tired and there was nowhere else for them to lie except in the bottom of the trench. Carrying parties and relieving troops coming up and wounded and returning parties coming down all tried to force a passage.

Although the battalion reached their objective, casualties were heavy; 148 men were killed, 276 wounded and twenty missing. Billie Nevill never got to see if his footballs made it to the German trenches – he was killed leading the advance and is buried in Carnoy Military Cemetery. Frank Long's name is also inscribed on the memorial in St Barnabas church.

Overall, the gains from the first day's fighting were limited. The expected breakthroughs had been achieved in only a few places, and in the northern sector the front line remained almost as it had at the start of the day. The British had suffered nearly 60,000 casualties, of whom almost 20,000 had been killed. Nineteen of Carshalton's men lay dead on the battlefield, and it is hard to imagine the impact on the village when reports of these men's deaths reached home.

Despite the heavy casualties incurred on 1 July, Haig took the decision to persist with the attacks the following day, reasoning that:

In view of the general situation at the end of the first day's operations, I decided that the best course was to press forward on a front extending from our junction with the French to a point halfway between La Boisselle and Contalmaison, and to limit the offensive on our left for the present to a slow and methodical advance. North of the Ancre such preparations were to be made as would hold the enemy to his positions, and enable the attack to be resumed there later if desirable.[40]

STEVENS, Frederick John

Age:	18
Rank:	Private
Regiment/Service:	The Queen's (Royal West Surrey Regiment)
Unit:	1st Battalion
Service Number:	L/10984
Died:	3 July 1916
Cemetery/Memorial:	Béthune Town Cemetery
Reference:	V.F.41

CWGC Notes: Son of John and Ada Stevens, of 'Ferndale', Butter Hill, Carshalton.

Born in Carshalton and worked as a grocer's assistant. It is possible Frederick lied about his age when he joined up; he said he was exactly 18 when he enlisted in April 1915. At the end of June and beginning of July the battalion was in the line at Cuinchy and suffered a steady trickle of casualties from enemy trench mortars, shelling and rifle grenades. On 3 July they suffered four killed and two wounded by German 'minnies' before being relieved and coming out of the front line at 10.30 p.m.

On 7 July the 38th (Welsh) Division, one of the New Army divisions, assaulted Mametz Wood.

BROWN, Herbert Leslie

Age:	25
Rank:	Lance Corporal
Regiment/Service:	Welsh Regiment
Unit:	16th Battalion
Service Number:	24165
Died:	7 July 1916
Cemetery/Memorial:	Thiepval
Reference:	7A & 10A

CWGC Notes: Son of the late William and Jane Brown.

Herbert lived at 33 Sutton Grove and worked as a bricklayer. He went to France in December 1915. On 7 July the battalion was situated in Carnoy:

8.30am- Battalion, under orders, drawn up on their own side of slope facing Mametz Wood in lines of platoons with a two platoon frontage … Our artillery ceased firing at wood at 8.30am, and first lines of battalion proceeded over the crest of the slope but came instantly under heavy machine gun frontal fire from Mametz Wood, and enfilade fire from Flat Iron Copse and Sabot Copse and the German second system, which was between Mametz Wood and Bazentin Le Petit Wood. Battalion suffered heavily and had to withdraw to their side of crest. Battalion made two more attacks, but position was much too exposed for any hope of success, and orders were received to cease operations … Our losses – six officers killed, six wounded, 268 other ranks killed, missing and wounded. Weather very wet, this adding greatly to exhaustion of troops.

Herbert is also commemorated on the Sutton and St Barnabas church memorials.

The attack had failed. Two brigades attacked Mametz Wood from the south three days later and succeeded, but with heavy casualties.

STANBRIDGE, Thomas Henry

Age:	21
Rank:	Private
Regiment/Service:	Queen's Own (Royal West Kent)
Unit:	C Company, 7th Battalion
Service Number:	G/2266
Died:	13 July 1916
Cemetery/Memorial:	Thiepval
Reference:	11C

CWGC Notes: Son of Albert Henry and Sarah Elizabeth Stanbridge, of 2 Greenside Breech Lane, Walton-on-the-Hill, Tadworth.

Thomas was born in 1895 in Balham. By the time of the 1901 census the Stanbridge family were living on Avenue Road, Carshalton. By 1911 they had moved again to Little Woodcote Farm, Upper Wallington, where Thomas worked as a shepherd. He enlisted in Croydon on 8 September 1914 and went overseas in July 1915. Thomas was assumed dead on 13 July 1916; he was probably killed that night when the 250 men of the 7th Battalion were attacked numerous times by German forces. In the early hours of that day the battalion had moved into positions near Trônes Wood, despite the Germans shelling the wood and the approaches to it. Later that morning orders were received that the battalion was to attack the wood. British artillery started their bombardment at 4 p.m., prompting a retaliatory barrage from the Germans. The attack commenced at 7 p.m. and at first progressed satisfactorily, but owing to the determined resistance of the enemy and the dense undergrowth, matted with fallen trees, the men were split up and had difficulty keeping in touch. This was accentuated by the heavy casualties among officers and NCOs. The men became scattered in small parties, in some cases with the Germans both in front and behind. Attempts were made to reorganise them, and a series of strongpoints were established inside the northern boundary of the wood. From these, patrols pushed out to the apex. However, some pockets of men were still surrounded by the enemy and were attacked throughout the night. The wood was finally cleared by 8.30 a.m. on 14 July with the help of reinforcements. Casualties over the two days were thirty-three killed, 182 wounded and thirty-three missing.

In June 1917 Private Stanbridge's mother, now living at 26 St John's Road, Carshalton, wrote to the War Office:

> Dear Sir,
>
> I am writing to know if you could give me any information of my son Thomas Henry Stanbridge 2266 Royal West Kent Regiment who has been reported wounded missing since last July 13th 1916 and we have never heard anything of him since. Being his mother I feel very worried about him. If you could kindly give me any satisfactory answer about him I should be very much obliged.

It is not clear whether Mrs Stanbridge received a response, but on 26 July 1917 a note was placed in her son's service record stating 'Regarded for official purposes as having died on or since 13.7.16.'

The second 'phase' of the Battle of the Somme, the Battle of Bazentin Ridge, started on 14 July. Following a short artillery barrage, the German troops were surprised by the dawn attack.

The 7th Division, of which the 2nd Battalion The Queen's was part, quickly captured their objective and moved on to take Bazentin Le Petit. They then went on to attack High Wood in the early evening.

ROGERS, Frederick Charles

Age:	39
Rank:	Private
Regiment/Service:	The Queen's (Royal West Surrey Regiment)
Unit:	2nd Battalion
Service Number:	G/814
Died:	14 July 1916
Cemetery/Memorial:	Caterpillar Valley Cemetery, Longueval
Reference:	XVI.G.22

Born in Usk, Monmouthshire, Frederick was married in 1909 and had three daughters and a son. He lived in Southdown Road, Wallington and worked as a builder's labourer. His battalion's attack on High Wood began on the evening of 14 July and successfully captured most of it, but the Germans doggedly held on to portions of the wood in the north. Several casualties in the battalion were caused by British artillery trying to drive the Germans

(Cheryl Rogers)

out through shell fire – unfortunately, many of their shells fell short. The battalion's casualties on 14–16 July were in excess of 300. Frederick was the brother of Carshalton casualties Percival and Albert Rogers.

On the right flank of the attack the 18th Division assaulted Trônes Wood, near Guillemont.

SEYMOUR, Leonard Maurice

Age:	21
Rank:	Private
Regiment/Service:	The Queen's (Royal West Surrey Regiment)
Unit:	7th Battalion
Service Number:	G/1897

Died: 14 July 1916
Cemetery/Memorial: Thiepval
Reference: 5D & 6D

CWGC Notes: Son of Isaac Seymour, of 13 Hale Cottages, Carshalton Rd, Carshalton.

Born in Streatham, Leonard was a gardener before joining the army in September 1914 and being sent to France in July 1915. The 7th Queen's began their assault of Trônes Wood at 7 p.m. over a front of 750 yards:

> Battalion, on assaulting was met by very heavy rifle, machine gun and shell fire and the advance was definitely checked owing to no supporting troops being to hand. The enemy would appear to have suffered very little damage from our bombardment as he developed very heavy rifle fire ... At 8.50pm a message was received that northern portion of Trones Wood would be re-bombarded and that attack was not to be pressed if success seemed unlikely. At 9pm remainder of battalion and 7th Buffs reorganised for defence of Longueval Alley in conjunction with present garrison. At 12.30am 14th July Instructions were received that battalion might withdraw to German old front line system if Longueval Alley was sufficiently held. At 2.30am battalion withdrew to Bedford Trench. Casualties, officers 13, other ranks 216.

Leonard's name is also on the memorial in St Barnabas church.

Whilst the day's assaults had been successful, the casualties were still high – over 9,000 in total. The following day the attack on High Wood continued.

PICKERING, Frank

Age: 21
Rank: Rifleman
Regiment/Service: King's Royal Rifle Corp
Unit: 16th Battalion
Service Number: C/1600
Died: 15 July 1916
Cemetery/Memorial: Thiepval
Reference: 13A & 13B

CWGC Notes: Son of Merrishaw and Frances Pickering, of Littleworth, Wing, Leighton Buzzard, Beds.

Born in Wing, Frank lived in Leighton Buzzard but enlisted in Sutton, where he had been living with his aunt and uncle in Wrythe Lane and

(Roger Pickering)

working as a gas fitter. He fell in action at High Wood, where his battalion was in support of the attack. They were ordered to advance at 9 a.m. after the artillery barrage lifted, and had to cross 1,000 yards of open ground. C Company on the left immediately came under machine gun fire, causing heavy casualties. Upon reaching the sunken road between the north-east corner of Bazentin Le Petit and the north-west corner of High Wood, the lead battalions could not advance due to the wire being uncut and heavy enfilade fire, so the company remained in this position the rest of the day. B Company on the right fared little better, with only two of their number being uninjured. In the late morning D Company was sent up as reinforcements and made it to the south edge of High Wood, where they remained all day under shell and sniper fire until withdrawing at 8 p.m. and being relieved at 3 a.m. A Company made it to the south-east edge of the wood, advancing over the open towards it once the artillery barrage lifted. Many casualties were caused by German machine guns in the wood. By the end of the day the company was spread out around the edge of the wood but had not gained a foothold inside it. Casualties amounted to ninety-one killed.

Frank had been a bell ringer at All Saints church, Carshalton, and in February 1919 the church bells were rung in his memory. His name is in the Great War Memorial Book of Church Bell Ringers, which is on display at St Paul's Cathedral; in addition he is commemorated on the Willie Bird cross and the war memorial at All Saints church, Wing.

Not all of Carshalton's casualties during this period occurred in the Somme offensive. In the Ypres sector the line was still being held and casualties incurred.

HAMLYN, Alfred Ernest
'Love is stronger than death'

Age:	29
Rank:	Second Lieutenant
Regiment/Service:	Duke of Cornwall's Light Infantry
Unit:	7th Battalion
Died:	16 July 1916
Cemetery/Memorial:	Lijssenthoek Military Cemetery
Reference:	IX.A.4

CWGC Notes: Son of Frederic and Alice Hamlyn, of 'Beechwood', Carshalton Rd, Sutton. Born at Hackney.

Alfred was educated at Hackney Downs School and King's College, London. He was Managing Director of Hamlyn and Co., and was a Freeman of the City of London. He joined up at the outbreak of the war and was commissioned in August 1915. He went overseas just eight weeks before he was killed near Potijze, 2 miles north-west of Ypres. The battalion war diary recorded 'Fairly quiet here, some shelling. Unfortunately working party in muddy lane under Second Lieutenant Hamlyn were shelled, one shell killing Second Lieutenant Hamlyn and wounding two sergeants and one man.' Alfred is also commemorated on Sutton war memorial and St Barnabas church memorial.

Back on the Somme, the fighting continued.

MADDER, Robert
'Duty and sacrifice'

Age:	28
Rank:	Second Lieutenant
Regiment/Service:	Gloucestershire Regiment
Unit:	3/5th Battalion
Died:	20 July 1916
Cemetery/Memorial:	Bapaume Post Military Cemetery, Albert
Reference:	I.F.10

(Whitgift School)

CWGC Notes: Son of Allan G. and Emily J. Madder, of Westcroft Farm House, Carshalton. Attached 145th Brigade, Machine Gun Corps.

Born in Tooting Graveney and attended Leicester House School (Carshalton) and then Whitgift Grammar School between 1903 and 1904. Robert joined the Peninsular and Oriental Steamship Company (P&O) in 1907 as a clerk. He was a passionate musician and a member of the choir at All Saints church. He enlisted in the London Rifle Brigade in September 1914 whilst living in Prince of Wales Road, Carshalton, and was commissioned in July 1915. He went to France November 1915 and the month before his death had been attached to the Machine Gun Corps. Robert was killed by shell fire as he left a German dugout near the Usna Redoubt, just off the Albert–La Boisselle road. His captain said, 'I have lost an excellent officer, of a type that cannot be easily replaced, and as a man and a member of our mess we had a great affection for him.' A plaque in All Saints church reads:

> To the glory of God and in proud and loving memory of Robert Madder, 2nd Lieut. Gloucestershire Regt, attd Machine Gun Corps, who was born 11th Dec. 1887 & fell in the Battle of the Somme 20th July 1916, the Lenten Cross was given by his Father Mother & two Sisters, to be borne before the Choir, of which he was a member. All Saints Day 1916. RIP.

Robert is also commemorated on the City of Gloucester war memorial. His sister Emily Winifred Madder painted a picture of the war memorial being unveiled, which is in the London Borough of Sutton's art collection and has previously been on display at Honeywood Museum.

From 15 July troops fought bitterly over Delville Wood near Longueval, commonly referred to as 'Devil's Wood'. The wood needed to be cleared to secure the British right flank prior to launching further attacks on the German lines. The battle for the wood proved extremely costly, particularly to the South African troops who fought there.

CROCKER, Albert George

Age: 28
Rank: Private
Regiment/Service: East Surrey Regiment
Unit: 1st Battalion
Service Number: 9241
Died: 23 July 1916
Cemetery/Memorial: Thiepval
Reference: 6B & 6C

CWGC Notes: Son of Albert George and Clara E. Crocker of 11 Mill Place, Mill Lane, Carshalton.

Albert was an unmarried labourer who was born in Wallington and lived at 11 Mill Place, Carshalton, before signing up in May 1915. His battalion was in the front line from 19 July, and was heavily shelled over the next few days. Albert was reported missing following an attack to take back parts of Delville and Longueval woods, which the Germans had captured on 19 July. The battalion war diary for 23 July states:

> Our function as a battalion was to capture and hold the two strongpoints … known to contain machine guns. The latter, as it was considered to be partially responsible for the heavy casualties incurred by the 2nd Suffolks on the morning of the 20th, was to be attacked at 3.15am … The former post … was attacked as part of the general assault at 3.40am with great judgement and skill by … a composite party of battalion snipers, sappers and Royal Engineers supported by two platoons of No 4 Company and a Lewis Gun team. The post was captured, one MG was captured and five others put out of action. In addition, it was estimated that some 30 to 40 Germans were killed by grenades and the post successfully consolidated … Our Lewis Guns did good work against the Germans, who seizing their opportunity secured as much ground as possible while our units were reforming … This small but important raid was well planned and equally well executed.

However, the captured post was isolated and the troops had to withdraw. Casualties to 12 noon on 23 July were five officers and an estimated 119 other ranks. The Germans in Delville Wood held on, and the fight for it continued into September.

Another phase of the Somme had also commenced on 23 July: the Battle of Pozières. This village sits on the Albert–Bapaume road and is a high point in the area. Control of the village was thus key for observation. The ridge was bitterly fought over, particularly by the Australians. However, it was not taken until 4 August.

During this period the 7th Battalion East Surrey Regiment was holding trenches north of Ovillers-la-Boisselle, about 1.5 miles down the road towards Bapaume. They clashed several times with the nearby German troops, and the war diary notes the level of artillery bombardments around Pozières at this time.

ULYET, Henry Edward

Age:	36
Rank:	Private
Regiment/Service:	East Surrey Regiment
Unit:	A Company, 7th Battalion
Service Number:	11778
Died:	4 August 1916
Cemetery/Memorial:	Thiepval
Reference:	6B & 6C

CWGC Notes: Son of Henry Edward and Emma Ulyet, of Hoxton, London; husband of Frances Ellen Powell (formerly Ulyet), of 14 Green Close, Carshalton.

A collier stoker, Henry was born in Hoxton and lived at 93 Westmead Road. He enlisted in September 1915 and had been in France for nearly four months when he was killed. The battalion returned to the front line near Ovillers on 30 July and during the night of 3–4 August were in reserve for an attack carried out by the 6th Buffs on some German positions. At 1 a.m. they were ordered to support the Buffs, and by 2.40 a.m. the objectives had been captured. The battalion's A Company returned early in the morning having had one man killed and two wounded whilst consolidating and holding Ration Trench. A further five casualties were caused by German shelling as the battalion was being relieved in the afternoon. Henry left a widow and two young sons, and is also commemorated on Sutton war memorial and St Barnabas church memorial.

The following day the battalion's B Company had to go back into the line to act as reserve.

ADAMS, Albert John

Age:	32
Rank:	Private
Regiment/Service:	East Surrey Regiment
Unit:	7th Battalion
Service Number:	15948
Died:	7 August 1916
Cemetery/Memorial:	Puchevilliers British Cemetery
Reference:	II.D.33

CWGC Notes: Son of Albert and Henrietta Adams, Berkshire.

Born in Ealing, Albert lived at 36 Cranfield Road, Wallington, and was a milk-man. He had moved to Carshalton when his sister married a local coal merchant, and joined up in November 1915. He died of wounds received in action – the battalion war diary for 7 August records that 'B Company under Captain Garnett return from the trenches having had a rather bad time. Casualties two men killed and six wounded, on one occasion 11 men were buried in a dugout but were dug out after about two hours hard work.'

The battalion went back into the front lines on the afternoon of 10 August. Despite enemy shelling and a night time patrol into no-man's-land, no casualties were suffered on 10 or 11 August.

WATKINSON, Edward

Age:	21
Rank:	Corporal
Regiment/Service:	East Surrey Regiment
Unit:	7th Battalion
Service Number:	919
Died:	13 August 1916
Cemetery/Memorial:	Thiepval
Reference:	6B & 6C

CWGC Notes: Son of the late Mr and Mrs C. Watkinson.

Edward was born in Carshalton and in 1911 was living in Sutton working as a draper's assistant before enlisting in September 1914. He was killed in action when the battalion attacked north of Ovillers on 12 August. At 10.30 p.m.:

> The artillery opened an intense bombardment on the enemy's lines until 10.33pm when our companies assaulted the positions ... Both our front line companies went out under cover of our bombardment and worked up as close to our barrage as possible. B Company on assaulting were met with machine gun fire and the enemy put up a barrage of bombs all along their trench, ren-dering it impossible to get near, the men having to get into shell holes and remain where they were ... Two more assaults were made by men of C and B Company neither met with success owing to the bomb barrage ... No more information has been received of D Company ... as far as can be ascertained it appears that D Company worked too much to the left ... D Company's supports never found any trace of the front platoons except a few wounded. All men who saw into the German trench agree that the enemy was in great strength in his trenches and that many had overcoats or packs on, so it is thought that a relief may have been in progress. The ground was exceedingly difficult to keep direction on, on account of the huge craters caused by our bombardment and trench mortars.

There were 169 casualties and missing. Edward was the brother of Oliver Watkinson, who was killed in 1918.

Bertram Caine and Samuel Currier were both serving with the 9th Battalion East Surrey Regiment. The war diary for the day they were killed records that C and D Companies were part of an attack on a German strongpoint (a concrete dugout surrounded by a trench) south-west of Guillemont, a village just over a mile to the south-east of Longueval. The attack was made in three waves of eighty men each. The artillery bombardment commenced at 5.10 p.m. and lasted for half an hour. The war diary states that:

> During the bombardment several of the 18 pounders fired short and caused casualties among our own attacking party in the trenches, during the whole of this bombardment the enemy's machine guns were very active and never ceased firing … At 5.42pm all our three waves left their trenches and advanced in perfect lines towards their objective. No sooner had the first wave left its trenches they were surprised to see the enemy looking over their parapet … The first two waves on approaching the enemy's line first came under very heavy rifle fire, and as they approached still closer to the enemy's trench by a tremendous volley of bombs. Nearly all the men when within a few yards of the trench were either killed or wounded, and only two officers and one or two NCOs actually succeeded in getting into the German trench, they were never seen again. Wounded men and a few that were not wounded jumped into the nearest shell hole and threw bombs at the enemy until exhausted, they crawled back to our trenches during the hours of darkness. The right of the third wave joined the first two waves, the left came under machine gun fire from the direction of Guillemont and were withdrawn … as the first two waves had not been successful.

Casualties were 190 killed, wounded, or missing.

CAINE, Bertram Claude

Age:	19
Rank:	Private
Regiment/Service:	East Surrey Regiment
Unit:	9th Battalion
Service Number:	16236
Died:	16 August 1916
Cemetery/Memorial:	Thiepval
Reference:	6B & 6C

It is possible Bertram's name has been mis-transcribed on the memorial; some sources record his name as Caine and others Came. He was born in Thornton Heath in 1897. In 1911 he was living at 36 Witford Road, West Croydon, with his father (a widower) and two boarders. He was living in Wallington at the time of his enlistment; he may have enlisted underage and only been 18 at the time of his death. His father Claud also enlisted in 1915, giving his address as Chestnut Cottage, Lavender Road.

CURRIER, Samuel Charles

Age:	38
Rank:	Private
Regiment/Service:	East Surrey Regiment
Unit:	9th Battalion
Service Number:	2289
Died:	16 August 1916
Cemetery/Memorial:	Thiepval
Reference:	6B & 6C

CWGC Notes: Husband of Annie L. Currier, of 25 St Andrew's Rd, Carshalton.

(Susan Wicks)

Samuel was born in Sutton in 1878. He grew up in Morland Road, was a Band of Hope cadet, and became an errand boy. As a young man he moved to Marylebone with his brothers where in 1901 he was working as a bus conductor. In 1902 he married and had three children born between 1902 and 1911. By this time he was back in Sutton with his young family, working as a general labourer in the building trade. He entered the war at the end of September 1915. He died of wounds, and is also commemorated on the Willie Bird cross and Sutton war memorial.

The 8th Buffs had moved into front line trenches between Delville Wood and Guillemont. On 18 August they attacked south-east towards the village.

YOUNG, Harry

Age:	34
Rank:	Private
Regiment/Service:	The Buffs (East Kent Regiment)
Unit:	8th Battalion
Service Number:	G/6635
Died:	18 August 1916
Cemetery/Memorial:	Thiepval
Reference:	5D

Harry was born in Hook and in 1911 he and his wife and three daughters were boarding with a family in Avenue Road, Wallington, where Harry worked as a gardener. He had previous service with the 3rd Dragoons. He was killed in action on 18 August. The attack commenced at 2.45 p.m. The assaulting party (C Company plus two platoons of B Company) moved out of their trenches and, keeping under the barrage, successfully reached their objective with very few casualties. One officer and a machine gun towards the southern end of the German trench put up a fight but they were quickly overwhelmed with bombs; the machine gun was captured and at once turned against the enemy. Reinforcements were now ordered up, and the men then attacked 'Machine Gun House', a strongpoint on the road towards Guillemont; this was occupied but the trench was strongly held. Twenty prisoners surrendered in the neighbourhood of this position. The left bombing party then proceeded to work up the trench but met with considerable resistance, especially around the machine gun near the trench junction. This machine gun they captured, as well as forty prisoners. A few casualties were caused by a sniper lying in a shell hole near MG House, but he was quickly dealt with by one of the bombing squads. A third bombing squad blocked and held the enemy trench running towards Guillemont. The position at MG House was quickly consolidated and the communication trench cleared and deepened. The old communication trench back to the left-hand bombing post was found choked with dead from previous attacks and the work on this post was very slow and difficult. Consolidation went on all night. A fresh communication trench was dug from Bosky Trench to the centre of the captured position. Three Vickers and five Lewis guns were placed in the front line. Altogether, about 120 prisoners were captured (including two officers), three machine guns (two of which were subsequently destroyed by shell fire) and many trophies such as automatic pistols, rifles, binoculars, and helmets. Casualties were one officer killed and six wounded, thirty-eight other ranks killed, 297 wounded and sixteen missing.

The Battle of Guillemont took place on 3–6 September, a consolidation exercise in preparation for the next planned offensive at Flers-Courcelette.

GROOMBRIDGE, John Granville

Age:	26
Rank:	Rifleman
Regiment/Service:	Rifle Brigade
Unit:	10th Battalion
Service Number:	S/1318
Died:	3 September 1916
Cemetery/Memorial:	Thiepval
Reference:	16B & 16C

CWGC Notes: Son of James and Susan Groombridge, of 27 Harold Rd, Sutton.

John was born in Sutton and was a member of the Carshalton Athletic football team. He enlisted on 4 September 1914, giving his occupation as 'attendant'. He was killed during the fighting around Guillemont, his brigade tasked with capturing two sunken roads branching out from the south-west corner of the village:

> Up to noon on this day the two battalions waited in the assembly trenches suffering considerable discomfort from overcrowding and casualties from shell fire. At noon, which was zero hour the advance began and proved completely successful ... By 2.30pm the brigade had reached the line of the Ginchy-

Wedgewood road, where they remained. The rest of the day was spent in consolidating the position gained. The night was uneventful.

This brief war diary entry hardly does justice to the difficulties the attacking troops faced. After capturing the first objective, the advancing troops were caught in the open by machine gun fire from a German trench that had not been marked correctly on their maps. The soldiers tried to pin down the Germans with rifle fire until a machine gun could be brought up to provide enfilade fire along the opposing trench. Once this had been done the advance to the second objective continued, one report of the action noting that every German in the resisting trench was killed. The following day the battalion suffered further casualties from shelling. Losses for both days were forty-one other ranks killed, 195 wounded and fifty-four missing. John is included in the casualty report for 3 September, initially reported as wounded. He was the brother of Herbert Groombridge, who died two years later, and is also commemorated on Sutton war memorial and St Barnabas church memorial.

WYATT, Ernest R.

(Liz Moss)

Age:	21
Rank:	Rifleman
Regiment/Service:	King's Royal Rifle Corp
Unit:	11th Battalion
Service Number:	R/2306
Died:	3 September 1916
Cemetery/Memorial:	Thiepval
Reference:	13A & 13B

Son of Havelock and Julia Wyatt, Ernest was born in Carshalton and lived in William Street, the Wrythe, working as a greengrocer. He enlisted in September 1914 (possibly underage) with his cousin Thomas Wyatt. His battalion was part of the 59th Brigade, the same brigade as John Groombridge's battalion, and Ernest was killed in the same attack. The battalion had reached their objective by 1.15 p.m. The war diary notes that 'The German losses must have been considerable as in the first and second sunken roads approximately 150 German dead were counted.' The battalion's losses amounted to twenty-two killed, seventy wounded and two missing. Ernest is also commemorated on the Willie Bird cross.

The attack against Guillemont was a success but the advance in the area continued for three more days.

PALMER, Alfred John

'He is absent from those that loved him, 'twas Jesus that called him away; he is come to the Lord who redeemed him, from night to the splendour of day'

Age:	18
Rank:	Private

Regiment/Service:	The Queen's (Royal West Surrey Regiment)
Unit:	8th Battalion
Service Number:	11877
Died:	17 September 1916 (wounded 5 September 1916)
Cemetery/Memorial:	Benhilton (All Saints) Churchyard
Reference:	62 (SW of church)

CWGC Notes: Son of George and Margaret Palmer, of 13 Stronsa Rd, Shepherd's Bush, London. Born at Sutton.

Alfred was a labourer and lived at 33 Harold Road, Sutton. In the 1901 census he was 2, making him 16 when he enlisted in September 1915 giving his age as 19 years 1 month. He landed in France in June 1916, and on 17 August was admitted to hospital with shellshock. He returned to his battalion and they went into front line trenches at Delville Wood on 30 August. On 5 September he was severely wounded whilst the battalion was being relieved, suffering gunshot wounds to his right leg and arm. He died on 17 September at East Leeds war hospital, and is also commemorated on Sutton war memorial and St Barnabas church memorial.

Three Carshalton men lost their lives on 9 September during the Battle of Ginchy. This village, close to Delville Wood and Guillemont, had to be captured to bring the British line closer to the Germans in further preparation for the major offensive at Flers.

ALLEN, Arthur John

Age:	21
Rank:	Private
Regiment/Service:	London Regiment (Royal Fusiliers)
Unit:	1/4th Battalion
Service Number:	7013
Died:	9 September 1916
Cemetery/Memorial:	Thiepval
Reference:	9D & 16B

In 1911 the family were living at 43 William Street, the Wrythe, and Arthur was working as an errand boy. He later lived in Bunhill Row, St Luke's (London), and worked as a postman. He initially served with the 8th London Regiment (The Post Office Rifles). Arthur died during a confused assault on German trenches at Leuze Wood near Combles, during which many men overshot their intended objectives and were killed by the British artillery barrage. Arthur's name also appears on the Willie Bird cross, Sutton war memorial, and the Sutton Post Office memorial.

Alfred Greenslade and Arthur Sutton were both in the 1/12th London Regiment (The Rangers). The Rangers' record of the attack reads:

On the night of the 8th–9th, the battalion moved up into assembly trenches at the head of Angle Wood Valley just below the crest along which runs the road from Leuze Wood to Guillemont, preparatory to an attack on the enemy's position at Ginchy Telegraph next morning. The attack started at 4.45am on the 9th. Immediately on crossing the ridge in front of the assembly trenches all companies came under very heavy machine-gun and rifle fire. This fire was coming from a German position half left from the line of advance ... The right leading company (C) encountered no enemy during their advance to the first objective except a small party of about twenty in a listening post, the survivors of whom were captured. The left leading company (D) advanced under heavy machine-gun and rifle fire and by the time the company reached the crest of the slope their strength had been reduced considerably. The men were ordered to lie down and open fire on the German trenches which were sited in a basin on the left front of the company ... D Company then advanced to the trench ... which was unoccupied and which they proceeded to consolidate, at the same time keeping up rifle fire on the enemy trenches.[41]

GREENSLADE, Alfred William

Age:	21
Rank:	Rifleman
Regiment/Service:	London Regiment (The Rangers)
Unit:	1/12th Battalion
Service Number:	7528
Died:	9 September 1916
Cemetery/Memorial:	Thiepval
Reference:	9C

CWGC Notes: Son of Mrs Alice E. Harrold, of 111 Westmead Rd, Sutton, Surrey.

Born in Slinfold in Sussex, Alfred was a domestic gardener and a St Barnabas Band of Hope cadet. His name is also on Sutton war memorial and the memorial in St Barnabas church.

SUTTON, Arthur

Age:	28
Rank:	Rifleman
Regiment/Service:	London Regiment (The Rangers)
Unit:	1/12th Battalion
Service Number:	4889
Died:	9 September 1916
Cemetery/Memorial:	Thiepval
Reference:	9C

Born in Twickenham and lived at 1 West Street Lane, Carshalton. Employed as a boot maker.

The village of Ginchy was finally taken that day by men of the 16th (Irish) Division, but casualties were high.

One week later, 15 September saw the start of the largest full-scale attack since the opening of the Somme offensive over two months previously. The Battle of Flers-Courcelette also heralded the introduction of another new weapon: the tank. The attack commenced at dawn and, whilst the advance on the village of Flers itself (supported by the tanks) was successful, in part because many of the Germans simply fled in the face of these new machines, elsewhere the advance faltered and did not reach all of its intended objectives.

Arthur Smith's and Bernard Tate's battalions were both part of XV Corps on the right flank of the attack, which reached most of its objectives.

SMITH, Arthur John

Age:	21
Rank:	Private
Regiment/Service:	East Surrey Regiment
Unit:	12th Battalion
Service Number:	17400
Died:	15 September 1916
Cemetery/Memorial:	Bulls Road Cemetery, Flers
Reference:	III.A.20

CWGC Notes: Son of Samuel and Sarah Smith, of North Road, Amberley, Arundel, Sussex.

Arthur was born in Hardham in Sussex, and in 1911 was living in Amberley working as a sub post office boy. He later lived at 29 West Street, and enlisted in Carshalton. His battalion was not part of the first day of the Somme offensive but moved into the front line trenches on 8 July. It had a 'quiet' period until mid-September. On 15 September seventeen officers and 634 men assembled north-west of Delville Wood:

> At 2am the battalion had taken up its position … The formation was lines of half platoons in file. A Company on the right, D Company on the left. The half platoons were concealed in shell holes … The battalion advanced at 6.15am and took the enemy's first and second line trenches. Although it suffered heavy casualties, losing nearly all the officers, it continued to advance to about 200 yards in front of Flers and occupied enemy trenches there. Casualties: officers 16, other ranks 286.

Arthur is also commemorated on Amberley war memorial.

TATE, Bernard George

Age:	23
Rank:	Rifleman
Regiment/Service:	King's Royal Rifle Corp

Unit:	8th Battalion
Service Number:	A/1284
Died:	15 September 1916
Cemetery/Memorial:	Thiepval
Reference:	13A & 13B

CWGC Notes: Son of William and Victoria Tate, of 21 Cowper Avenue, Sutton.

Bernard was born in Benhilton and had been a patrol leader with 1st Sutton Troop Boy Scouts. He also played football for Carshalton Athletic, and was linked by marriage to Robert Cairns. He enlisted soon after war broke

(Glenys Rands)

out giving his occupation as 'pyrotechnist'. He was killed in action during an operation to capture Switch Trench, located south of Flers, supported by two tanks. The battalion had to advance over 1,000 yards taking another trench (known as Tea Support) on the way. Although the attack was a success the enemy continued to harass the troops with sniper and machine gun fire and artillery barrages. Casualties were 331, including ninety-eight missing. Bernard's name is also inscribed on Sutton war memorial and St Barnabas church memorial.

Although the use of tanks was a breakthrough in terms of mechanised warfare, they were not without their problems; prone to breaking down, very slow and often becoming bogged down in mud or trenches that they were unable to traverse. However the gains made on 15 September were as much as 2,000 yards; several key villages had been taken and High Wood had finally been cleared. It was a huge advance, but not the strategic breakthrough that had been hoped for. Progress over the next few days was minimal as the British needed time to reorganise. Bad weather also hindered further operations and added to the misery of those in the front line.

During the period 25–28 September the Fourth Army attacked along a 6-mile front towards Morval, Lesboeufs and Gueudecourt, capturing all three villages.

DAWSON, Wilfred Charles

'Greater love hath no man than this'

Age:	34
Rank:	Corporal
Regiment/Service:	Royal Field Artillery
Unit:	B Battery, 190th Brigade
Service Number:	46262
Died:	26 September 1916
Cemetery/Memorial:	Longueval Road Cemetery
Reference:	C.8

CWGC Notes: Son of Charles William and Margaret Rachael Dawson, of Great Yarmouth; husband of Marion Dawson, of Florence House, Pakefield, Lowestoft. Headmaster of Carshalton School, Surrey.

Wilfred was educated at Birmingham University and had previously been head-master of a school in Shackleford, near Godalming. His battery of guns was located near Longueval and had begun bombarding the German lines around Gueudecourt on 24 September in preparation for the attack on the village. One man was wounded on 24 September, one killed and one wounded on 25 September, and four wounded on 26 September. Wilfred lies buried alongside another man from his battery who died the same day. He is also commemorated on the Birmingham University and Wallington war memorials.

HACK, John Frederick Charles

'Gone from my sight but memory lives my darling my beloved husband'

Age:	38
Rank:	Lieutenant
Regiment/Service:	Royal Garrison Artillery
Unit:	117th Heavy Battery
Died:	26 September 1916
Cemetery/Memorial:	Longueval Road Cemetery
Reference:	B.16

(The War Illustrated)

Born in Bermondsey, John had worked as a clerk before enlisting in the army in 1897 aged 18. Rising through the ranks he saw service in South Africa and India. He was married in May 1915. The battery war diary states '25/9/16- Advanced to positions left of Trones Wood where centre section rejoined 28/9/16. During the period 13th–30th the battery was heavily engaged but despite adverse circumstances ammunition supplies etc all above moves were successfully carried out.' There is no casualty information, although the diary does confirm that John was with the battery in July. He is also commemorated on Sutton war memorial (his father lived in Thicket Crescent at the time of his son's death), and St Barnabas church memorial.

On 26 September General Gough's Reserve Army attacked Thiepval, one of the objectives from the very first day of the Somme offensive. A high point on the battlefield, its capture would have allowed the British a commanding view of the area and opened the way for further advances. Although the fighting was heavy, Thiepval was captured that day. However, the Schwaben Redoubt, a German strongpoint near Thiepval Wood consisting of a series of trenches and dugouts, still resisted attempts to capture it.

SCOTT, Frederick George

Age:	20
Rank:	Corporal
Regiment/Service:	The Queen's (Royal West Surrey Regiment)
Unit:	7th Battalion
Service Number:	G/7294

Died: 28 September 1916
Cemetery/Memorial: Thiepval
Reference: 5D & 6D

CWGC Notes: Son of George Alfred and Amy Scott, of 27 Victoria Rd, Sutton.

Frederick was born in St John's Wood but later moved to 15 Gordon Cottages, West Street Lane. He worked as a van guard and horse keeper before joining the army, but also cited previous service in the King's Royal Rifles when he joined up. On 14 July he suffered shellshock, most likely incurred during the battalion's attack on Trônes Wood the previous day, and spent several days in hospital. He returned to his battalion and was killed in action on 28 September during their attack on the Schwaben Redoubt:

> The battalion started to leave Blighty Valley at 10.15am. On debouching from north-east corner of Authuille Wood it was seen that all movements between here and Thiepval were in full view of enemy observation balloon … From about 11.30am till after the hour of attack, enemy maintained fairly heavy shrapnel barrage and long range rifle and machine gun fire on the forming up place of the battalion which luckily caused few casualties. At 1pm our artillery barrage opened and the battalion moved forward to the attack. Bulgar Trench was found to be weakly held and the occupants were disposed of without much difficulty. After crossing this trench it was seen that direction, which was extremely difficult to maintain owing to the lack of landmarks and ignorance of the ground of almost the whole battalion, was likely to be lost, as the battalion was inclining slightly to its left and there was an inclination to bunch in the centre. Some opposition was encountered in Martin's Lane and by this time heavy rifle and machine gun fire was coming from south face of Schwaben Redoubt, which caused casualties and checked the leading waves, and [causing] waves to become mixed. The assaulting companies got over Market Trench with some difficulty and were shortly afterwards checked by a strongpoint … the battalion being held up by this point for over an hour … On the battalion's right enemy strongpoint still held out. A projected attack on it by men of the battalion and 8th Suffolk Regiment under cover of Stokes gun[42] fire was not persisted in as Stokes gun fired very short and was ineffectual … No further attempts were made to take it that night … It was now beginning to get dark and … further advance that night was clearly impracticable. The battalion therefore consolidated ground gained. During the night there was continuous bomb fighting on western face of the redoubt and finally battalion's left was driven back where touch was gained with 7th Royal West Kent Regiment … Except for the reserve company which was held back in Bulgar Trench till about 5pm the battalion suffered little from enemy shell fire from zero till about 7pm. After this hour a fairly heavy though not very accurate shell fire was maintained on the ground captured throughout the night … The moppers up who were allocated to each of the first four waves did not reach Schwaben Redoubt except

two men. The going was very slippery and great difficulty was experienced in keeping up to the barrage. This gave the enemy time to get machine guns into action. From the number and positions in which some of the enemy dead lay in their trenches it seems probable that many manned the parapet and risked the barrage. The enemy, though a number of them were of poor physique, fought well when encountered hand to hand. The men of the battalion, a considerable majority of whom had little or no experience, on the whole showed good fighting qualities but little initiative and required much leading. The following incident which occurred during the fight may be of interest – in Bulgar Trench there were few Germans but those who surrendered were very quick to again pick up arms and shoot our leading waves in the back unless quickly dealt with.

The following day was spent fighting off counter-attacks. The battalion suffered forty-six killed, 262 wounded and eighty-seven missing.

1 October saw another renewed offensive, the Battle of the Ancre Heights, an ambitious plan by Haig to reduce the German salient round the River Ancre.
   Maurice Cook's battalion had already been in action for several days before the start of this stage of the campaign, fighting in the battle for the Thiepval Ridge.

COOK, Maurice Percival

Age:	21
Rank:	Private
Regiment/Service:	Queen's Own (Royal West Kent)
Unit:	7th Battalion
Service Number:	G/2507
Died	1 October 1916
Cemetery/Memorial:	Thiepval
Reference:	11 C

(Sutton Grammar School)

Born in Brenchley in Kent, Maurice lived at 12 Byron Avenue. He attended Sutton County School from 1909–10, and had been in the local Band of Hope cadets. He worked as an office clerk before joining the Royal West Kents in September 1914, and went to France at the end of August 1915. He was wounded at Loos less than a month later, when he was shot in the stomach, but after a period convalescing at home he returned to France in April 1916.

In the early hours of 30 September, after participating in an attack the previous night, the battalion took over the old German line from the Pope's Nose[43] near Thiepval northward along the British front as far as the River Ancre. They held about 1,800 yards of the front line, which meant every man was needed and there was no reserve. Shortly after the relief had been completed the Germans started a bombing attack on the right flank, and after some sharp fighting succeeded in pushing the British back 100 yards. This was attributed to the better performance of the German grenades (in terms of throwing distance) and a shortage of rifle grenades amongst the British. A counter-attack was immediately organised and succeeded in driving the Germans back some 50 yards, when without warning a shrapnel barrage from their own artillery started landing amongst the British troops. This disorganised the counter-attack and caused twenty-five casualties. When the artillery ceased the British continued their attack and pushed the Germans back to their own lines.

That afternoon orders were received to attack the notorious Schwaben Redoubt. This attack commenced at 4 p.m. Owing to the extraordinary broken nature of the ground and the fact that no opportunity had been given them for reconnoitring no-man's-land, the attackers veered to the right leaving one objective unattacked. Seeing this, the officer commanding the men of the Royal West Kents led his men forward to attack. The British artillery barrage lifted when these men were still 50 yards away from the German trenches; the enemy soldiers quickly manned their parapet and opened heavy rifle and machine gun fire on the advancing troops. A retaliatory bombardment by the Germans commenced a few minutes later on the British front and rear lines and on no-man's-land. The officer then noticed a German bombing party working round his left flank. He therefore collected the remains of his platoon, engaged them and drove them back. The main attack was faltering, and with only nine men remaining, they withdrew to the British trenches. Casualties were twenty-four killed, 103 wounded and eight missing.

The next day the battalion again saw action, a reconnaissance party encountering enemy bombing parties, driving them out with bombs and stokes mortars. There is no mention of casualties from this action, although the war diary states 'Our heavy artillery dropped several shells into our trenches during the afternoon, causing some casualties.' The Sutton Grammar School magazine *The Suttonian* reported that Maurice was shot by a sniper whilst part of a bombing party, which could have occurred in the action of 30 September or 1 October. His name is also on the Sutton Grammar School and St Barnabas memorials.

Elsewhere along the front, further attempts were made to press home the attack. Towards the south of the sector the Germans had built a fourth line of defences on the Transloy ridge, and the British Fourth Army needed to capture these as a precursor to the planned breakthrough.

HOLLINGSWORTH, John Frederick

Age:	31
Rank:	Second Lieutenant
Regiment/Service:	Royal Sussex Regiment
Unit:	14th Battalion, attached GHQ 7th Battalion
Died:	2 October 1916
Cemetery/Memorial:	Grove Town Cemetery, Méaulte
Reference:	I.M.2

CWGC Notes: Native of Wallington. Son of Frederick J. and Rebecca Hollingsworth, of Strawberry Lodge, Carshalton.

Although he worked as a lace buyer, John also had previous military experience with the Oxfordshire and Buckinghamshire Light Infantry and the Honourable Artillery Company. After joining up in November 1915 he was quickly promoted to Second Lieutenant in January 1916, and at the time of his death was attached to the 7th Battalion East Surrey Regiment. They were situated in Gueudecourt, a village close to Le Transloy that had been captured towards the end of September:

> The enemy keeps up an incessant barrage on the front and back of the village but luckily most of his shells go over our front line trench which is just in front of the village and is a single very narrow, but deep trench. Battalion HQ appears to be rather an unhealthy spot and catches more than its fair share of shells. During the early morning Second Lieutenant Hollingsworth was buried and sustained severe injuries to his head and later died of wounds.

John was taken to the 2/2 London Casualty Clearing Station in Méaulte on the outskirts of Albert, but died there later that day, exactly one week before his 32nd birthday.

Even those troops not directly taking part in the new attacks were not out of danger.

COTTER, James Thomas

Age:	30
Rank:	Private
Regiment/Service:	Middlesex Regiment
Unit:	19th Battalion
Service Number:	PW/5179
Died:	4 October 1916
Cemetery/Memorial:	Thiepval
Reference:	12D & 13B

CWGC Notes: Brother of Mrs M. W. Choules of 10 Seymour Rd, Beddington Corner, Mitcham.

James was born in Carshalton, worked as a labourer, and lived at 2 Parkside Green. The 19th Battalion of the Middlesex Regiment was a pioneer battalion responsible for carrying out various general labouring tasks. In late September and early October the battalion was busy digging trenches and cutting trench frames around Turks Lane and Goose Alley trenches, about 2,000 yards west of Gueudecourt. Although the war diary does not mention casualties, this was dangerous work and the men were susceptible to enemy shelling. Private Cotter's name is also on the Willie Bird cross.

British troops were still holding other sectors of the Western Front, and fighting continued in these areas too. Frederick Smith was killed during a trench raid near Chalk Pit Wood in the Loos sector.

SMITH, Frederick John

Age:	23
Rank:	Lance Corporal
Regiment/Service:	East Surrey Regiment
Unit:	13th Battalion
Service Number:	15917
Died:	5 October 1916
Cemetery/Memorial:	Philosophe British Cemetery, Mazingarbe
Reference:	I.B.35

Born in Carshalton and lived at 4 Alexander Cottages, Sutton, Frederick was a storekeeper before joining the army in November 1915. His battalion arrived in France in early June 1916. He was killed in action, his commanding officer writing:

> The patrol under Lieutenant Davis which left my lines on the night of the 4th–5th October and was reported by me on the morning of the 5th as missing has since returned. Lieutenant Davis is slightly wounded; one other rank killed, two other ranks slightly wounded. This patrol consisting of one officer and three other ranks left … on the night of the 4th–5th October at 12.30am and proceeded to the enemy's lines … for the purpose of keeping the enemy wire which had been cut by our trench mortars under observation and to prevent it being repaired; also if possible, to capture a prisoner or bring back an identification. On reaching the gap in the wire Lieutenant Davis discovered that some coils of fresh concertina wire had been placed close to the gap. He anticipated that this had been so placed for the purpose of repairing the gap, so waited on the chance of capturing a prisoner from a working party. He heard no sign of life in the enemy's trenches, and as daylight was approaching he decided to withdraw. On reaching the neighbourhood of our wire a machine gun opened fire, and inflicted the casualties mentioned. Lieutenant Davis being uncertain of his whereabouts, withdrew the party into a neighbouring shell-hole and awaited daylight. They remained there without food or water until 7pm when it was dark enough to return to our lines. The man killed has been located today and will be brought in during the night. I consider the conduct of Lieutenant Davis, under very trying circumstances, is very praiseworthy, for the coolness and resource shown by him in a sudden emergency. He states that the men behaved excellently under the very trying circumstances in which they were placed.

The soldier killed during the raid is almost certainly Frederick. His name is also on the Willie Bird cross.

Back on the Somme worsening weather hampered the offensive; however, on 7 October the attack on the Transloy Ridge was renewed. Although the village of Le Sars was captured the attack stalled, achieving only limited success.

COOPER, Charles Henry

Age: 27
Rank: Rifleman
Regiment/Service: King's Royal Rifle Corps
Unit: 10th Battalion
Service Number: R/32888
Died: 7 October 1916
Cemetery/Memorial: Thiepval
Reference: 13A & 13B

CWGC Notes: Son of Mr D.W. Cooper of 'Endwood', Carshalton Park Rd, Carshalton.

Charles was born in Battersea and worked as a clerk prior to enlisting in May 1916, five months before he died. The circumstances in which Charles lost his life are unclear. The battalion took part in the attack which captured Guillemont in early September, at a cost of 100 men, and suffered further casualties throughout September during the Somme offensive, most notably on 17 September when they suffered another 117, in an unsuccessful attempt to secure a 'jumping off' position for the proposed attack on Lesboeufs the next day. By early October the battalion was stationed in Bernafay Wood and although there were a small number of casualties mentioned in the war diary Rifleman Cooper does not appear in this list. He is also commemorated on Sutton war memorial and the memorial at St Barnabas church, where he had been a Band of Hope cadet.

DE WARBURG, Hermann Vivian

'God's will be done'

Age: 24
Rank: Second Lieutenant
Regiment/Service: Machine Gun Corps (Infantry)
Unit: 122nd Company
Died: 7 October 1916
Cemetery/Memorial: AIF Burial Ground, Flers
Reference: VII.H.10

CWGC Notes: Son of Charles H. and Annie de Warburg, of 'Lyndhurst', Stanley Park Rd, Carshalton.

Hermann's grave at the AIF Burial Ground, Flers. (Author's collection)

Hermann was born in Wandsworth and worked as a clerk. After joining up in November 1914 he initially served as a trooper with the Royal Horse Guards before being commissioned as a temporary second lieutenant with The Queen's in March 1915 (stating that he could only ride 'slightly'; perhaps the reason for the change of regiment). From there he was transferred to the Machine Gun Corps in December 1915 and went to France in May 1916. The first few days of October had seen his company engage the enemy on several occasions. On 7 October they were positioned north-east of Flers. At 2 p.m.:

> The general offensive was continued, in which the guns took part. Four guns were detailed to follow up the advance on the left flank and to assist in consolidating the ground won, and to pay special attention to the sunken road … to enfilade the enemy on the left, should he attempt to counter-attack. These guns advanced up the sunken road and when no longer able to advance further, two positions were taken up on the road … About 5pm the gun on the right was moved to the left of No 2 gun. These gun positions were then joined up by a trench and the trench was then manned by infantry belonging to the division on our left. This position was maintained until relieved. Four other guns were ordered to follow up the advance on the right hand flank. Unfortunately both officers of these sections were killed as soon as they got over the parapet, and one gun was put out of action. The remaining guns then manned the old line until the morning, when the guns were sent up to the new position which had been dug … The chief damage was done by enemy machine guns which enfiladed our line from the left. The guns seemed to be located about 300 yards on our left.

Hermann was one of the officers killed, along with six other men. His remains were recovered in December 1917.

HENTON, Alfred Edward

Age:	26
Rank:	Rifleman
Regiment/Service:	London Regiment (Post Office Rifles)
Unit:	8th Battalion
Service Number:	4711
Died:	11 October 1916
Cemetery/Memorial:	Dernancourt Communal Cemetery Extension
Reference:	III.F.2

CWGC Notes: Son of Mr and Mrs D. Henton, of 6 Court Farm, Manor Green Rd, Epsom. Native of Sutton.

In 1891 Alfred and his family were living in Sutton Grove. By 1911 his family were living at Glenwood, Ringstead Road, while Alfred was boarding with the Weston family at 36 Myrtle Road and working as an assisting postman. Unsurprisingly, when he enlisted he joined the Post Office Rifles, a battalion of the London Regiment comprised mostly of Post Office employees. He may have died of wounds received during the battalion's action of 7 October, when they 'made a somewhat disastrous attack on the famous Butte de Warlencourt, a mound which bristled with unsuspected machine guns. Two companies were completely wiped out, only seven men returning'.[44] The battalion suffered over 400 casualties. The Butte de Warlencourt is a prehistoric burial mound situated close to the Albert–

Bapaume road 'about 70 feet high, cunningly tunnelled by the enemy, and used as an observation post from which machine gun and artillery fire from positions echeloned in depth was directed with devastating effect on the western slopes up which our men had to advance'.[45] Due to the flat nature of the terrain it had commanding views of the local area and was the object of many British attacks, being briefly captured in November. It marked the furthest advance of the British during the Somme offensive and was not taken until February 1917, when the Germans retreated to the Hindenburg Line. The Germans then retook it during their offensive of March 1918. Alfred is also commemorated on Sutton war memorial, the Sutton Post Office memorial and St Barnabas church memorial. His brother George served in the same battalion, and their other brother Frank had been killed the previous year.

GIBSON, John Seear

Age:	32
Rank:	Second Lieutenant
Regiment/Service:	Bedfordshire Regiment
Unit:	8th Battalion, attached 16th Trench Mortar Battery
Died:	15 October 1916
Cemetery/Memorial:	Thiepval
Reference:	2C

CWGC Notes: Fourth son of the late Edward Morris and Martha Gibson, of Sutton; husband of Elsie May Gibson, of Maidstone, Kent.

(Dulwich College Register)

Born in Camberwell, John was educated at Dulwich College. He then joined the Merchant Service and was at sea for just over a year. He trained as an electrical engineer and held several positions prior to the outbreak of war. He originally joined the Royal Naval Volunteer Reserve as an ordinary seaman in September 1914. In March 1915 he was discharged to a commission in the Regular Army, and was married at St Barnabas church on 15 April 1916, two days before being posted to France. He served at Ypres and took part in the Somme offensive, being temporarily attached to the Royal Engineers Tunnelling Company on two occasions. He joined the Bedfordshire Regiment in August 1916 and was attached to the 16th Trench Mortar Battery. He died of wounds received during an enemy barrage whilst in trenches near Lesboeufs. His commanding officer wrote to his wife:

> It is with the deepest regret I have to inform you of the death in action of your husband, Second Lieutenant John S. Gibson, who was wounded by a fragment of shell on the evening of 15th October, and died a few hours afterwards without regaining consciousness, so that he suffered no pain. We buried him quite near to where he fell, where we have erected a little wooden cross bearing his name and regiment. He had been transferred to the Trench Mortar Battery

three days previously, and happened to be on duty with his mortar quite near to his own company when he fell. Second Lieutenant Gibson did very valuable work always with the battalion, and will be greatly missed by all ranks. All are heroes out here; the fighting just now is very severe.

Like many men buried on the battlefield, John's grave was later lost and he is now commemorated on Thiepval memorial to the missing. His name is also on Sutton war memorial, Dulwich College war memorial, St Barnabas church memorial, and on a plaque in St Nicholas church, Sutton.

On 21 October a successful attack was carried out against two long German trenches north of Thiepval and Courcelette known as Stuff Trench and Regina Trench.

JOHNSON, Robert Worthington

Age:	34
Rank:	Company Sergeant Major
Regiment/Service:	Norfolk Regiment
Unit:	8th Battalion
Service Number:	13760
Died:	21 October 1916
Cemetery/Memorial:	Thiepval
Reference:	1C & 1D

Robert was born in Southport, Lancashire, but by 1911 was living with his parents at 1 Loughborough Villas, West Street, Carshalton, and working as a wine merchant's clerk. He was awarded the DCM for gallantry in the vicinity of Thiepval between 16 and 29 September, the citation in November 1916 reading 'For conspicuous gallantry in action. He marked out the line of a trench under intense fire, and got every man to his work. He displayed great courage and determination throughout, and set a splendid example to his men.' Robert was killed during the battalion's attack on Regina Trench. Casualties were twenty-nine killed, eighty-nine wounded and thirteen missing.

The following week the German positions east of Lesboeufs were the subject of British attention. The 1st Middlesex Battalion took part in the attack:

During the night of the 27th–28th preparations were made for the attack which was timed at 6am. By 5.30am the whole four companies of the battalion were in position east of Lesboeufs ... The objectives to be gained by the brigade were the German positions in front of Le Transloy, known as Rainy Trench, Dewdrop Trench, and the dugouts north-east of the latter with strongpoints. At 6am the two leading companies A and C went forward in the assault preceded by an intense artillery barrage on the German position. Much opposition was met with from rifle and MG fire from the flanks, but the attack was pushed forward, and the first objective Rainy Trench gained. Further progress was held up by a strong German point on our right, and by the Germans still in possession of Dewdrop Trench on our left. Bombing tactics were employed with success, and by 9.30am the whole objective was in our hands. The German strongpoint on the right fell to the remainder of C Company ... The work of consolidating the captured position was put in hand, and rapid progress made. German snipers were active against our wounded. The enemy did not attempt to counter-attack, and the battalion was relieved that night ... The losses of the battalion that day were 36 killed, 143 wounded 29 missing.

LOVEGROVE, Charles George Gordon

Age:	27
Rank:	Private
Regiment/Service:	Middlesex Regiment
Unit:	1st Battalion
Service Number:	G/43824
Died:	28 October 1916
Cemetery/Memorial:	Thiepval Memorial
Reference:	12B & 13B

CWGC Notes: Son of John and Frances Lovegrove, of 'St Margarets', Highfield Rd, Sutton.

(Sutton Local Studies)

Born in Carshalton, Charles lived in Sutton and attended Sutton County School. When war broke out he was in West Africa and took part in the successful invasion of the German Kameruns colony. It is not clear who he was serving with at this point, but he ended up in France with the Middlesex Regiment. The school magazine reported that he was killed in action going over the top. He is also commemorated on Sutton Grammar School's memorial.

STEVENS, Roderick John

Age:	23
Rank:	Private
Regiment/Service:	Middlesex Regiment
Unit:	1st Battalion
Service Number:	PW/5530
Died:	2 November 1916
Cemetery/Memorial:	St Sever Cemetery Extension, Rouen
Reference:	O.I.B.3

CWGC Notes: Son of John and Martha Stevens, of 96 Stanley Rd, Carshalton.

Born in Beckenham and a labourer, Roderick had only enlisted six months prior to his death. He likely died of wounds received in the action on 28 October, being evacuated to Rouen, where there were several hospitals. His brother George served in the Royal Garrison Artillery and survived the war.

Despite some successes, many of the German trenches (particularly Boritska) were not taken and the battalion fell back. These trenches were the subject of further attacks over the following days and were finally taken on 5 November.

GRAY, Joseph

'In my father's house are many mansions. I go to prepare a place for you'

Age: 24
Rank: Private
Regiment/Service: The Queen's (Royal West Surrey Regiment)
Unit: 1st Battalion
Service Number: G/13383
Died: 5 November 1916
Cemetery/Memorial: AIF Burial Ground, Flers
Reference: II.K.30

CWGC Notes: Born in London. Son of Marie Annie Gray, of 109 Stanley Rd, Carshalton, and the late William Gray.

Born in Camberwell, in 1911 Joseph was living with his mother, a storekeeper, and working as her assistant. On 5 November 1916 C Company of the battalion was in support of the attack on Boritska Trench. At 3.15 p.m. they advanced to assist with the consolidation before being relieved in the evening. In five days in the trenches they had lost forty-four killed, 135 wounded, and fifty-five missing. The battalion war diary notes the difficulty in getting rations to the men during this time, with the ration parties frequently becoming lost and the men having to use their reserve 'iron rations'.

The final phase of the Somme offensive began on 13 November. The Battle of the Ancre was intended to capture objectives that should have been taken on the first day back in July. The attack was preceded by a huge artillery bombardment, but the effect of the shelling combined with the weather meant that much of the ground had turned to thick mud.

PERRYMAN, Frederick William

Age: 20
Rank: Private
Regiment/Service: Middlesex Regiment
Unit: 17th Battalion
Service Number: G/44046
Died: 13 November 1916
Cemetery/Memorial: Thiepval
Reference: 12D & 13B

Frederick was born in Caterham but by 1914 was living at 13 Holly Cottages, Lodge Road, Wallington. The 17th Middlesex was known as the 'football battalion' as many of its original members were professional football players.

On 12 November the battalion had marched to Mailly, leaving there late at night to reach the forming-up area for the next day's operations, an attack on Pendant Copse near Serre:

> At zero hour namely 5.45am the British artillery began its preliminary bombardment of the German lines and at 5.51am the battalion went over in waves … The morning was very misty and it was impossible to see more than 25 to 30 yards. Pendant Copse our objective was invisible. All ranks were extremely cheerful and success seemed inevitable. Two of the companies B and D went over playing mouth organs.

However, by 7.20 a.m. the attack had faltered. Various units were mixed up in no-man's-land and, although the German retaliatory artillery bombardment was slight, their machine guns caused a lot of trouble. B Company became held up by uncut wire opposite the German trenches and experienced great difficulty owing to the fog, which helped to conceal the advancing troops but also led to many becoming disoriented. Some of the men started to return. Seventy-nine were collected and ordered to hold Legend Trench. In the early afternoon orders were received to hold the front line by strong posts and machine guns, and the position remained the same for the rest of the day. The enemy heavily shelled various parts of the line and the trenches were in an extremely bad condition, forcing the men to use the top for getting about. Throughout 14 November the battalion continued to hold the line and suffered further casualties from shell fire before being relieved the following day. They had suffered just over 300 casualties killed, wounded and missing. The failure of the attack was attributed chiefly to the fog (causing loss of direction and confusion of units) and, the uncut German wire. Frederick had initially been reported as missing, and according to the local newspaper, was not confirmed killed until July 1917.

Some limited success was achieved on 13 November, including the capture of Beaumont Hamel, and General Gough (commander of Fifth Army) decided to renew the attack the following day.

CARPENTER, Cecil Henry

Age:	23
Rank:	Private
Regiment/Service:	Honourable Artillery Company
Unit:	D Company, 1st Battalion
Service Number:	4740
Died:	14 November 1916
Cemetery/Memorial:	Thiepval
Reference:	8A

(Whitgift School)

CWGC Notes: Son of Henry William and Emelie Carpenter of 'St Heliers', Carshalton Park Rd, Carshalton. Educated at Whitgift Grammar School, Croydon. Enlisted, November 1915. Went to France, June 1916.

Cecil attended Homefield Prep School in Sutton then Whitgift Grammar School from 1905 to 1910. After school he became a bank clerk. His battalion had been in action during the Somme campaign at the Ancre and Beaumont Hamel. On the morning of 14 November the battalion had carried out an attack on Beaucourt and, despite initial resistance from the Germans, the village was taken by 7.45 a.m. The battalion then proceeded to dig in on the outskirts of the village, but were heavily shelled in the afternoon. Cecil was initially listed as missing following the action and was not officially confirmed dead until August 1917, when one of his fellow soldiers stated:

> On the morning of November 14th, 1916, while digging in on the outskirts of Beaucourt, I saw No 4740 Pte. Carpenter C.H., enter a shell hole immediately in front of my position distance some ten yards away. During the day we were subject to heavy shelling and at about 4pm, a large shell exploded either in or very close to the shell hole which Pte. Carpenter had not been seen to leave. The force of the explosion blew me out of the back of the trench and covered me with earth. I feel quite convinced the Pte. Carpenter was in the shell hole at the time and must have been killed by the explosion.

Beaucourt had been successfully taken. Cecil Carpenter was the last of Carshalton's casualties in the Somme campaign, although it continued for several more days. The final attack on 19 November was made in heavy snow and ultimately the decision was made to end the campaign. It had lasted five months; barely 6 miles of ground had been gained, but one objective at least had been achieved – the French still held Verdun. This achievement had come at a terrible price for the British: over 400,000 casualties, including nearly 100,000 dead. The campaign had cost Carshalton fifty-nine of its men and boys, with no doubt many more wounded during the course of the offensive. In February 1917 the Germans gave up the area to withdraw to the Hindenburg Line.

Although the offensive was over, the British held a dangerous position around the Aisne.

GABB, Stanley Frederic

Age:	19
Rank:	Second Lieutenant
Regiment/Service:	Machine Gun Corps
Unit:	76th Company
Died:	8 December 1916
Cemetery/Memorial:	Gézaincourt Communal Cemetery Extension
Reference:	II.D.16

CWGC Notes: Son of George Byers Gabb and Eliza Mary Gabb, of 1 Carshalton Rd, Carshalton. Native of Croydon. Brother of Richard Gabb.

Stanley was educated at Sutton Valence School from 1910 to 1913 and then attended the Collège Mariette in Boulogne. He worked as a marine insurance broker's clerk and had joined the Inns of Court Officer Training Corps in September 1915, the month after his brother Richard had been killed in Gallipoli. Commissioned to the Machine Gun Corps in September 1916, he landed in France on 18 November and only joined his company four days before he was wounded. On 4 December his company was in trenches in the Serre sector. They were relieved by the 9th Machine Gun Company but Stanley was wounded during the relief, suffering gunshot wounds to the chest and back. He died four days later at the 29th Casualty Clearing Station at Gézaincourt.

The winter months were traditionally a 'quiet' period as both sides settled down for the winter and began preparing their plans for the following year. Nevertheless, with the front line held all the way to the North Sea, casualties were still a daily occurrence.

CAIRNS, Robert Arthur

Age:	35
Rank:	Private
Regiment/Service:	East Surrey Regiment
Unit:	9th Battalion
Service Number:	22714
Died:	22 December 1916
Cemetery/Memorial:	Philosophe British Cemetery, Mazingarbe
Reference:	II.B.6

(Barbara Holmes)

CWGC Notes: Husband of M.A. Cairns of 4 Baden Villas, Waterloo Rd, Sutton.

Robert was born in Carshalton and worked as a plasterer. He married in 1903 and had one daughter. Robert enlisted in December 1915 and was killed in action near Hulluch a year later. The war diary for that day states that the Germans launched two 'minnies' into the battalion's trenches, killing one man and wounding seven. Robert is also commemorated on the memorial in St Barnabas church. He was the cousin of Frank Chalcraft and was also linked by marriage to Bernard Tate.

McDONOUGH, John Sholto

Age:	42
Rank:	Lance Corporal
Regiment/Service:	Royal Fusiliers
Unit:	23rd Battalion
Service Number:	981
Died:	25 December 1916
Cemetery/Memorial:	Bois Guillaume Communal Cemetery
Reference:	II.C.2A

Born in Portsea, Hampshire, in June 1874. Whilst no record can be found of John in the 1901 or 1911 census, in 1911 his mother was living at 'Eydonholme', Alma Road. John had been in France for just over a year before he died. In December 1916 his battalion was located in Oneux, undergoing training. The cemetery he is buried in is some 75 miles from Oneux, and was attached to No. 8 General Hospital. He died from an ulcer so was probably taken ill some time earlier and transferred out of the line.

1917

The early stages of the Battle of the Somme had been famously filmed by the official British cinematographers Geoffrey Malins and John McDowell. Malins was a Carshalton resident and lived with his wife and daughter at Holmwood, 18 Beeches Avenue. The later stages of the Somme campaign were also filmed and released under the title The Battle of the Ancre and the Advance of the Tanks. *In January 1917 the local paper wrote about the film:*

The Tanks in Action – Can you imagine yourself being suddenly transferred from your home, with all its comforts, to the vast battlefield of France with its perilous surroundings and its seeming isolation from places where at the moment there is no war? Can you conceive in the smallest degree what your feelings would be if you were to stand amidst thousands of khaki-clad men with their clothes heavily encumbered with mud and bullets ever whistling around them threatening to destroy the lives of some of the best specimens of manhood? Verily it is a difficult thing to do, but you can assist yourself in giving the reply by seeing the film portraying the battle of the Ancre and the advance of the 'Tanks'. No! There will be no necessity to go on a railway journey; the picture is almost at your very door, for it is at the Cheam Road Picture Theatre for the whole of next week, and you ought to be there to get a little insight into the conditions under which our brave soldiers live for the preservation of our freedom … There is abundant evidence of the jeopardy in which the photographer placed himself in every inch of the film, and all the more because that man resides in the locality will Sutton be proud of him. Lieutenant Malins, who was responsible for recording 'The Battle of the Somme', resides at The Beeches, Carshalton, and probably he will pay a visit to Cheam Road Picture Theatre and narrate some of his experiences, in addition to witnessing the production.

In January Kaiser Wilhelm II agreed to Germany conducting a campaign of unrestricted submarine warfare against all shipping, irrespective of nationality – a move that would ultimately contribute to the USA entering the war.

The year opened relatively quietly on the Western Front. In early February Germany moved back to more fortified positions known to the British as the Hindenburg Line. This move shortened the length of front line that the Germans had to defend and removed the salients in the line that had been created during the Somme offensive. British forces were now free to advance unopposed over the ground they had so bitterly fought over in 1916. The routine of trench life, including raids and patrols, meant that danger was never far away.

BROWN, Walter Frederick

Age: 28
Rank: Private
Regiment/Service: East Surrey Regiment
Unit: 9th Battalion
Service Number: G/16200
Died: 2 February 1917
Cemetery/Memorial: Boulogne Eastern Cemetery
Reference: VIII.B.205

CWGC Notes: Son of Mercy Brown of Flora Villas, Brickfield Lane, Carshalton; husband of K.G. Brown of 32 Orchard Road, Sutton.

Walter was born in Carshalton and worked as a labourer before he enlisted in November 1915. He died of wounds received in a trench raid on 25 January near Hulluch:

> The battalion carried out a successful trench raid against the enemy ... Purposes were (1) To obtain identifications (2) To inflict losses on the enemy (3) To secure a sample of German ration bread.[46] Strength of party – three officers and 50 other ranks, six sappers ... Their advance was apparently not observed, as no fire was directed at them ... and they entered the enemy's trench without casualty ... About 60 yards from the point of entry ...   Second Lieutenant Thomas came upon two sentries with their hands in their pockets standing on the firestep: he called on them to surrender, but as they made a movement to raise their rifles he shot them both; it was evident that these men had not, previous to the appearance of Second Lieutenant Thomas, the slightest idea that anything unusual was occurring. At this point there was a dugout, the entrance of which was covered with a canvas screen; a German came out and was shot by Second Lieutenant Thomas, the latter then ordered several of the enemy, who were sitting on the steps leading down to the dugout, to surrender, as they were screaming with terror and apparently paralysed with fear. Second Lieutenant Thomas fired a shot into the entrance upon which three Germans surrendered; shortly afterwards some of the enemy were seen escaping by the other entrance; Second Lieutenant Thomas shot one of these and the bayonet men two others. By this time the alarm had evidently been given as the party were being bombed. Second Lieutenant Thomas decided to withdraw ... Near the junction of Sap 45 with the enemy's front trench, the entrance to a dugout was seen, and near to it a German was seen looking through a periscope; the latter was shot by the leading bayonet man. The dugout had three entrances; Sergeant Summers shot one of the enemy escaping by the third entrance. All the entrances were then guarded. From sounds it was certain that there were a considerable number of the enemy in the dugout, but, in spite of Mills' and SK[47] bombs being thrown down, they refused to come out ... The order for withdrawal was then received, and the party withdrew, Sapper Wilkes having meanwhile blown in the dugout with a mobile charge.

Two of the sappers were wounded during the withdrawal. Total casualties were three killed and four wounded (three sappers and Walter Brown). The regimental history conflicts with this account slightly and states that two men were killed by machine gun fire whilst crossing the 110yd of no-man's-land. Walter's name also appears on the Willie Bird cross and Sutton war memorial.

WARREN, William Henry

Age:	18
Rank:	Private
Regiment/Service:	The Queen's (Royal West Surrey Regiment)
Unit:	8th Battalion
Service Number:	G/24323
Died:	2 February 1917
Cemetery/Memorial:	Béthune Town Cemetery
Reference:	VI.B.10

CWGC Notes: Son of Henry and Kate Warren, of Vine Cottage, 7 Harold Rd, Sutton. Born at Torquay, Devon.

William gave his age as 19 years 2 months when he enlisted in September 1915, and his occupation as chauffeur. However, based on census information he was more likely 16 or 17 when he enlisted. He initially served in the East Surrey Regiment before being transferred to the 8th Queen's. In early February 1917 the battalion was based in Hulluch and although enemy artillery and '*minenwerfer*' were active, the battalion's war diary does not mention any casualties. However, some casualties had been caused by shell fire in mid-January, when the battalion was in the trenches at Philosophe, 4 miles from Hulluch. Béthune was an important railway and hospital centre just 10 miles from Hulluch, so it is likely William was brought there due to illness or wounds. His name is also on the Sutton and St Barnabas memorials.

SKELTON, William Alfred

'*Dearly loved and sadly missed*'

Age:	33
Rank:	Private
Regiment/Service:	Middlesex Regiment
Unit:	21st Battalion
Service Number:	6620
Died:	22 February 1917
Cemetery/Memorial:	Bray Military Cemetery
Reference:	II.C.41

CWGC Notes: Son of David and Annie Skelton, of Carshalton; husband of Florence Miriam Skelton, of 42 Lakehall Rd, Thornton Heath.

Born in Carshalton, William lived at 4 West Street Lane and worked as a general labourer in the building trade. His brother Henry was a jockey, known as the 'The Sparrow King of Sutton'. William died from pneumonia. In January his battalion spent time in Maricourt and Rancourt, just 10 miles from Bray; in February they were based in Maurepas, over 100 miles from where he is buried. It is possible he was admitted to hospital near Bray in January, succumbing to the illness the following month.

As the Germans retreated the British advanced further east, testing the new German line. On 4 March the 8th Division launched an attack against the German positions on the 'Hogs Back', overlooking Bouchavesnes.

KNIGHT, Francis Ernest

Age:	34
Rank:	Captain
Regiment/Service:	Northamptonshire Regiment
Unit:	2nd Battalion
Died:	4 March 1917
Cemetery/Memorial:	Thiepval
Reference:	11A & 11D

CWGC Notes: Son of Samuel and Sarah Elizabeth *(The Sphere)* Knight, of The Corner House, Old, Northants.

Francis was educated at Wellingborough School, where he was head boy and a colour sergeant in the Cadet Corps. He then attended the University of London before becoming the head of the general stores department for the Crown Agents for the Colonies. He lived at 'Briarbank', Hawthorn Road, Sutton. Enlisting in September 1914, Francis joined the Royal Fusiliers as a private. In April 1915 he received his commission and joined the 8th Battalion Northamptonshire Regiment before being attached to the 2nd Battalion. He was overseas from August 1915 and was promoted to captain in February 1917. On 4 March 1917 the battalion attacked the enemy trench system on the Moislains Ridge, about 17 miles east of Albert. All objectives were taken and held against repeated counter-attacks. Casualties were seven officers, including Captain Knight, and 235 other ranks. His commanding officer wrote to his parents:

Captain Knight was killed by a shell on the afternoon of the 4th March 1917 after a successful attack on the German trenches. His company had done very well indeed in the attack and he had himself been wounded but refused to leave his company early in the day. His loss is an irreparable one to the battalion where he was beloved of officers and men, whilst I personally looked on him as one of my most trusted company commanders. My deepest sympathies go with you in a loss which the whole regiment shares with you.

Francis is also commemorated on Sutton war memorial. One of his younger brothers was also killed during the war.

The 8th Division suffered over 1,000 casualties during the attack, many caused by the German shelling. As the British moved towards the outposts of the Hindenburg Line, the village of Écoust had to be taken in order to then take the village of Bullecourt.

COOKE, Edward Ralph

Age:	38
Rank:	Private
Regiment/Service:	Honourable Artillery Company
Unit:	2nd Battalion
Service Number:	9281
Died:	31 March 1917
Cemetery/Memorial:	H.A.C. Cemetery, Écoust-St-Mein
Reference:	I.A.28

(Whitgift School)

CWGC Notes: Son of Alfred E. and Leila Cooke; husband of Kathleen Cooke of High Barn, Middleton, Bognor, Sussex. Born at Wimbledon.

Edward was educated at Collegiate School, Wallington, and then Whitgift Grammar School from 1892 to 1894. His parents lived at 'The Cottage', West Street, Carshalton. He worked as a clerk on the Stock Exchange then worked at the Admiralty and as a special constable in Carshalton. He married in Carshalton on 14 February 1915 and his son was born in December 1915. Edward was a resident of Tilehurst, and enlisted in Reading at the end of October 1916 before arriving in France in January 1917.

On 30 March the battalion had relieved the Border Regiment in the line near Écoust, north-east of Bapaume. The relief was completed by 6.50 a.m. on the morning of 31 March, but that night the line was heavily shelled, attacked in force and the British defenders driven out. Edward was killed by machine gun fire during the attack. He is also commemorated on Tilehurst war memorial, the Stock Exchange war memorial, and a plaque in All Saints church, Carshalton.

THOMPSON, Rupert Archibald

Age:	30
Rank:	Sergeant
Regiment/Service:	The Queen's (Royal West Surrey Regiment)
Unit:	6th Battalion
Service Number:	22548
Died:	4 April 1917
Cemetery/Memorial:	Faubourg d'Amiens Cemetery, Arras
Reference:	III.N.6

CWGC Notes: Son of Henry and Mabel Sophia Thompson, of 9 Station Rd, Carshalton.

Before the war Rupert worked as a fishmonger. Strangely, in the 'Soldiers Died in The Great War' database his name is recorded as Robert Arthur Thompson. It seems that for some unknown reason he gave different forenames when he enlisted. In an bizarre twist, his death plaque (dead man's penny) was dug up in a field near Flitton, Bedfordshire, by a metal detectorist in 1999. This plaque also gave his name as Robert Arthur, but quite how it ended up buried in the field is a mystery.

Rupert Thompson, centre. (June Davies)

In April 1917 his battalion was in Arras:

> The night was quiet, we found large working parties. Our artillery fire opened at 6.15am, bombardment was heavy but not intense. Enemy shelled Arras during the morning, one shell burst in Museum Trench burying some men of C Company. Six other ranks killed and 26 wounded, we also had four men killed and three wounded by a shell when they were fetching rations.

Rupert was the brother of Eric Thompson, who was killed a little over a month later.

On 9 April the Battle of Arras commenced. Widely known for the Canadian success at Vimy Ridge, attributable largely to thorough preparation and training, this was just part of a wider move to break through the new German defensive line.

DELLER, Arthur Lewis

Age:	25
Rank:	Private
Regiment/Service:	The Buffs (East Kent Regiment)
Unit:	6th Battalion
Service Number:	G/13079
Died:	9 April 1917
Cemetery/Memorial:	Arras Memorial
Reference:	Bay 2

CWGC Notes: Son of Mrs Mary Ann Deller, of 17 Green Wrythe Lane, Carshalton.

Arthur was born in Carshalton and lived at 3 Parkside, Green Wrythe Lane. His pre-war occupation is given as 'painter's assistant' before he joined the East Surrey Regiment in December 1915. He was killed in action and was initially declared missing:

> At zero hour, 5.30am our artillery and machine guns opened fire on the German lines and at the same time the battalion left the trenches, moving to the attack in artillery formation … The first objective (the Black Line) … was quickly captured by the battalion without much loss. A two hour bombardment of the enemy's second system (the Blue Line) followed, and the advance was resumed as the barrage lifted forward. More opposition was encountered than before, snipers and machine guns being active on both flanks. After some stiff hand-to-hand fighting D Company were able to get around to the flank, and by rifle grenading concealed machine guns, pushed forward in shell holes, captured Houlette Work, their objective on the Blue Line. C Company on the right were troubled by enfilade machine gun fire operating from the right flank from the ruins near Estaminet Corner. By means of Lewis Gun fire and rifle grenading these were however eventually silenced, and this company was able to proceed. The Blue Line was then consolidated. Lewis Guns pushed forward, and strongpoints [were] dug.

Only officer casualties are mentioned: three killed and seven wounded.

The Hindenburg Line was characterised by a series of defensive lines and although success was achieved in some areas, the German third line (the Brown Line) held.

BROWN, Leonard Reuben

Age:	28
Rank:	Private
Regiment/Service:	Royal Fusiliers
Unit:	10th Battalion
Service Number:	61579
Died:	10 April 1917
Cemetery/Memorial:	Houdain Lane Cemetery, Tilloy-Les-Mofflaines
Reference:	E.6

CWGC Notes: Son of Mrs W.R. Brown, of Avondale, Butter Hill, Carshalton, and the late W.R. Brown.

Born in Carshalton, Leonard was a clerk before he joined up in December 1915. The battalion war diary for the day he died states:

> At 4am the battalion withdrew to Feuchy Chapel. About 10am moved to Brown Line by railway. Advanced under slight enemy artillery fire and machine gun fire until checked by intense machine gun fire about 600 yards west of Monchy-Le-Preux. Our casualties by this time were fairly heavy.

The battalion's casualties in the period 9–11 April were twelve officers and twenty-four other ranks. Leonard's name is also on the Royal Fusiliers memorial at St Michael's church, Cornhill, in the City of London. He was the brother of Charles Brown.

Monchy-Le-Preux was not captured until the following day. In the meantime The Queen's had made their own attack on 9 April under the cover of a new tactic – the creeping barrage. This entailed the artillery barrage moving gradually forward with the infantry following close behind, giving the enemy little time to man their defences once the barrage stopped.

KING, William Thomas James

Age: 29
Rank: Private
Regiment/Service: The Queen's (Royal West Surrey Regiment)
Unit: 6th Battalion
Service Number: G/3513
Died: 10 April 1917
Cemetery/Memorial: Arras Memorial
Reference: Bay 2

CWGC Notes: Husband of Lucy Sarah Webb (formerly King).

William was born and lived in Carshalton and is likely to have died of wounds received in action near Arras on 9 April when: 'The battalion attacked the German trenches at 5.30 a.m. The battalion was in the front line of the attack. The final objective was Glasgow Trench … this was gained with relatively few losses.' Casualties were six killed, ninety-five wounded and nineteen missing. William is also commemorated on Wallington war memorial and the memorial chapel in St Barnabas church.

BROWN, Herbert Walter

Age: 27
Rank: Private
Regiment/Service: Royal Fusiliers
Unit: 8th Battalion
Service Number: 7600
Died: 25 April 1917 (wounded *c.*11 April 1917)
Cemetery/Memorial: Étaples Military Cemetery
Reference: XVIII.A.6A

CWGC Notes: Son of Walter and Emma Brown, of South Kensington, London; husband of A.G. Brown, of 6 Croft Rd, Godalming.

Born in Earl's Court, Herbert worked for a press agency before the war and was superintendent of the Sunday school at Emmanuel church, Park Lane,

Carshalton, as well as the minister's warden and a member of the choir. He joined the Public Schools Battalion of the Royal Fusiliers in 1915 and saw active service as a stretcher bearer. On 9 April the battalion, part of 36th Brigade, had participated in the main Arras offensive. Due to the creeping barrage they suffered no casualties prior to reaching the German lines. Although held up for some time by two strongpoints, the attack was successful, and by 10 a.m. all objectives had been taken along with 129 prisoners and two machine guns. The battalion's war diary reports the casualties as 'slight', with forty-three killed, 203 wounded and seven missing. The following message was received from Brigadier General Owen, commander of 36th Brigade:

> Please convey my very best congratulations to all ranks who took part in the attack today. They did magnificent work. They went forward and carried out their job as if they had been in the practice trenches at Ligneneuiel. Whilst one cannot but regret the number of casualties experienced, yet considering the successful results achieved they have on the whole proved remarkably small.

On 11 April the war diary records that there was not much shelling, though two other ranks were killed and three wounded. Herbert was shot in the abdomen by a sniper on or around 11 April; he started to recover and was able to write to his wife, but suffered a relapse and died on 25 April.

TREHEARN, Alfred William

Age:	31
Rank:	Private
Regiment/Service:	Machine Gun Corps (Infantry)
Unit:	111th Company
Service Number:	25427
Died:	12 April 1917
Cemetery/Memorial:	Duisans British Cemetery, Etrun
Reference:	I.Q.19

CWGC Notes: Son of Mrs E. Trehearn, of Beaulah Mount, Titchfield, Surrey.

Alfred was born in Hatcham, Kent, although the family later moved to 'Glendennig' in Blakehall Road, Carshalton. Alfred worked as a clerk before he went overseas in July 1915 and initially served with the Royal Fusiliers. On 9 April the company was in Arras, covering the advance of troops attacking Monchy-Le-Preux to the south-east. The attack continued on 10–11 April, the company finally being relieved on 12 April once the village had been captured, returning to Arras. Although no casualties are mentioned it is likely Alfred was wounded at some point during this action; the local paper noted he died of wounds received the same day, and Duisans cemetery is located on the north-west outskirts of Arras. Alfred is also commemorated on the Addey and Stanhope school war memorial, Deptford.

The first phase of the Battle of Arras had been very successful, advancing up to 4 miles and with particular success at Vimy Ridge.

BAKER, Harold William

Age:	18
Rank:	Private
Regiment/Service:	Royal Fusiliers
Unit:	20th Battalion
Service Number:	PS/10635
Died:	16 April 1917
Cemetery/Memorial:	Heninel-Croisilles Road Cemetery
Reference:	II.E.34

The Baker family lived at 5 Park Avenue, Wallington. (St Olave's School)
Harold was born in Lewisham and attended St Olave's School between 1910 and 1915. The record of Olavian Fallen declares:

> Harold William Baker excelled at cricket and rugby and was an NCO in the school cadet corps. He is mentioned frequently in the Olavian magazine between the years 1910 and 1915. In his spare time, not content with his strong religious beliefs, he had become an unofficial street preacher, taking the world of God into the slum areas – an often thankless task. His best school friend was Harold Grose, a fellow rugby player, with whom he enlisted in the Fusiliers. Grose, who survived the conflict, would retain affectionate memories of 'the Preacher'. The Allied line gradually pushed seven miles south-east of Arras with men from Northumberland capturing the high ground of Wancourt tower. The 15th April saw desperate German counter-attacks almost all repulsed. Private Baker was involved in all of these infantry actions at the tender age of eighteen. On the 16th, he was advancing with his friend Jimmy Wilde, a Welsh school-master, and their officer, Lieutenant CE Powell, when all three men were cut down in one sweep of an enemy machine gun from the high ground. The three men were buried alongside each other by an officer of the Kings (Liverpool) Regiment, who later found them, after their brigade had pushed the reinforcing troops forward. The clean white stones of these brave men sit in the sunshine at the Heninel-Croisilles Road Cemetery, on a road that crosses a plateau south-west of Arras.

The battalion war diary confirms the details of the action in which Harold died:

> Night march successfully carried out and arrived at place of assembly at 2.45am. Attacked enemy's position ... A, D and B Companies formed up and proceeded about 100 yards when heavy machine gun fire was opened from front and flanks. Progress then was slight and the attack was inclining too much to the right.

The advance was stopped and C Company entered the trenches. The attack would have been successful but MG fire was too severe and the attack failed.

PARSONS, Frederick Charles

Age:	38
Rank:	Corporal
Regiment/Service:	East Surrey Regiment
Unit:	No. 9 Platoon, C Company, 13th Battalion
Service Number:	19388
Died:	23 April 1917
Cemetery/Memorial:	Thiepval
Reference:	6B & 6C

(Rowena Preston)

Fred was born in Lambeth and although he obtained work as a draper's assistant, from an early age harboured an ambition to join the army. He eventually enlisted underage in 1895 at 16. He joined the 1st Battalion Prince of Wales's Regiment, a Regular Army battalion, and saw service in India. Upon completion of his service he returned to England, married and had two children. He then joined the Great Northern and City Railway (part of the London Underground), starting as a signalman and ending up as station master of Highbury station. However, in 1915 his brother-in-law Frank Glanville died, and Fred took over the running of the family fishmonger business at 38 West Street, Carshalton, most likely working with his nephew Sidney Glanville, who also died in the war. Fred re-enlisted into the army in May 1916 – his son later recalled Fred telling his mother that 'his greatest wish was to be decorated for bravery on the field of battle'.[48] On 15 April 1917 Fred wrote to his wife:

> I have been very busy yesterday and today at clerical work for the Captain doing company reorganisation etc, although we have got an acting Company Sergeant Major whilst our CSM is on leave the Captain and in fact all come to me for everything as also the acting Company Sergeant Major asks me to do everything for him. I have been promoted to Lance Sergeant last night and the Colonel when promoting me, spoke very well to me on my work since I joined the 13th. I am also helping the Quartermaster Sergeant as his clerk in my spare time with a view to taking his place when he comes home on his ten days leave, and also as so few can do that job properly. I am looking forward to a QMS job should a vacancy occur. We are going on a long march tomorrow and shall see the Germans' latest dirty work, also don't expect a letter for about three days but I might be able to write; not quite sure about the despatch of the mail, had a rotten wet day, and a cold wind sort of blows through you. I am not taking over a platoon yet, am too useful at Company Headquarters and it is better for me as I am more comfortable and get things better (food etc). I cannot stop to write a longer letter today.

On 17 April he sent another short letter:

> Just a line to let you know I shall not be able to write for a few days, cannot say
> how many, had fine weather for our march but it poured all night and we were
> in a large roofless barn so the majority got wet somewhat. I have been put in
> charge of a platoon today and we are now after Jerry's tail again. I am very well
> and busy. No chance of writing long letter.

Frederick was killed instantly by a shell on St George's Day, in a trench near
Gouzeaucourt, 10 miles south-west of Cambrai. Nine of his comrades were
wounded in the same blast. His commanding officer Captain Launton wrote to
Frederick's wife:

> I had formed a very great opinion of him, so much so, that he went into the
> line last time as Platoon Sergeant. He was a very capable, industrious, and
> brave NCO and both officers and men of my company liked and admired him
> immensely, and were very sorry indeed that he was taken away from us.

Frederick was initially buried in Gouzeaucourt Wood, but at some point his grave
was lost as he is now one of the missing listed on Thiepval memorial.

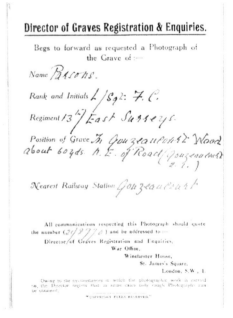

A picture of Frederick Parson's original grave, which would have been requested by his family.
(Rowena Preston)

*On 23 April the assault was renewed in an effort to relieve the pressure on the beleaguered
French troops attacking to the south as part of the Nivelle offensive.*

PENN, Harry Watson

'Their glory shall not be blotted out'

Age:	27
Rank:	Lance Corporal
Regiment/Service:	Royal Fusiliers
Unit:	10th Battalion
Service Number:	1083
Died:	23 April 1917
Cemetery/Memorial:	Chili Trench Cemetery, Gavrelle
Reference:	Sp. Mem. A.4

(Wendy Pogmore)

Born in Southwark, Harry worked as an electrical draughtsman and lived with his parents and siblings in Beech Tree Road, Carshalton, before he went to France in July 1915. During his training he wrote to his younger brother, Edgar:

Monday evening

Well Edgar boy how are you? And how's the soldiering going on.

Do you know we had a nice new rifle served out to each of us today with our own numbers stamped on them, and they will be the ones that we shall use on those rotten Germans. Expect to get the long new bayonets in a few days.

Talking about bayonets I got a nasty dig in the ribs while bayonet fighting on Saturday. They thought I had broken one at first but it seems I haven't. Am going to have it well looked at tomorrow by the doctor. Don't think that it was a real bayonet point, it was one of those we use for practice, but was quite enough I can tell you, as I've had a bad cough as well. Hope to sleep all right tonight have taken something for it.

This won't do now will it telling you all my silly little troubles its nothing serious really. Don't forget to tell Ma that. It's just been enough to keep me off parade.

All our company have gone out tonight trench digging etc but this is when I don't go ... I've used the sponge bag and have been quite nice and clean since I had it and am just using that piece of Pears Soap that Mary gave me last Christmas. Have had it in my kitbag all this time.

The boys are gambling all round me and there's such a chink of money that I can hardly hear the tune the lad is playing on the piano. Some yarn but tis true.

Well how are the chicks, the garden, and the W.C. worms I mean.

Just kiss Ma and Pa, Auntie Bertha and the girls for me won't you, and be a good boy like you always are you rascal.

Good night boy,
Harry

Harry died during an offensive on the German line north of the River Scarpe:

> At zero hour (4.45am) the battalion advanced in accordance with the artillery barrage programme until the German second line was taken and here considerable confusion arose owing to men of the 63rd Brigade getting over too much to the left. About this point it was found difficult to make a further immediate advance owing to enemy enfilade machine gun fire and snipers. The battalion on our left was slightly in rear of us and we had to wait until they came up in line before the machine guns and snipers were silenced. The advance then continued up to the road ... A patrol was pushed out to find if Cuba Trench was occupied. The patrol returned and reported that Cuba Trench was clear of the enemy. The battalions then consisting of three officers and about 50 OR's occupied Cuba Trench at 9.30am ... Patrols were immediately sent out to get into touch with the 63rd Brigade on our right, but returned having failed to do so, a defensive flank was then formed by machine guns on our right. Immediate consolidation of Cuba Trench was started. Patrols were periodically sent out to get into touch with the 63rd Brigade but it was not until 9.55pm that we succeeded in doing so ... At 1pm a patrol was sent out to reconnoitre the crossroads ... but was unable to approach owing to very active enemy snipers. Fifty prisoners were captured during the day. Patrols were sent out during the night. All through the advance the enemy barrage was very intense.

The battalion's casualties in the period 22–29 April amounted to forty-six killed, 198 wounded and twenty-two missing.

WARNER, Daniel
'Faithful unto Death'

Age:	28
Rank:	Private
Regiment/Service:	Royal Fusiliers
Unit:	D Company, 4th Battalion
Service Number:	25657
Died:	23 April 1917
Cemetery/Memorial:	Étaples Military Cemetery
Reference:	XIX.H.17A

(Nick Fairbrother)

Daniel was born in Croydon and lived at 2 Riverside Villas, Mill Lane, Carshalton, and was a labourer before he enlisted in December 1915. He died of wounds probably received during the battalion's assault on 13 April near Arras:

> 6.45pm- On leaving the assembly position the battalion came under a hostile artillery barrage ... As it advanced it went through two more barrages the latter of which was very heavy consisting of high explosive and gas shells ...

The battalion came under very heavy MG and rifle fire from both flanks but chiefly from our right flank in the direction of Guemappe and Wancourt … The battalion continued to advance and reached the sunken road where they were held up by very heavy MG and rifle fire … There were now only three officers left with the companies … This was about 8pm … The battalion received orders to withdraw at about 1am.

None of the objectives were taken and casualties included fifteen killed, forty-two wounded and thirty-four missing.

ROGERS, Percival Richard

Age:	32
Rank:	Private
Regiment/Service:	East Surrey Regiment
Unit:	7th Battalion
Service Number:	G/24344
Died:	30 April 1917
Cemetery/Memorial:	Feuchy British Cemetery
Reference:	II.A.15

Percival was born and lived in Thornton Heath. He joined the army in December 1915 having previously worked as a general labourer. His battalion suffered no casualties towards the end of April so it is likely that Percival succumbed to wounds received at the start of the Arras offensive earlier in the month. At this time the battalion was based in Arras and had suffered few casualties due to lightly holding the line and having good dugouts. Early on the morning of 9 April the battalion carried out a successful attack:

> Our barrage opened at zero i.e. 5.30am and by that time all the waves were in or near the front trench ready to go over. The enemy barrage did not descend for three minutes and the whole battalion got away without, I think, one casualty. All the lines detailed to us were taken in excellent style the whole affair being carried off like a parade!

From 6.15 a.m. messages, wounded and prisoners started to trickle back, but reports as to progress were conflicting. The first German line of defence (the Black Line) had been captured and this was being consolidated under fire from machine guns and snipers situated in the Blue Line (the third German line). By the afternoon all the objectives in the Blue Line had been captured; the Brown Line (fourth line) was captured in the evening, with the exception of one redoubt which was taken early the next day. Casualties during the attack were 218 killed, wounded and missing out of a strength prior to the attack of 674 – nearly a third of their total. Percival was the brother of Carshalton casualties Albert and Frederick Rogers, the last of the three to be killed.

On 3 May the Third Battle of the Scarpe was launched, part of a two-pronged attack coinciding with the Australian assault at Bullecourt, 11 miles south-east of Arras.

DEELEY, George

Age:	21
Rank:	Gunner
Regiment/Service:	Royal Field Artillery
Unit:	B Battery, 124th Brigade
Service Number:	48893
Died:	3 May 1917
Cemetery/Memorial:	Cojeul British Cemetery, St-Martin-sur-Cojeul
Reference:	C.58

George was born in Wallington and lived at 92 Stanley Road. A farm labourer, he enlisted in January 1915. On 3 May the 124th Brigade was supporting the assault, bombarding Fontaine Wood: '9.20am- At this hour O.C. B Battery reported a direct hit on one of his guns, which killed two men (including the no. 1), wounded two seriously (one died later) and two slightly.' George is also commemorated on Wallington war memorial.

FRYER, Frederick William

Age:	27
Rank:	Corporal
Regiment/Service:	King's Shropshire Light Infantry
Unit:	5th Battalion
Service Number:	8795
Died:	3 May 1917
Cemetery/Memorial:	Arras Memorial
Reference:	Bay 7

Born in Marylebone, Frederick had previously served in the army but left before the war started, securing a job with the Birmingham police force in November 1913. He or his family later lived at Rose Cottage, Mill Lane. He was called up on reserve on 4 August 1914 and went to France with the 1st Battalion on 20 September. Although on one occasion he had a lucky escape when a shell killed the sergeant standing next to him, he was later wounded in the leg at Hooge in 1915. However, he recovered sufficiently to return to France. On 28 April 1917 Frederick's battalion moved into Niger Trench near Wancourt in the Arras sector. On 3 May orders were given for an attack to be made on the German-held Ape Trench in order to straighten the line. The battalion was detailed to occupy and hold Ape Trench once the initial assaulting force had captured the position. The attack was a success and Frederick's battalion maintained possession until relieved on the night of 4 May 1917. Twelve men were killed during the attack. Frederick was initially reported missing and was not confirmed killed until December 1917.

THOMPSON, Eric Stewart

Age:	35
Rank:	Private
Regiment/Service:	East Surrey Regiment
Unit:	1st Battalion
Service Number:	31050
Died:	7 May 1917
Cemetery/Memorial:	Arras Memorial
Reference:	Bay 6

Eric was born in Streatham and lived at 21 Station Road in Carshalton. A butcher, he was married with four children. The battalion war diary for the day he was killed records 'Enemy again put up a barrage about 3.15am on the front line. His artillery was active all day and his aeroplanes very bold, flying low over our trenches especially during the afternoon. Lewis gun fire was opened on them but did not prove very effective.' Three men were killed and eleven wounded. Eric's brother Rupert had been killed the previous month.

(June Davies)

The Arras offensive officially ended on 16 May. Although gains had been made, particularly at the start of the offensive at Vimy Ridge, the German system of elastic defence had prevented the hoped for breakthrough. British and Commonwealth casualties amounted to over 150,000 men.

The British next carried out a successful operation on the Messines Ridge on 7 June. This included the detonation of nineteen mines under German lines, and by mid-June the whole of the ridge was in British hands. Although none of Carshalton's men were killed in this battle, casualties continued to occur elsewhere along the Western Front.

HOOKER, David

Age:	30
Rank:	Private
Regiment/Service:	Border Regiment
Unit:	8th Battalion
Service Number:	19738
Died:	5 June 1917
Cemetery/Memorial:	St Quentin Cabaret Military Cemetery
Reference:	II.N.10

David, a labourer, was born in Mitcham and lived at 2 Palmerston Road. Carshalton. He had three brothers who also served in the war. Whilst there was a heavy German bombardment reported on 5 June, no casualties are mentioned. However, the previous day B Company suffered one casualty wounded at Neuve-Église. The previous week on 30 May, C and D Companies had supplied 200 men for a working party; as C Company was travelling down the Neuve-Église road a shell burst amongst them, killing four and wounding six. It is likely that David was wounded in one of these incidents.

GARROD, Herbert Henry

'Their glory shall not be blotted out'

Age:	26
Rank:	Gunner
Regiment/Service:	Royal Field Artillery
Unit:	D Battery, 102nd Brigade
Service Number:	122398
Died:	17 June 1917
Cemetery/Memorial:	Railway Dugouts Burial Ground
Reference:	Sp. Mem. B.15

Born in Clapham, Herbert lived at 17 St John's Road, Carshalton, and was married with one son. A leather hand by trade, he joined up in November 1914, initially serving with The Queen's, and was overseas from April 1915. His brigade had a steady number of men wounded throughout June caused by counter-battery fire. On 16 June three men were wounded whilst moving to new positions and four were wounded on the following day. His name is also on the Willie Bird cross.

EDWARDS, Lawrence Granville

Age:	20
Rank:	Lance Corporal
Regiment/Service:	The Queen's (Royal West Surrey Regiment)
Unit:	10th Battalion
Service Number:	G/6392
Died:	27 June 1917
Cemetery/Memorial:	Ypres (Menin Gate) Memorial
Reference:	Panels 11-13 & 14

CWGC Notes: Son of Harriett Sarah Edwards, of 25 Godstone Rd, Whyteleafe, and the late Samuel Pearce Edwards.

Born in Cross In Hand, Sussex, and lived at Laundry Cottage, High Street, Carshalton. Lawrence was a waiter before he enlisted in August 1915. He was probably killed or died of wounds whilst the battalion was holding trenches near Hollebeke, south-east of Ypres. On 27 June the battalion was relieved after four days in the front line trenches. Lawrence's brother Albert served in the 7th Queen's and was awarded the DCM.

GLANVILLE, Sidney Frank

Age:	29
Rank:	Private
Regiment/Service:	Border Regiment
Unit:	11th Battalion
Service Number:	28642
Died:	29 June 1917
Cemetery/Memorial:	Nieuwpoort Communal Cemetery
Reference:	I.B.7

(Stephen Glanville)

CWGC Notes: Son of Frank and Sarah Glanville, of West St, Carshalton; husband of Nora Glanville, of 34 Goodinge Rd, Holloway, London.

Born in Edmonton, Middlesex, when he enlisted he gave his occupation as baker; previously, according to the 1911 census, he was working as a fishmonger. Sidney lived at 47 Mill Lane, Carshalton, joined the Army Service Corps in January 1915 and was sent overseas in November 1915. It is believed he was killed on 29 June; although the battalion war diary does not record any action that day, they relieved the 17th Highland Light Infantry in the trenches near Nieuwpoort, right on the Belgian coast. Sidney was the nephew of Frederick Parsons.

HALL, William George

Age:	24
Rank:	Private
Regiment/Service:	East Surrey Regiment
Unit:	7th Battalion
Service Number:	6181
Died:	11 July 1917
Cemetery/Memorial:	Arras Memorial
Reference:	Bay 6

William was born in Carshalton and worked as a fireworks labourer. He married in 1910, had a daughter in 1911 and lived at 54 William Road. He went to France in June 1915. Just prior to his death, in the period 5–9 July, the battalion was in the front line (Arras Museum trenches) and suffered three other ranks killed and two wounded. On 11 July 'at 5.30am the enemy launches a determined attack on Long Trench with his storm troops and *flammenwerfen*.[49] They took Long Trench and inflicted 90 casualties on the 6th Buffs ... we lost our outpost line in Long Trench'. However there is no mention of whether the East Surreys also suffered any casualties that day. William's name is also on the memorial chapel in St Barnabas church.

CAISBROOK, James Henry

Age:	28
Rank:	Sergeant
Regiment/Service:	East Surrey Regiment
Unit:	13th Battalion
Service Number:	13027
Died:	27 July 1917
Cemetery/Memorial:	Fins New British Cemetery, Sorel-Le-Grand
Reference:	I.E.14

Born in Clifton, Worcestershire, James worked as a market gardener and had previously boarded with the family of another Carshalton casualty, Alfred Greenslade. At the end of July 1917 the 13th Battalion was near Gouzeaucourt where each company spent two days in the camp near Dessart Wood, obtaining baths and firing on the range. At night the companies were posted to the battalion front, and it is likely that James died of wounds received on 26 July when seven other ranks were wounded and three killed. His name is also on the memorials at Sutton and St Barnabas church, where he had been a Band of Hope cadet.

Buoyed by the success of the earlier offensive at Messines, on 31 July the Third Battle of Ypres campaign began, advancing towards the village of Passchendaele (the name of the village now synonymous with the campaign) and attempting to break out of the Ypres salient and capture the ridge that overlooked Ypres from the east. However, the preliminary bombardment lasted for ten days, and gave the Germans ample opportunity to prepare for the imminent attack.

Wounded soldiers arriving at Carshalton station for a concert at the Grove, 1917. (Sutton Local Studies)

SPEAR, Ernest

Age:	32
Rank:	Private
Regiment/Service:	Royal Fusiliers
Unit:	17th Battalion
Service Number:	G/52579
Died:	13 August 1917
Cemetery/Memorial:	Béthune Town Cemetery
Reference:	VI.F.71

Born in Yeovil and lived at 15 St John's Road. A leather dresser by trade, Ernest joined up in December 1915. He died of wounds near Béthune; in 'Canal Section' on the night of 10–11 August a mine was exploded, creating a crater which the Germans occupied. The following night a party was ordered to retake the crater. Seventy-five men attacked and the Germans retreated. Casualties to Ernest's battalion were three killed and ten wounded. He is also commemorated on the Willie Bird cross.

On 15 August the Canadians engaged the Germans in the Battle of Hill 70, near Lens. The objective was to draw German troops away from the fighting of the Third Battle of Ypres campaign further north. The capture of Hill 70 would also have provided an excellent observation post.

JAY, Douglas Pierce

Age:	26
Rank:	Private
Regiment/Service:	Canadian Machine Gun Corps
Unit:	2nd Company, 34th Battalion
Service Number:	602213
Died:	15 August 1917
Cemetery/Memorial:	Vimy Memorial

CWGC Notes: Mentioned in Despatches.

(Sutton Grammar School)

Douglas was born in Sutton and attended Sutton County School from 1905 to 1908. The family lived at 'Lancaster', Croft Road, Sutton, and his father was a prominent figure in the local council and parish committee. Douglas was in Canada for three years working as a farm labourer before joining the Canadian Expeditionary Force soon after the outbreak of war. He trained there for a year before coming to Britain in October 1915. He spent nine months in England then thirteen months in France. His death is mentioned in the battalion war diary although the date is recorded as 16 August:

> Barrage opens at 4.25am. A and B sections went forward in support of infantry and reached positions in red and blue lines. Enemy made a series of counter-attacks during the day. Our final objective consolidated by evening. Brigade suffered heavy casualties. Our casualties as follows: one other rank (Private Lane) killed. Three other ranks wounded. 16th- weather remains fine, our guns firing almost continuously on SOS barrage. Artillery kept up terrific bombardment all day. Three other ranks (Ptes Downes, Jay, and McAfee) killed, seven other ranks wounded.

After Douglas' death, his commanding officer Lieutenant Ferrie wrote:

It is my sad duty to inform you how your son Douglas was killed in one of the most severe actions the Canadians have ever been in. After the man in charge of the gun was wounded your son – the coolest man in the crew – took charge and handled it with the greatest bravery until shot through the head by a sniper. One consolation is that he never knew what hit him as he was killed instantly. Your son had been with A section (my section) a long time, and was one of the best men we have ever had. He was known throughout the whole company for his coolness and courage, and had a warm place in the hearts of all of us. He died doing his duty, which is all a man can do.

A comrade, Ronald Smith, also wrote to Private Jay's brothers:

Just a few lines to express to you my deepest sorrow in losing your brother who, as you know, was my dearest friend. I was not with him at the time he met with his death, but from what the boys tell me Doug did not suffer one moment's pain. He was regaining the trench with his gun when he was sniped by a German. He had just been forward with his gun to repulse a counter-attack, and in the position which he took up he did some wonderful work, and anything that is coming to Doug for his grand work will be more than earned. On the morning of the 15th he was the life and soul of the three crews, and on the way out to his objective he gave first hit to three men. He is sadly missed by his section and the rest of the Machine Gun Company. I cannot put into writing my own feelings in losing such a one in a million friend.

Douglas was mentioned in despatches for his actions on the day he was killed. He is also commemorated on Sutton war memorial, the Sutton County School memorial and the memorial chapel at St Barnabas church.

In an effort to retake the hill, the Germans deployed large quantities of poison gas, but the Canadians repulsed the German counter-attacks. Despite this, in ten days the Canadians had suffered over 9,000 killed, wounded and missing.

Although the start of the Third Battle of Ypres campaign had been promising with large gains made, heavy rain broke out and the attack literally became bogged down in a quagmire of mud. On 16 August an attack was made on the village of Langemarck, 6 miles north of Ypres.

SAVAGAR, George Leonard

Age:	19
Rank:	Private
Regiment/Service:	Royal Inniskilling Fusiliers
Unit:	8th Battalion
Service Number:	41017
Died:	16 August 1917
Cemetery/Memorial:	Tyne Cot
Reference:	Panels 70 to 72

CWGC Notes: Son of James George and Kate Savagar, of 'Somerton', Upland Rd, Sutton.

Born in Balham, George was a clerk prior to enlisting in January 1916. His address is given as 'Glencoe', Blakehall Road. On 16 August the battalion went into action with nineteen officers and 462 other ranks. A and B Companies were on the left and C and D Companies on the right:

> At zero the troops advanced and were not affected by enemy's artillery barrage, which was put down behind our front line … Machine gun fire was encountered about 200 yards west of Borry Farm causing very heavy casualties … We advanced another 100 yards were then completely held up. This was about 5am. Right leading company made an attempt to take Borry Farm from front by rushing it under cover of Lewis gun fire. This was unsuccessful and two flank attacks were made by same company endeavouring to get in from north side of the farm which consists of three concrete dugouts linked up by a breastwork and was strongly garrisoned by about 100 men and at least three MGs. The remnants of C Company took cover in shell holes about 100 yards west of Borry Farm and held this position all day. D Company were about 50 yards north-west of C Company. As far as can be ascertained the left companies advanced about 800 yards, in conjunction with battalion on left which fell back after a time. Germans advanced from dugouts and made an encircling movement on A and B Companies who stood their ground until almost surrounded, and then fought their way slowly back; only about 15 men were left in each of these companies … From about 10am onwards enemy filtered over ridge from direction Delva Farm and Hill 35 and appeared to take some of our men prisoner. Troops near Low Farm were able to fire on enemy who made no organised counter-attack.

Casualties were forty-five killed, 198 wounded and 101 missing.

By the end of the day the 16th Division, of which the 8th Royal Inniskilling Fusiliers was part, was back at its original start point.

On 27 August the 1/6th Royal Warwickshire Regiment attacked towards Langemarck Ridge.

COMYNS, Charles

Age:	24
Rank:	Private
Regiment/Service:	Royal Warwickshire Regiment
Unit:	1/6th
Service Number:	260092
Died:	27 August 1917
Cemetery/Memorial:	Tyne Cot
Reference:	XII.A.19

(Sutton Grammar School)

CWGC Notes: Son of Mr J.R. and Mrs A.D. Comyns.

Born in Halifax, Charles attended Sutton County School between 1903 and 1908. He entered the army under the Derby scheme in February 1916, but *The Suttonian* notes that his work as a chemist at his father's shop on Carshalton High Street prevented him from being called up for over a year. He initially joined the Essex Regiment but was then transferred to the Royal Warwicks. He went to France in June 1917 and was shot by a sniper shortly after climbing over the parapet of his trench, the battalion war diary stating: 'Moved into position north and south of St Julien–Winnipeg Road ... and dug in. Attacked at 1.55 p.m. enemy position at Winnipeg Farm and cemetery ... Advance impossible due to state of ground and fire from machine guns and snipers in concrete emplacements.' Casualties were twenty-eight men killed, 123 wounded and fourteen missing. Charles is also commemorated on the memorial at Sutton Grammar School.

RAYMOND, George

Age:	33
Rank:	Private
Regiment/Service:	Royal Fusiliers
Unit:	C Company, 13th Battalion
Service Number:	63795
Died:	10 September 1917
Cemetery/Memorial:	Outtersteene Communal Cemetery Extension, Bailleul
Reference:	I.A.42

CWGC Notes: Son of Mrs Susan Raymond, of 4 Limes Cottages, Green Wrythe Lane, Carshalton.

George was born in Bermondsey and worked as a leather dresser before he joined up in January 1917. The regimental history records that:

> After the attack on August 16th the wet weather and the arrangement of new tactics to suit the new elastic defence of the Germans imposed a long interval in the operations; and, although minor assaults were delivered here and there, no further concerted movement took place in this area until September 20th. There was minor activity on other parts of the line.[50]

George died of wounds possibly received on 8 September, when the battalion went into the line near Hollebeke (two killed, two wounded), or 9 September, during a German night raid on their battalion outpost in which two men were wounded. He is also commemorated on Wallington war memorial.

Due to the horrendous weather the battlefield had become a sea of mud and water-filled shell holes, and it was decided to delay any further offensive until 20 September.

KEEBLE, William

Age:	38
Rank:	Gunner
Regiment/Service:	Royal Garrison Artillery
Unit:	208th Siege Battery
Service Number:	130668
Died:	22 September 1917
Cemetery/Memorial:	Outtersteene Communal Cemetery Extension, Bailleul
Reference:	I.B.34

CWGC Notes: Son of Mrs S. Keeble, of 11 Talbot Rd, Carshalton. Native of London.

Born in Peckham, William joined the army in February 1916. He lived at 11 Talbot Road in Carshalton, and his occupation is given as 'traveller'. In September 1917 his battery was based near Dickebusch (about 10 miles from where he is buried); they were firing on 'harassing tasks' in preparation for an attack by the Second Army on 20 September. William was reported 'dangerously wounded' on 18 September, his injuries possibly the result of retaliatory shell fire. He died on 22 September at No. 1 Australian Casualty Clearing Station. In early October his brother John wrote to the Australian Red Cross Society asking for further information about William's fate; whilst it is clear from the records that he received a reply, the contents remain unknown.

The attack on 20 September was a success and plans were made for a further operation on 26 September.

FREEMAN, John William

'Remembering you we will be brave and strong'

Age:	23
Rank:	Lieutenant
Regiment/Service:	Royal Engineers
Unit:	X Corps, Signal Company
Died:	24 September 1917
Cemetery/Memorial:	Klein-Vierstraat British Cemetery
Reference:	III.E.4

CWGC Notes: Son of Florence Freeman, of 'Kingsweir', Carshalton Rd, Sutton, and the late Frank Freeman.

(Whitgift School)

John attended Whitgift Grammar School between 1908 and 1911 and then Malden College. He joined the Royal Engineers Signals in October 1914 as a second lieutenant and was promoted to lieutenant in July 1917. He specialised in field telegraphy and signalling and had proceeded to the front only ten weeks before his death. He died of wounds received on the Ypres–Menin Road whilst in charge of a signals working party carrying out general maintenance to the buried cable system. His colonel wrote:

> He was perfectly splendid, always cheerful, and a grand worker. In the short time he was at the front he had already done so well that I had sent his name for the charge of divisional artillery signals with the acting rank of captain. He would certainly have won the Military Cross had he survived. He was one of the best of my boys.

John is also commemorated on Sutton war memorial and St Barnabas church memorial.

WOOD, John Batty

Age:	28
Rank:	Rifleman
Regiment/Service:	Rifle Brigade
Unit:	16th Battalion
Service Number:	S/29750
Died:	27 September 1917
Cemetery/Memorial:	Spoilbank Cemetery
Reference:	I.P.10

John was born in Leeds and lived in Carshalton at Flora Villas, Brickfield Lane, the Wrythe. He was married with a child and worked as an electrical clerk. His battalion had been in action on 20 September 1917. The German lines had been successfully captured but casualties had been heavy due to snipers and machine gun fire, with over 200 men killed and wounded. The following week, on 27 September, the battalion was at Ridge Wood in support to 118th Brigade. They were relieved in the evening by the Yorks and Lancs Regiment and proceeded by buses to Dranoutre. Casualties were two killed in action, thirteen wounded, and two missing. It is possible John was a casualty either on 20–21 September and died of wounds, or was killed on 27 September during this relief. His name is also on the Willie Bird cross.

The British and Commonwealth troops were slowly making advances towards the Passchendaele Ridge. A rethink of tactics helped to achieve this, with a shift from large-scale offensives to assaults designed to capture small parts of the German line then hold out against any counter-attacks.

STRACEY, John William

Age:	21
Rank:	Lance Corporal
Regiment/Service:	The Queen's (Royal West Surrey Regiment)
Unit:	3/4th Battalion
Service Number:	T/201638
Died:	4 October 1917
Cemetery/Memorial:	Tyne Cot
Reference:	Panels 14 to 17 & 162 to 162A

CWGC Notes: Son of Mrs Frances E. Field, of
1 Rochester Rd, Carshalton.

John was the brother of Thomas, who had died in
Mesopotamia in 1916. The 1911 census shows the
brothers living in Mill Lane and John working as a

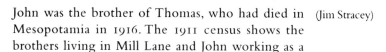

(Jim Stracey)

garden boy. On the night of 2–3 October 1917 his battalion had moved into front
line trenches to the south-east of Polygon Wood, a difficult manoeuvre due to the
muddy terrain, which affected not only troop movements but also the provision
of essential supplies. The following day the Second Army attacked:

> At 6am the battalion advanced to the assault … only slight opposition was
> offered to our advance which proceeded quickly except on the centre of B
> Company where a concrete fortress put up a show of resistance which was
> soon overcome … The enemy artillery maintained a continuous barrage over
> the whole area captured until 4pm. Great difficulty was experienced in clearing
> the wounded. At 9am the enemy made a counter-attack on the right which
> was however dispersed by our artillery fire. The enemy shelled the back area
> throughout the night thus rendering communications and removal of casualties
> extremely difficult.

Over 260 men from the battalion became casualties that day.

LIDDELL, Arthur John

Age:	29
Rank:	Second Lieutenant
Regiment/Service:	King's Own Yorkshire Light Infantry
Unit:	8th Battalion
Died:	5 October 1917 (wounded 23 September 1917)
Cemetery/Memorial:	Calais Southern Cemetery
Reference:	Plot B. Row Officers. Grave 12

CWGC Notes: Son of William Joseph and Elizabeth Liddell, of Woodside,
Carshalton Park Road, Carshalton.

Arthur worked as a clerk for the London, Brighton and South Coast Railway. He joined the Honourable Artillery Company in December 1915 and was attached to the 2nd Artists' Rifles OTC. He was posted to the KOYLI after he was commissioned in March 1917. He died at the No. 9 Red Cross hospital in Calais, after suffering shell wounds to both thighs and a bayonet wound to the thigh on 23 September when the battalion had been in Tor Top Trench at Hill 62 to the east of Ypres. He is commemorated on the London Brighton and South Coast Railway Company memorial at London Bridge station.

KIRBY, David

Age:	31
Rank:	Private
Regiment/Service:	Machine Gun Corps (Infantry)
Unit:	55th Company
Service Number:	72596
Died:	10 October 1917
Cemetery/Memorial:	Bard Cottage Cemetery
Reference:	V.A.22

(Hazel Kirby)

Born in Carshalton and a labourer, David lived at 21 St James Road. He played football for Carshalton Athletic, enlisted in September 1914 and initially served with The Queen's (Royal West Surrey Regiment). In October 1914 he wrote home from Purfleet camp:

> Thanks very much for the cigarettes, which were very acceptable to the members of the club. It has been beautiful weather until today but it is now raining, which makes it very miserable, especially getting about in the clay. I am sorry to say we do not get much time for football except on Sunday, when we sometimes have a kick about on purpose to keep our eyes in. I shall be very glad when we shift into barracks as the nights are very cold. I wonder if we shall all be playing together next season? I hope so, when we can all recall our different experiences. I think this is all now as I hear the bugle blowing for cookhouse and I must be off.

The 55th MGC had been in training at the beginning of October. On 9 October they moved to 'Dirty Bucket Camp' near Vlamertinghe. On 10 October, 'at 2pm A and D sections proceeded up line in motor lorries to Hurst Park (north-east of Ypres). A section had the following casualties as limbers were being unloaded: six killed, 11 wounded. D section had the following casualties: two killed, three wounded.' David is also commemorated on the Willie Bird cross. He was the brother of Thomas Kirby.

SHIRLEY, Horace Charles

Age:	33
Rank:	Private
Regiment/Service:	East Surrey Regiment
Unit:	1st Battalion
Service Number:	33766
Died:	10 October 1917
Cemetery/Memorial:	Tyne Cot
Reference:	Panels 79 to 80 & 163A

(Jim Shirley)

Born in Carshalton, Horace was a bricklayer who lived at 94 Stanley Road before signing up in December 1915. He was married with a son born in 1912 and was linked to the Kilty family by marriage. He may have been wounded in action during the battalion's offensive on 8–9 October near Polygon Wood and Sanctuary Wood, where the battalion attacked the Polderhoek Spur as a subsidiary attack to the Battle of Poelcapelle. The attack was unsuccessful, the Germans in Polderhoek Chateau pushing them back. The battalion war diary also reports that, on 7 October, '20 men of No 2 Company in a pillbox were heating a petrol tin supposed to contain water.[51] Actually it was full of petrol, exploded and the men were all burnt, some badly.' It is possible that Horace was one of these men and later succumbed to his wounds.

TYLER, Herbert

'Yet again we hope to meet thee when the day of life has fled'

Age:	34
Rank:	Private
Regiment/Service:	West Yorkshire Regiment (Prince of Wales's Own)
Unit:	11th Battalion
Service Number:	52402
Died:	17 October 1917
Cemetery/Memorial:	Lijssenthoek Military Cemetery
Reference:	XXI.H.20

CWGC Notes: Son of William and Hannah Tyler, of Lower Green, Tewin, Welwyn, Herts; husband of Annie Tyler, of 137 Stanley Rd, Carshalton.

Born in Tewin, Herbert was a gardener. He enlisted in October 1916, initially joining 2/1st Hunts Cyclist Battalion. He transferred to the West Yorkshire Regiment in early September 1917 just a month before his death, and had fought in the 'Battle of Menin Road' in which the 23rd Division was engaged in the period 18–24 September, and which cost his battalion 288 casualties. On 16 October the battalion moved from Clapham Junction Trench to Zillebeke Bund, an embankment on the side of a lake west of Zillebeke that had been emptied of water by shell fire and hence was an ideal place to seek cover. However, Herbert was admitted to the 17th Casualty Clearing Station near Lijssenthoek that day with a shell wound to his abdomen and arm. He had a son, also named Herbert, born in May 1918, after his death.

Heavy rainfall in mid-October meant that the offensive again had to be postponed. Towards the end of October the 'Second Battle of Passchendaele' was launched, a final attempt to break through and capture the Passchendaele Ridge.

ALLUM, John

Age:	35
Rank:	Private
Regiment/Service:	London Regiment (Artists' Rifles)
Unit:	1/28th Battalion
Service Number:	764960
Died:	30 October 1917
Cemetery/Memorial:	Tyne Cot
Reference:	Panel 153

John was born in Ludlow in Shropshire. After moving to Carshalton he lived in Gordon Road then at 'Ivydean', Beeches Avenue. He was married and worked as a hospital steward at the 'Poor Law' hospital. He joined up in January 1917 and had gone over to France in May 1917. He was killed in action during the battle for Passchendaele Ridge. The regimental history records that:

> Early on the 30th our brigade attacked ... under a very heavy barrage: the British artillery averaged one gun to every nine yards of front. To reach our objective we had to cross the Paddebeeke, on the map an insignificant stream-let, but in fact by this time a wide and almost impassable swamp. The instant our attack started, the forward troops came under intense machine gun fire from an almost invisible enemy who had taken refuge in their pillboxes during our bombardment, and were now posted in carefully chosen tactical posi-tions. Simultaneously our supporting troops suffered heavy casualties from enemy artillery, while the ground to be traversed was a deep sea of mud, which drowned wounded men and clogged rifles and Lewis guns in the first few min-utes, rendering them entirely useless. Consequently it was not long before the attack was brought to a complete standstill ... On this day the Artists went into action about 500 strong and suffered 350 casualties.[52]

The journalist and writer Philip Gibbs also described the conditions suffered by the men of the Artists' Rifles:

> It is idle for me to try to describe this ground again, the ground over which the London men and the Artists had to attack. Nothing that I can write will convey remotely the look of such ground and the horror of it. Unless one has seen

vast fields of barren earth, blasted for miles by shell fire, pitted by deep craters so close that they are like holes in a sieve, and so deep that the tallest men can drown in them when they are filled with water, as they are now filled, imagination cannot conceive the picture of this slough of despond … The shell craters yesterday were overbrimmed with water, and along the way of the becks, flung out of bounds by great gun-fire, these were not ponds and pools, but broad deep lakes in which the litter and corruption of the battlefield floated.[53]

BILLETT, John Henry

Age:	18
Rank:	Private
Regiment/Service:	Royal Warwickshire Regiment
Unit:	14th Battalion
Service Number:	29893
Died:	31 October 1917
Cemetery/Memorial:	Tyne Cot
Reference:	Panels 23 to 28 & 163A

John was born in Blandford, Dorset, but the family later moved to Carshalton Place. He enlisted underage and went overseas in June 1915 when he was just 16. His battalion took over front line trenches in Polderhoek on 24 October 1917. The war diary describes the trenches and shell holes as half full of mud. In the period 24–25 October the battalion lost four men killed, sixteen wounded, and two missing. On 26 October they attacked the German position at Polderhoek Chateau. The chateau and surrounding area were taken after some heavy hand-to-hand fighting, and about 250 prisoners were captured. However, the battalion had to withdraw after coming under heavy flanking machine gun fire from another position. Casualties were thirty killed, 141 wounded and fifty-nine missing, and John died of wounds received in this action. His father also served in the war, as a sergeant in the Somerset Light Infantry; in November 1924 he wrote to the *Ypres Times*[54] saying 'My son was killed in the Ypres Sector on about the 20th October, 1917 … at a place called Polderhoek Chateau, Gheluvelt … I should be glad to hear from any of your readers if they know anything about him.'[55] Like countless others whose loved one's bodies were never found, it is clear that seven years later John's fate was still a cause of anguish for the family.

The Canadians finally captured Passchendaele village on 6 November and the campaign officially ended on 10 November. However, the Germans still held the northern tip of the ridge.[56]

Despite the losses of the Third Battle of Ypres campaign, further operations began on 20 November at Cambrai. This battle is famous as it was the first time tanks were used on a large scale. The German troops were caught by surprise and in many places retreated in the face of the tank attacks. In some places the British advanced as much as 6 miles.

STEVENS, Frederick

Age:	19
Rank:	Private
Regiment/Service:	East Surrey Regiment
Unit:	13th Battalion
Service Number:	23730
Died:	26 November 1917
Cemetery/Memorial:	Cambrai Memorial, Louverval
Reference:	Panel 6

CWGC Notes: Son of William and Annie Emma Stevens, of 32 Lodge Rd, Wallington.

Frederick was born in Croydon but by 1911 the family were living at 15 Shorts Road. His battalion was part of the 40th Division which was a Bantam division where the men were all shorter than the normal regulation height of 5ft 3in. On 25–27 November the battalion was involved in heavy fighting trying to clear Bourlon Wood and village just to the west of Cambrai. As the regimental history records 'The importance of Bourlon Ridge and its menace, if held by the British, to the German defences south of the Sensee River were, of course, obvious to both sides.'[57] Casualties amounted to 229.

Once again the initial British successes were not consolidated and the attack became bogged down. The Cambrai operations ended on 27 November, but three days later the Germans counter-attacked, by early December driving the British back to the positions held at the start of operations. Despite highlighting the tactical benefits of utilising tanks, casualties during the campaign were over 40,000 men.

STEVENS, Herbert Henry

Age:	36
Rank:	Private
Regiment/Service:	Cameron Highlanders
Unit:	6th Battalion
Service Number:	201193
Died:	23 December 1917
Cemetery/Memorial:	Duisans British Cemetery, Étrun
Reference:	V.D.56

CWGC Notes: Husband of R.E. Stevens, of 152 Stanley Rd, Carshalton.

Herbert was born in Sutton and worked as a labourer. His address when he enlisted in December 1915 is given as 11 Cranfield Road, Wallington. His battalion was in front line trenches near Étrun, just outside Arras, from 16 December. Trench mortars caused eight casualties on 18 December. Some other ranks were also admitted to hospital during this time but the war diary does not state whether through illness or injury.

1918

1918 opened with the eerie lull characteristic of the winter. Whilst raids and attacks were carried out, no major offensive was launched as each side resupplied and prepared for the coming year. Carshalton was largely unaffected during this time, with no reported casualties until March, the longest such period since the war had started.

WHITE, Harold Edward

Age:	24
Rank:	Sapper
Regiment/Service:	Royal Engineers
Unit:	Y Corps Signal Company
Service Number:	245717
Died:	3 March 1918
Cemetery/Memorial:	Tyne Cot
Reference:	Panels 8 & 162

CWGC Notes: Also served RAMC.

Harold was born in Peckham, lived in Bethnal Green and was a junior clerk. It is believed his mother Grace moved to 5 North Street sometime after 1911; she was certainly living there by 1919. Harold served initially with the Royal Army Medical Corps before transferring to the Royal Engineers. At the time of his death his company was employed near Abeele (south-west of Poperinge) burying about 350 yards of communication cable per day, which had to be buried deep to avoid being cut by shell fire. Although it is unknown how Harold died, there was a constant risk when burying cable of being exposed to enemy artillery bombardments.

NICHOLLS, James Frederick

'In loving memory of our dear son, never forgotten by Father, Mother and all at home'

Age:	18
Rank:	Private
Regiment/Service:	The Queen's (Royal West Surrey Regiment)
Unit:	1st Battalion
Service Number:	60992
Died:	7 March 1918
Cemetery/Memorial:	Nine Elms British Cemetery
Reference:	XIII.F.17

CWGC Notes: Son of James Nicholls, of Carshalton.

James enlisted in June 1915 and gave his age as 17 years exactly. However, the 1901 census gives his age as 2, so it is likely that he was only 16 when he signed up. He gave his occupation as baker and address as 11 St James Road, and, as he was too young to serve overseas, he was assigned to the 29th Training Reserve Battalion before later being posted to The Queen's. He probably died of wounds received on 2 or 3 March whilst in the line at 'Hamburg' trenches in the Ypres area; the battalion suffered four other ranks wounded during this time. Nine Elms British Cemetery is located to the west of Poperinghe, near Ypres. James was the nephew of Thomas George Wyatt and Ernest Baker.

James Nicholls, far right. (Mario Fuller)

Meanwhile, the Germans had been planning their next offensive. At the beginning of March they had signed a peace treaty with the Russians, removing the threat to the east and enabling them to commit further troops to the Western Front, where they hoped to make a decisive breakthrough before the USA could build up an effective fighting presence on the continent.

The offensive was launched on 21 March and swept through the British defences in many areas, aided by dense fog. The confusion experienced at this time is reflected in many of the British battalions' war diaries, which often do not contain much information about this period. The Fifth Army was particularly affected and over 20,000 men were taken prisoner. German tactics contributed greatly to the successes. They utilised 'stormtroopers' who were trained to skirt round strongpoints that were causing problems and leave them to be dealt with by the supporting troops. But many of the British battalions put up a bitter defence and, despite their gains, German casualties were also high.

BROOKS, Caleb James

Age:	19
Rank:	Private
Regiment/Service:	Queen's Own (Royal West Kent)
Unit:	7th Battalion
Service Number:	G/23762
Died:	21 March 1918
Cemetery/Memorial:	Pozières Memorial
Reference:	Panels 58 & 59

CWGC Notes: Son of James Charles and Emma Brooks, of 'Waverley', 32 Stanley Rd, Carshalton.

Caleb was born in Maidstone and worked as a hairdresser. He was the brother of Reginald and William Brooks; all three brothers were to lose their lives in the space of just over a month, with Caleb the first to be killed. On 20 March information had been received that the enemy was massing in large numbers.

The following day they advanced under cover of dense fog and surrounded the battalion headquarters at about 11 a.m. A, B and C Companies were also surrounded at about 10.30 a.m. Approximate casualties were twenty officers and 577 other ranks.

PINKS, Harry Ambrose

Age:	18
Rank:	Rifleman
Regiment/Service:	King's Royal Rifle Corp
Unit:	9th Battalion
Service Number:	A/205132
Died:	21 March 1918
Cemetery/Memorial:	Pozières Memorial
Reference:	Panels 61 to 64

CWGC Notes: Son of Mr and Mrs W. Pinks.

A cleaner, Harry lived at 18 West Street Lane, Carshalton. His father was assistant superintendent of the Carshalton Urban District Council Fire Brigade. Harry joined the 22nd Training Reserve Battalion in March 1917, aged 17. A year later he was in France. On 21 March:

> At about 4.45am an intense bombardment was opened on the battalion front and on back areas. Wires to brigade headquarters were broken at once, and a heavy ground mist made visual signalling impossible. The bombardment continued until about 9.30am, gas shells being extensively used for the last two hours. The German infantry then came over in small columns. Information as to what actually happened is almost entirely lacking but it would appear that the enemy came in on our left flank, and not on our front, as the first warning of the attack was the appearance of Germans moving down the St Quentin Road. C and A Companies were killed or captured to a man. A few men of B Company escaped … The Germans would seem to have lost direction in the mist and to have remained in some force round our front line for several hours … The red smoke signal for the closing of barrage lines had been sent up but it is almost certain that the gunners were unable to see this signal or the SOS which had been sent up from battalion headquarters at 10am. D Company in Lambay Switch had seen no signs of the enemy at 11.20am, but very shortly after this small columns of his infantry began to press forward into the Bois de Lambay, and over the Ovillers Lambay ridge. A pigeon message from Col Berry stated that battalion headquarters were still holding out at 12.20pm but no further information was received from the front line, or from D Company, one or two men escaped from D Company and it would appear that the Lambay position was not seriously attacked, at any rate until about 2pm by which time the enemy had occupied Benay and had reached the battle zone and had thus entirely cut off Lambay Farm. Sounds of MG fire were heard later in the day

from the direction of Lambay which would suggest that the company held out for some time after being surrounded. By the evening of March 21st the battalion had apparently ceased to exist.

The battalion's casualties amounted to nearly 650 men.

BROWN, Percy George

Age:	19
Rank:	Rifleman
Regiment/Service:	King's Royal Rifle Corps
Unit:	1st Battalion
Service Number:	A/203517
Died:	24 March 1918
Cemetery/Memorial:	Dernancourt Communal Cemetery Extension
Reference:	X.D.13

CWGC Notes: Son of Harry Robert Brown, of 31 Sutton Grove, Sutton, and the late Bertha Brown.

Percy lived at 31 Sutton Grove and in 1911 was working as a newsboy. On the opening day of the offensive the battalion reported a heavy bombardment all along the front. During the afternoon of 22 March they received reports of an enemy breakthrough to the south and in the evening were moved up to plug the gaps near Equancourt and Fins. On the morning of 23 March the battalion withdrew to ensure line was kept straight. Some casualties were caused by shell fire, machine guns and planes whilst withdrawing over 1,000 yards of open ground. Their new position on top of a hill was subjected to heavy machine gun fire causing many casualties whilst digging in at the eastern edge of Valluhart Wood, with the enemy trying to flank and enfilade them. During the evening they withdrew to the village of Bus. Enemy fire continued through the night, and the men had no rations or water and were running low on ammunition. They also suffered from confusion over lack of orders and continual shelling. Again they withdrew, but by this time D Company had been entirely wiped out, and the other companies had suffered heavily. The war diary also reports that British guns were shelling the line where some troops were still in place. The battalion moved to Gueudecourt and then on to Destremont Farm. There is no mention of total casualties. Percy is also commemorated on Sutton war memorial.

MUNDAY, William Thomas

Age:	34
Rank:	Rifleman
Regiment/Service:	King's Royal Rifle Corps
Unit:	8th Battalion
Service Number:	29361
Died:	24 March 1918

Cemetery/Memorial: Grand-Seraucourt British Cemetery
Reference: IV.E.1

Born in Folkestone, William was a porter who lived at 13 Southdown Road, Carshalton. He enlisted in November 1915. Due to the disorganisation caused by the offensive no battalion war diary exists for this period; on 21 March the Germans had attacked and the battalion had fought a rearguard action from Jussy to Flavy, many of the troops being surrounded and overrun. Due to the number of casualties in this and other battalions it was reformed into a composite battalion in April before being officially disbanded in July.

TURNER, Arthur

Age: 26
Rank: Private
Regiment/Service: East Surrey Regiment
Unit: 9th Battalion
Service Number: 16104
Died: 24 March 1918
Cemetery/Memorial: Pozières Memorial
Reference: Panels 44 & 45

CWGC Notes: Son of Mrs Elizabeth Turner, of 16 St John's Rd, Carshalton.

Arthur was a farm labourer who enlisted in November 1915. He was reported as wounded and missing at some point in the period 21–27 March. On 21 March the battalion was near Vermand and suffered from enemy artillery. The battalion war diary records that on 25 March it was defending Fonches and suffered considerably due to the enemy artillery barrage. Arthur is named in the list of battalion wounded; during March they suffered over 400 killed, wounded and missing. In late 1918 or early 1919 a comrade of Arthur's wrote to his mother, and although the original letter is lost, some correspondence still remains on Arthur's service record:

> Dear Mrs Turner,
> your letter to hand am pleased to hear you got my report through alright and I cannot say how sorry I am to have to tell you that it is all too true as he was one of the best youngsters I have seen you should have known long ago that he was killed as there was plenty more beside myself that knew there was a Sergeant Wyatt I think he lives somewhere near you he knows more than I do about it if he is home now I believe he got hit the same day as I did last October. I am quite alright myself and am home for good with my wife and children and hope you have got your other sons home alright that I have heard Arthur speak about will close with my deepest sympathy.
> Yours,
> Mr C. Smith.

It appears Charles Smith was asked to confirm these details to the War Office. His report from January 1919 stated:

> Saw him lying dead: On or about March 24th 1918 I was carrying up ammunition close to Vermand when I saw Turner laying with Captain Lester of D Company and one other (I cannot remember his name) they had been caught by a shell in the back. They were lying in no-man's-land, we were not able to stop, so cannot say if they were buried.

His description of Arthur was 'Little short fellow, fresh complexion always jolly and bright, and most willing. He was the Captain's runner, Captain Dymond of D Company. Turner came from Carshalton near Sutton. He was a carter on a farm.' In February 1919 Arthur's mother wrote to the War Office: 'As I have had the letter from Mr Smith I thought I would send it on to you for you to see that he saw my son killed … I should be glad if you could let me know any more about him as the anxious time I am having is making me ill.' It is not clear if she received a reply to this letter, but in June 1919 the War Office declared that Arthur was killed on or around 24 March 1918. Captain Lester, who was seen lying with Arthur, has a date of death of 25 March and is buried in Bellicourt British Cemetery.

BATCHELOR, Charles

Age:	27
Rank:	Private
Regiment/Service:	Leinster Regiment
Unit:	2nd Battalion
Service Number:	5527
Died:	26 March 1918
Cemetery/Memorial:	Pozières Memorial
Reference:	Panel 78

CWGC Notes: Son of Mr and Mrs Batchelor, of 39 St James Rd, Carshalton; husband of Florence Batchelor, of 37 Green Wrythe Lane, Carshalton.

It is probable that Charles was wounded or killed during the chaotic few days of the initial German advance. On 21 March his battalion was situated near

(Jean Lambert)

Villers Faucon. The war diary records that the German bombardment started in the early morning and caused many casualties. On 22 March the division on their right retreated, leaving their flank open. The Germans were therefore able to push through and inflicted heavy casualties, forcing the battalion to withdraw. By 11.30 a.m. most officers were casualties and the British counter battery fire was proving an added risk as it was very close to their own lines. The following day further casualties were caused by enemy shell fire. During the offensive the

16th (Irish) Division, of which the battalion was part, suffered over 7,000 casualties. Charles was the brother-in-law of Thomas Wyatt, and his name also appears on the Willie Bird cross.

CARTER, William Maurice

Age:	22
Rank:	Private
Regiment/Service:	The Queen's (Royal West Surrey Regiment)
Unit:	10th Battalion
Service Number:	G/9940
Died:	26 March 1918
Cemetery/Memorial:	Arras Memorial
Reference:	Bay 2

CWGC Notes: Son of Annie Bessie Carter, of Perryvale, Alberta, Canada, and the late John Carter.

Born in Croydon, the 1911 census shows William working as a shop boy at a chemist's and living in Thornton Heath with his mother, father, uncle, eight brothers and one sister. He later lived in Carshalton at 5 Mill Lane. He signed up in November 1915 and was killed in action in March 1918. From 21 March the battalion was in the vicinity of Favreuil, north of Bapaume, and carried out a fighting withdrawal during this time, often harassed by enemy artillery and planes. The battalion war diary for 26 March is not available; however, the records of the 12th Brigade show that in the period 21–31 March the 10th Queen's suffered 385 casualties killed, wounded and missing. Out of a strength at the beginning of the month of 902 this equates to a casualty rate of over 40 per cent. The brigade as a whole suffered over 1,000 casualties during the same period.

FULLER, James

Age:	20
Rank:	Lance Corporal
Regiment/Service:	East Surrey Regiment
Unit:	9th Battalion
Service Number:	9343
Died:	27 March 1918
Cemetery/Memorial:	Pozières Memorial
Reference:	Panels 44 & 45

James was born in Carshalton and lived at 16 William Street. Known to his family as 'Jumbo', he worked as a labourer and joined up underage in May 1915. He was appointed Lance Corporal in October 1917 and was awarded the Military Medal on 29 December 1917, although it is not known for what act. Prior to his death he had been wounded once before. He was killed in action in the Fonches/Hallu area of the Somme. On 26 March:

At 1am the battalion withdrew to a line 2,000 yards east of Fonches between Hallu and Hattencourt. This was an old enemy front line that had been evacuated by the enemy in 1916. At 7.45am a message was received that our right flank had given and had withdrawn, at 8am another messenger reported that the trench 30 yards immediately in front of the battalion was full of enemy. There was a good deal of machine gun firing on both sides, the battalion inflicting many casualties in the enemy ranks. At 8.30am the enemy launched a violent attack all along the front. The battalion was garrisoning a front of about 1,400 yards and beat off the enemy again and again causing very heavy casualties in the enemy ranks. The battalion was determined to hold on at all costs and would not withdraw. The right flank had gone at 7.45am and the left flank went at 8.30am. Under Major C.A. Clark's command defensive flanks were at once formed and still we held the enemy back against terrific odds. The battalion continued this great stand against overwhelming numbers, every officer and man fighting to the last, until 9.30am when it was completely surrounded. Major C.A. Clark kept on fighting until the last and is believed to be a prisoner of war. Only three officers and about 30 men succeeded in getting away. This great stand by the battalion held the enemies [sic] advance up for over an hour, besides inflicting very heavy casualties in his ranks.

The surviving men were put into a composite battalion with the remainder of some other battalions, and saw further action the following day. In all, the battalion suffered 417 casualties during March. James Fuller's name is also on the Willie Bird cross.

The Germans attacked again on 28 March, towards Arras. However, the Third Army stood its ground.

BROWN, Charles Ernest

Age:	23
Rank:	Private
Regiment/Service:	Northumberland Fusiliers
Unit:	1st Battalion
Service Number:	56087
Died:	29 March 1918
Cemetery/Memorial:	Arras Memorial
Reference:	Bays 2 & 3

Born in Carshalton, Charles was the brother of Leonard Brown. He was a grocer's assistant and lived at 2 Butter Hill. He enlisted in February 1915 and went to France in April that year with the Army Ordnance Corps. On 28 March:

Enemy attack about 4.30am and capture front line. Enemy in very large numbers and supported by immense concentration of artillery, low flying aeroplanes, continue attack but were held up by reserve line until 3.30pm in spite of fact that both flanks were in the air. Order to evacuate position received. This was done. Battalion withdrew … and took up position in brigade support … 29th March- Enemy does not renew his attack but shells all lines very heavily.

Charles was killed in action.

ASTILL, Ernest William Richard Dearle

Age:	27
Rank:	Second Lieutenant
Regiment/Service:	London Regiment (Queen Victoria's Rifles)
Unit:	2/9th Battalion
Died:	30 March 1918
Cemetery/Memorial:	Pozières Memorial
Reference:	Panels 87 & 88

Born in Brixton, Ernest was employed as a ledger clerk for E.D. Sassoon and Co. trading house and lived with his family lived at 'Ediedene', Woodstock Road, Carshalton. He played cricket for Dulwich Hamlet Cricket Club. He enlisted at the outbreak of the war, went to France in May 1915 and had previously been wounded in action on the first day of the Somme (when his brother Reginald had been killed) and was sent back to England with shellshock. He was commissioned in August 1917 and at the time of his death was attached to III Corps training school. A note in his service record states that he was killed with 'Carey's force', 'date uncertain, probably 30.3.18.' Carey's was an irregular force thrown together during the March offensive when the German 'St Michael' attack looked to be threatening Amiens. Named after the officer in command, the unit was made up of any spare men who could wield a gun: engineers, surveyors, army schools staff, clerks and so on. Comprised of about 3,000 men, the force saw action until 31 March, when it was disbanded and the men returned to their normal units. Ernest is also commemorated on the Dulwich Hamlet Football Club memorial.

NOBLE, John Stanley

Age:	19
Rank:	Lieutenant
Regiment/Service:	Royal Berkshire Regiment
Unit:	5th Battalion
Died:	30 March 1918
Cemetery/Memorial:	Doullens Communal Cemetery No. 1
Reference:	VI.A.8

(Whitgift School)

CWGC Notes: Son of James and Emily Mary Noble, of 7 Grosvenor Avenue, Wallington.

John was born in Willesden and attended Whitgift Grammar School from 1907 to 1915. He trained at Sandhurst and was gazetted to the Royal Berkshire Regiment in July 1917. He went to France in August 1917, fought in the first battle of Cambrai, and was promoted to lieutenant in January 1918. On 27 March his battalion was near Martinsart, and sent troops to help try and stem a German attack. The situation was confused and attacks continued throughout the day as the battalion tried to hold the line. The following morning the Germans attacked again. A heavy artillery bombardment was brought down on them and the battalion repulsed the attack. The men were relieved on 29 March, but John was admitted to 3 Canadian Stationary Hospital at Doullens on the same day with a gunshot wound to his abdomen. He died of his wounds the following day. His entry in the Whitgift Book of Remembrance states 'At school and after, his keenness and modesty were notable and made him a general favourite.'

Friday 30 March marked the final day of the German 'St Michael' offensive. Their troops were becoming worn down and their supply lines overstretched; a successful Allied counterattack meant that no further gains were made.

JENKINS, Harry

Age:	40
Rank:	Private
Regiment/Service:	Cambridgeshire Regiment
Unit:	1st Battalion
Service Number:	327070
Died:	3 April 1918
Cemetery/Memorial:	Wimereux Communal Cemetery
Reference:	IX.D.7

CWGC Notes: Son of David and Esther Jenkins, of 39 Mill Lane, Carshalton.

Harry, a stoker by trade, died from tetanus, a common threat during the war due to the difficulty of keeping wounds clean. His battalion was not in action at the beginning of April but it is possible that Harry was wounded during the Germans' March offensive and then contracted the disease. This is borne out by the fact he is buried in a cemetery near Boulogne, where soldiers were treated prior to being shipped back to England. In the period 21–31 March the battalion suffered 383 casualties, over half of these missing. During this time the battalion covered the retreat of the British from Longavesnes to near Aubercourt, a distance of about 30 miles.

PAUL, Reginald Frederick

Age:	19
Rank:	Rifleman
Regiment/Service:	London Regiment (London Rifle Brigade), attached Artists' Rifles

Unit:	5th Battalion
Service Number:	304759
Died:	5 April 1918
Cemetery/Memorial:	Arras Memorial
Reference:	Bay 9

CWGC Notes: Son of Frederick Ernest and
Rosetta Amy Paul, of 'The Rookery',
31 Blakehall Rd, Carshalton.

Frederick attended Sutton County School, (Sutton Grammar School)
which he left in 1914. In January 1917 he joined
the London Rifle Brigade and went to France
on 1 March 1918. He died of wounds probably received at some point during the
German offensive. Between 20 March and 3 April his battalion suffered twenty-
four men killed, 143 wounded and 133 missing. He is also commemorated on the
memorial at Sutton Grammar School.

*After 5 April the German commander, Ludendorff, called off the Somme offensive. However,
he changed tactics and on 9 April the Battle of the Lys commenced with the aim of attacking
the southern sector of the Ypres salient and breaking through to the coast.*

GRAVES, Sidney

Age:	39
Rank:	Private
Regiment/Service:	Royal Fusiliers
Unit:	2nd Battalion
Service Number:	G/51216
Died:	13 April 1918
Cemetery/Memorial:	Ploegsteert Memorial
Reference:	Panel 3

Sidney was born Carshalton and lived at 19 Cambridge Road. He was married
at St Barnabas church in 1903 and had a daughter born in 1905. Before the war
he worked as an insurance agent. On 13 April the battalion was holding the front
line along the Vieux Berquin–Outtersteene Road:

> Early in the morning a heavy attack was launched by the enemy on our left
> which was finally held up. The ammunition dump … catching [sic] fire causing
> considerable confusion to the enemy who were forming up close by. A consid-
> erable number of Germans were killed with machine gun fire from our left post.
> Later on it was seen that the KOYLI on our right were retiring before a heavy
> German attack which was being launched against the village of Vieux Berquin.
> The Lancashire Fusiliers in support on our right also retired, thus leaving our
> right flank in the air. The defensive flank from our right post was immediately

formed towards Vieux Berquin. Shortly after this the troops on our left were seen to leave their trenches and retire. They were stopped by the Staff Captain of the 86th Brigade and led forward to their original trenches. Meanwhile the enemy attacked our line but was held up about 800 yards from it by machine gun and rifle fire. He then proceeded to dig himself in on a line 800 yards from our position. At nightfall the company commander of the company of the 31st Division on our left informed us that his battalion had moved off and had vacated all the trenches on our left. The position then was that we were holding a line in front with both flanks in the air and with the certain knowledge that the enemy held the village of Vieux Berquin. At dusk a withdrawal was duly carried out without confusion and in perfect order, and troops were found digging in on a line in the rear of Vieux Berquin. Rear headquarters prepared for relief of battalion, but could get no definite instructions from either brigade or division.

Casualties were fifteen officers and 234 other ranks incurred within just fifty-two hours in the front line: 'They were true to their fate in finding the hottest part in the battlefield; but their steadfast stand had played no small part in gaining time for the deployment of reinforcements.'[58]

JOHNSON, Charles

Age:	32
Rank:	Private
Regiment/Service:	South Wales Borderers
Unit:	2nd Battalion
Service Number:	45264
Died:	20 April 1918
Cemetery/Memorial:	Ploegsteert Memorial
Reference:	Panel 5

Born in Brixton, Charles had lived in both Wallington and Sutton. He was married and worked as a baker. On 20 April 1918 the battalion moved to the outskirts of Hazebrouck but there is no mention of any casualties. However, they had been involved in a large action on 11–12 April, when the Germans attacked Les Haies Basses, causing casualties of 533 out of a strength of 724. Following this battle the battalion had withdrawn to Doulieu on 12 April, then Ferme Labis the following day.

BROOKS, William Charles

'Safe home with Jesus'

Age:	19
Rank:	Private
Regiment/Service:	Bedfordshire Regiment
Unit:	7th Battalion
Service Number:	49218

Died:	24 April 1918
Cemetery/Memorial:	Crucifix Corner Cemetery, Villers-Bretonneux
Reference:	Sp.Mem.1

CWGC Notes: Son of James Charles and Emma Brooks, of 'Waverley', 32 Stanley Rd, Carshalton.

William was born in Bournemouth and enlisted in February 1917. On 24 April 1918 the battalion was in billets:

> Battalion ordered to 'stand to' at 4am. Moved up to line by stages during the day and took up position just South of Cachy. Battalion ordered to do counter-attack at 10pm. From information received the enemy had penetrated our defences to a depth of 2,000 yards (approx.) on a wide frontage. Battalion was formed up in position for attack with Royal West Kents on right and Australians on left. Night was intensely dark. Battalion moved forward to the assault and encountered slight opposition for first 1,000 yards. When battalion on our right was held up by heavy machine gun fire, the reserve company was ordered forward at this stage and thus reinforced. The assault was continued and final objective reached in spite of fierce enemy opposition and with two exposed flanks. The left company of battalion was ordered to withdraw in order to conform with line of battalion on left ... During this action the regiment alone took over 200 prisoners. Many enemy dead were observed on the captured ground. Five enemy machine guns were captured during this action and handed over to the French on relief ... The bearing of all ranks was most commendable, and deserving of the highest praise.

Casualties were sixteen killed, 112 wounded and seventy missing. William was the last of the three Brooks brothers to be killed.

SHORT, John Kenneth

Age:	23
Rank:	Lance Corporal
Regiment/Service:	King's Own Yorkshire Light Infantry
Unit:	6th Battalion
Service Number:	23358
Died:	24 April 1918
Cemetery/Memorial:	Pozières Memorial
Reference:	Panels 59 & 60

CWGC Notes: Attached 2/4th London Regiment (Royal Fusiliers).

The Short family lived at Westmead Farm, Westmead Road, where John worked as a farm hand. He went to France in August 1915 but in early 1918 his battalion had been disbanded and the men absorbed by the 2/4th London Regiment.

On the day John died the battalion was defending Villers Bretonneux against a German attack:

> All was ready to receive the advancing waves of German infantry, but it must be admitted that some of the stoutest hearts were filled with something approaching dismay when out of the fog, at a distance of 40 to 50 yards, loomed the weird forms of German tanks ... there is no doubt that the sudden appearance of these monsters shook our defence for a moment, and the men fell back a short distance. They remained perfectly under control, and were rapidly rallied by their officers a short distance in rear of the front trench, after which the German infantry, advancing in three waves close behind the tanks, were hotly engaged with rifle and Lewis gun fire, which inflicted heavy loss on them ... The first news of what was occurring in front was received at Battalion Headquarters in a message timed 6.30am: 'Tanks have crossed front line trenches, front line has fallen back, have rallied them at Company HQ line.' Steadily the tanks pressed our line back though our retirement was carried out gradually and at ghastly loss to the German infantry ... The heavy casualties sustained this day in 'missing' were due to the fact that in retirement the battalion was forced to leave many men, who might otherwise have been saved, in the enemy's hands.[59]

The casualties included twenty-four killed, 113 wounded and 205 missing. Lance Corporal Short was killed in action.

MERRITT, Frank Robert

Age:	21
Rank:	Private
Regiment/Service:	Tank Corps
Unit:	4th Battalion
Service Number:	75395
Died:	25 April 1918
Cemetery/Memorial:	Morbecque British Cemetery
Reference:	I.D.3

CWGC Notes: Son of Henry and Alice Merritt, of 45 St John's Road, Carshalton.

Frank was born in Carshalton and was a carman prior to enlisting in The Queen's in September 1915. Although in the Tank Corps, on 20–23 April the men were attached to the 31st Division and carried out reliefs of other troops near Morbecque. On 21 April they suffered one man wounded and on 22 April one killed and five wounded. Frank's name is also on the Willie Bird cross.

PENWILL, Douglas

Age:	19
Rank:	Private
Regiment/Service:	Essex Regiment
Unit:	10th Battalion
Service Number:	42853
Died:	26 April 1918
Cemetery/Memorial:	Hanguard Communal Cemetery Extension
Reference:	I.B.6

(Sutton Grammar School)

CWGC Notes: Son of Gertrude Penwill, of 'Highfield', 24 Elgin Rd, Wallington, and the late Charles Penwill. Born at Sutton.

Douglas attended Sutton County School between 1909 and 1913, lived at 'St Elmo', Highfield Road, Sutton, and worked as a clerk. In March 1917, when he was just under 18, he joined the 27th Training Reserve Battalion. He trained for a year in Britain before going to France in April 1918. Three weeks later he took part in the attack on Hanguard Wood, south-east of Amiens, from which he did not return. On 25 April the battalion had received orders to attack the wood. Arriving in position at 1 a.m. on the 26 April, they dug in for protection against the enemy shelling in the area. Their objective was the road running through the western and eastern positions of the wood. Zero hour was 5.15 a.m. at which time the battalion moved forward with 'indifferent' artillery support. Thankfully the German guns were equally inactive, but the leading companies suffered considerable casualties from hostile machine gun fire. The men were supported by three tanks, but they could not locate the German strongpoint at the northern edge of the wood whence most of the machine gun fire seemed to come. The battalion, considerably reduced, dug in on the track running north and south through the wood. This line was consolidated and they established contact with the units to their left and right. Casualties were twelve officers and 201 other ranks. The Sutton County School magazine speculated that Douglas had either been killed in action or died a prisoner. His name is also on the school memorial and Sutton war memorial.

At the end of April the Battle of the Lys drew to a close. Neither side had emerged victorious and combined casualties for both sides amounted to over 50,000 men.

MEARS, Walter

Age:	27
Rank:	Private
Regiment/Service:	Suffolk Regiment
Unit:	1/4th Battalion
Service Number:	201807
Died:	1 May 1918

Cemetery/Memorial: Étaples Military Cemetery
Reference: LXVII.A.29

CWGC Notes: Son of Thomas William and Eliza Mears of Carshalton. Native of Carshalton.

Walter was a labourer and lived at 58 Mill Lane. He served from December 1915. The 1/4th Suffolk Regiment was a pioneer battalion and at the beginning of May 1918 was based at Maison Rolland carrying out training and parades. With no casualties on 1 May, it is likely that Walter was wounded sometime earlier, during the German offensive, possibly towards the end of April. At this time the battalion was at the 'Gentilles Switch', where during the period 22–27 April, they suffered twenty-six men wounded by shells and gas.

BAKER, Ernest

Age: 27
Rank: Lance Corporal
Regiment/Service: East Surrey Regiment
Unit: 12th Battalion
Service Number: 15817
Died: 5 May 1918
Cemetery/Memorial: Ypres Town Cemetery Extension
Reference: III.F.9

CWGC Notes: Husband of E. Baker, of 13 St James Rd, Carshalton.

Born in Carshalton, Ernest was married and lived at 22 William Street. He worked as a coal porter and carman before joining up in November 1915. It is likely that he died of wounds received on 3 or 4 May, when the front and support lines were shelled causing several casualties. Private Baker's children laid wreaths on the Carshalton war memorial when it was unveiled in 1921. Ernest was the uncle of James Nicholls and brother-in-law of Thomas George Wyatt. His name is also on the Willie Bird cross.

(Sue Ealing)

A family memorial to Ernest Baker. (Sue Ealing)

BARNES, Harry

Age:	39
Rank:	Private
Regiment/Service:	Royal Fusiliers
Unit:	34th Battalion
Service Number:	26512
Died:	15 May 1918
Cemetery/Memorial:	St Sever Cemetery Extension, Rouen
Reference:	Q.II.H.14

CWGC Notes: Trans. to 60268 101st Company, Labour Corps.

Harry was born in Wickham and lived at Oxford Villas, Green Wrythe Lane. Previously a boiler maker at Southampton docks and a labourer in the mills, he enlisted in November 1915. He was wounded by a gas shell whilst serving with the Labour Corps and died the same day. He is also commemorated on the Willie Bird cross.

HAYES, John

Age:	30
Rank:	Private
Regiment/Service:	Royal Fusiliers
Unit:	34th Battalion
Service Number:	26474
Died:	15 May 1918
Cemetery/Memorial:	St Sever Cemetery Extension
Reference:	P.XI.K.15A

CWGC Notes: Son of John and Ellen Hayes, of 3 Swan Yard, West St, Carshalton. Transf. to (60382) 101st Company, Labour Corps.

Born in Woodmansterne, John was a labourer living at Swan Yard, West Street, and joined up on 11 December 1915, the day after his younger brother Patrick. He died in the same incident as Harry Barnes.

BADCOCK, Edward Salter
'Until the day break'

Age:	30
Rank:	Sergeant
Regiment/Service:	The Queen's (Royal West Surrey Regiment)
Unit:	D Company, 7th Battalion
Service Number:	200042
Died:	16 June 1918
Cemetery/Memorial:	Senlis Communal Cemetery Extension
Reference:	II.C.9

CWGC Notes: Son of George Edward Salter Badcock of 184 Holmesdale Rd, South Norwood, and the late Annie Badcock; husband of Winifred Badcock, of Slade St, Bayswater, Perth, Western Australia.

Edward was born in Southwark and attended Whitehorse Road School in Thornton Heath. He worked as a clerk in the goods manager's office at the London Bridge terminus of the London, Brighton and South Coast Railway. In 1911 he was married and living at 17 North Avenue, Carshalton. Before the war he had been a member of the Croydon Battalion Territorials and when war broke out he remained in England instructing new troops, until in 1917 he was sent to France. Whilst the battalion was holding the line near Albert he was shot in the head during a night patrol. The second of seven sons, four of his brothers also served, one of which was also killed in September 1916 whilst serving with the Canadians. Edward is also commemorated on the London Brighton and South Coast Railway Company memorial at London Bridge station.

WATKINSON, Oliver Barnet

Age:	32
Rank:	Sergeant
Regiment/Service:	Royal Garrison Artillery
Unit:	12th Brigade Heavy Artillery Group
Service Number:	24499
Died:	21 June 1918
Cemetery/Memorial:	Longuenesse (St Omer) Souvenir Cemetery
Reference:	V.B.79

CWGC Notes: Son of Charles and Amelia Watkinson, of Carshalton.

Oliver was born in Coulsdon and was the brother of Edward Watkinson. He served in the army before the war and at the time of the 1911 census was in Allahabad, India, with the 82nd Company, RGA. It is unknown which battery Oliver served in within the 12th Brigade Heavy Artillery Group during the First World War. In early June 1916 the brigade was based at Saint-Sylvestre-Cappel, east of St Omer. They were engaging targets in the Meteren sector, about 7 miles to the south-east. They suffered eleven casualties wounded up until 10 June (most likely through retaliatory shell fire) and it is possible that Oliver was one of these men. St Omer was a hospital town and he probably died of his injuries there later.

PARSONS, Harold Cope

'Not dead but living unto thee'

Age:	29
Rank:	Corporal
Regiment/Service:	London Regiment (Queen Victoria's Rifles)
Unit:	9th Battalion
Service Number:	390946
Died:	24 June 1918
Cemetery/Memorial:	Bavelincourt Communal Cemetery
Reference:	C.5

(Croydon in the Great War)

CWGC Notes: Son of George Keeble Parsons and Aimee Eliza Sarah Messenger; husband of Helen Riddle Parsons, of 8 Heathview Rd, Thornton Heath. Native of Thornton Heath. Enlisted Nov. 1914, wounded June, 1917.

Harold's parents lived at 53 The Beeches, Carshalton. Harold worked as a clerk before joining up. Although wounded in June 1917 he returned to active service. On the day he died his battalion was located at Baizieux, 7 miles west of Albert: '175th Infantry Brigade relieved the 174th Infantry Brigade on the right: the battalion relieved the 6th London Regiment in the right sub-sector. D Company sustained casualties on the way up to the line.' At the time Bavelincourt, where Harold is buried, was being used by the field ambulances of Harold's division.

CLARK, Frank William

'Even so them also which sleep in Jesus will God bring with him'

Age:	19
Rank:	Rifleman
Regiment/Service:	London Regiment (Queen Victoria's Rifles)
Unit:	B Company, 1/9th Battalion
Service Number:	394520
Died:	4 July 1918
Cemetery/Memorial:	Bavelincourt Communal Cemetery
Reference:	C.6

CWGC Notes: Son of William V. and Mary M. Clark, of 43 Morland Avenue, East Croydon.

Born in Clapham, in 1911 the family were living at 27 Franconia Road, Clapham, where Frank was a schoolboy. Prior to his enlistment in March 1917 (giving an address of 2 The Exchange, London Road, Thornton Heath) he worked as a clerk. On 4 July the corps to the right attacked enemy positions. The battalion front was bombarded by the enemy, causing casualties of four killed and six wounded. Frank's link to Carshalton is currently unknown – it is possible that he, his parents, or siblings lived in the area, but as Clark is quite a common name this has not been confirmed.

KING, Richard Reuben

Age:	21
Rank:	Private
Regiment/Service:	The Queen's (Royal West Surrey Regiment)
Unit:	2/4th Battalion
Service Number:	T/202051 (T/4460)
Died:	27 July 1918
Cemetery/Memorial:	Vauxbuin French National Cemetery
Reference:	IV.A.9

CWGC Notes: Son of Mrs Ada Matilda King, of 8 St John's Rd, Carshalton.

Richard was born in Carshalton and worked as a porter. He joined up in June 1915. On the day he died the battalion was near Villers-Hellon, forming up in preparation for an attack on the Parcy–Tigny line under the command of the French. Richard is likely to have died of wounds received from enemy shelling that began at 4.30 p.m., wounding six men. His name is also inscribed on the Willie Bird cross.

In August the Allies launched their own offensive, the Battle of Amiens, the start of the '100 days offensive' that would bring the war to a close. Dense fog on the opening day of the offensive helped the troops surprise the Germans and substantial gains were made.

JASPER, James Victor
'Greatly beloved, deeply mourned'

Age:	26
Rank:	Private
Regiment/Service:	Royal Army Medical Corps
Unit:	17th Field Ambulance
Service Number:	57340
Died:	14 August 1918
Cemetery/Memorial:	Lijssenthoek Military Cemetery
Reference:	XXV.G.22

CWGC Notes: Son of the Rev. James Edward and Maria Jasper, of 67 Park Lane, Wallington; husband of Mary Eleanor Jasper (nee Rogers), of Church Stretton, Salop. Clerk in Parr's Bank, Chelsea. Enlisted March 1915.

James was killed in action. The unit's war diary has no information on casualties, but at the time of his death they were based at Remy Siding near Lijssenthoek. This was an area next to the Poperinghe–Hazebrouck railway line used to house several casualty clearing stations.

STAINES, William Hugh

Age:	19
Rank:	Private
Regiment/Service:	Norfolk Regiment
Unit:	C Company, 12th Battalion
Service Number:	41836
Died:	15 August 1918
Cemetery/Memorial:	Le Grand Hasard Military Cemetery, Morbecque
Reference:	Plot 2. Row E. Grave 7.

CWGC Notes: Youngest son of William and Amelia Staines, of Sutton.

A milkman, William lived at 3 Harold Road, Sutton. He was 18 when he joined the 26th Training Reserve Battalion in August 1916 and served overseas from December 1917, initially with the Bedfordshire Regiment. The war diary of his battalion for 15 August makes no mention of casualties but states that they relieved the Royal Scots Fusiliers in the Grand Marquette/Sanitas Corner area. There was a trench raid that sustained casualties the following day, so it is possible that his death was not recorded in the war diary, he died of wounds received in the days or weeks before his death (although this does not tie in with the information contained in his service record), or his death has been recorded on the wrong date. He died two weeks before his 20th birthday and is also commemorated on Sutton war memorial and St Barnabas church memorial.

PERFITT, Richard

Age:	32
Rank:	Private
Regiment/Service:	Duke of Cornwall's Light Infantry
Unit:	1st Battalion
Service Number:	5385
Died:	10 September 1918
Cemetery/Memorial:	Abbeville Communal Cemetery Extension
Reference:	IV.E.19

Richard was born in Camberwell and by 1916 was living at 2 Gordon Cottages, West Street Lane. He died of wounds received in action on 31 August near Beugnatre, north-east of Bapaume:

Dull morning with light showers. About 5am the SOS was sent up by the New Zealand Division on our right. The enemy made a strong attack and the New Zealand Division withdrew leaving our right flank exposed. The situation was restored by a counter-attack by the New Zealand Division assisted by our A and B Companies. The enemy was completely repulsed and our companies took about 50 prisoners. The enemy retired over the high ground and was followed up by our patrols who reported a great number of enemy dead caught in our counter barrage.

Richard's name is included in the casualty list for this day – in total, there were sixty-three wounded, fourteen killed and nine missing.

COLLINS, Robert Henry

(Hazel Kirby)

Age:	35
Rank:	Driver
Regiment/Service:	Royal Field Artillery
Service Number:	97904
Died:	28 May 1919 (wounded 15 September 1918)

Born in Wycombe Marsh, Robert lived at 30 Station Road and worked as a labourer for the South Metropolitan Electric Light Company. He played football for Carshalton Athletic and Sutton United. He enlisted in 1915 and initially served with the 2nd Division Ammunition column before moving to the 41st Brigade Royal Field Artillery. He was discharged due to a bomb wound in his right thigh received on 15 September 1918. On that day the brigade had moved to new battery positions between Hermies and Doignies at dusk. The war diary reports that 'there was a good deal of bombing during the night'. Correspondence in his service record from his wife suggests that he died as a consequence of being gassed, but he is not recorded in the CWGC database.

DALE, Ernest David

Age:	46
Rank:	Rifleman
Regiment/Service:	King's Royal Rifle Corps
Unit:	2nd Battalion
Service Number:	R/500
Died:	18 September 1918
Cemetery/Memorial:	Bellicourt British Cemetery
Reference:	I.H.5

Ernest was born in Carshalton and was a labourer. He had four children and was the stepfather of Arthur Chandler, who was killed in April 1915. He was also second cousin of another Carshalton casualty, Richard Keattch. He lived at 8 William Street, Carshalton, and had served and been wounded in the Boer War. He joined up again in September 1914, stating that he had previously served with the Scots Guards and was sent overseas in March 1915. In a letter home in May 1915 he reflected, 'We have just got back from one of the biggest fights ever fought, it was something awful, thousands killed and wounded. I can't make out how any of us got back at all.'[60] Ernest was killed in action in the Battle of Épehy during the advance on the outposts of the Hindenburg Line. On 17 September the battalion had moved to Maissemy. The following day:

By 4.30am the battalion was formed up ready for the attack. The battalion was attacking on a front of about 800 yards which gradually narrowed down to about 500 yards at the final objective. Area extended from the impossible marsh ground of the River Omignon on the left to the road running north-east from Maissemy to Berthacourt … Our first objective was an enemy trench system along the high ground … halfway between Maissemy and Berthacourt. The second and final objective was Berthacourt. Zero was at 5.20am and the battalion moved forward. The morning was very wet and unpleasant but the weather got up towards noon. Prisoners soon began to come in but news was difficult to get on account of the heavy scotch mist which hung thickly in the valleys and this prevented any signalling or direct indication of the attack. The colonel went forward and got in touch with the company commanders of C and B Companies and learnt that the battalion was held up by machine guns on the left and right flanks. C Company was ordered to work around the left flank and B Company to gather with a portion of the left company of the Camerons to work around the right while A Company held the machine guns in front … All this caused considerable delay and as it was not till about 9.40 that the position was turned it was discovered that our barrage had gone far ahead. However without the aid of the barrage the battalion pushed forward quickly. They fought their way right through the village of Berthacourt to the eastern outskirts and finally consolidated there throwing out sentry groups in front of the main line of resistance. Throughout the offensive enemy shelling was practically negligible and most of the opposition was from machine guns … We had been told to expect a counter-attack from Pontruet a village 500 yards to the east of Berthacourt and sure enough much movement in the shape of small groups of enemy was observed working forward from that village at about 4.40pm. We had a telephone line back to brigade which was laid as we advanced and our Artillery Liaison Officer was able to get back to his brigade and within a few minutes an excellent barrage of shrapnel and high explosive was put down on the area where movement was seen with the result that the counter-attack failed to develop.

Casualties were twenty-five killed, ninety-nine wounded and six missing. Ernest was the oldest of Carshalton's men to be killed in action. His name is also on the Willie Bird cross.

The Battle of Épehy had been a moderate success with advances of up to 3 miles in the centre of the German line. Many German prisoners and weapons were also captured. Preparations continued for a final push against the defences of the Hindenburg Line.

KEATTCH, Richard Albert

Age:	25
Rank:	Private
Regiment/Service:	East Surrey Regiment
Unit:	1st Battalion
Service Number:	15918
Died:	24 September 1918
Cemetery/Memorial:	Lebucquière Communal Cemetery Extension
Reference:	II.G.27

CWGC Notes: Son of Mrs M.E. Keattch, of 1 Laburnum Villas, Brickfield Lane, Carshalton.

A carman who was born in Carshalton, Richard had enlisted in November 1915. His battalion was in the trenches in the period 20–25 September 1918, during which time the men carried out patrols in no-man's-land to ascertain the condition of their barbed wire and were subject to enemy artillery bombardments. Total casualties during the tour in the line were one officer wounded, six other ranks killed and twenty-five other ranks wounded. Richard was the second cousin of Ernest Dale, killed less than a week earlier. Richard's brother Frank also served and was wounded in 1915.

ELCOCK, James William

Age:	34
Rank:	Corporal
Regiment/Service:	Sherwood Foresters (Notts & Derby Regiment)
Unit:	1/8th Battalion
Service Number:	269872
Died:	26 September 1918
Cemetery/Memorial:	Vis-en-Artois Memorial
Reference:	Panel 7

(Hazel Kirby)

CWGC Notes: Son of Annie Elcock of 4 Bedford Villas, Wrythe Green, Carshalton, and the late James Elcock; husband of Amelia Frances Elcock of 55 Carshalton Rd, Carshalton.

James was a keen athlete and secretary of the local athletics club and Carshalton Athletic Football Club. He was employed as a law clerk before enlisting. On 24–26 September the battalion was involved in a small action near Pontruet designed to straighten the line and gain the high ground in the area. The objectives were taken on the 25 September although after that they suffered frequent enemy shelling until relieved on 26 September. Casualties were five killed and twenty-four wounded. James Elcock's name is also on the Willie Bird cross.

With the American Army now arriving in force on the Western Front and the German Army showing signs of weakness, on 28 September the final Battle of Ypres commenced, with the objective of breaking out of the Ypres salient.

CHANDLER, Reginald Victor

'He is gone we follow slowly; treasuring a memory holy'

Age: 19
Rank: Private
Regiment/Service: Seaforth Highlanders
Unit: 7th Battalion
Service Number: 204564
Died: 28 September 1918
Cemetery/Memorial: Ypres Town Cemetery Extension
Reference: II.F.27

Reginald Chandler, seated fourth from left on the front row.

CWGC Notes: Son of Joseph and Nancy Chandler of 8 Burton House, Myatt's Park, Camberwell, London.

A clerk for Carshalton Urban District Council, Reginald originally enlisted underage but was discharged when his true age was discovered. He re-enlisted in

June 1917 aged 18 years 1 month, giving his address as 55 Clapham Road, south-west London. On 28 September:

> Weather very wet. The battalion took part today in an attack which extended from Dixmude in the north to St Eloi in the south. The Belgian army cooperated with the Second British Army in the operation which was completely successful … At 5.30am the artillery barrage opened and five minutes later the infantry attack commenced. One battery of the artillery appeared to be firing two-three minutes late and our first wave suffered several casualties in consequence, these being practically the only casualties we had that day.

Despite the weather the assault was a success and seemingly caught the Germans by surprise, with the objectives taken by 8 a.m. Casualties totalled nine killed, eighty-three wounded, and seven missing. At a council meeting reference was made to 'Private Chandler's amiability and business capacity whilst on the council's employ'.

The Germans retreated and the Allies advanced up to 6 miles, pressing home the attack over the next few days.

AUSTIN, Alfred Charles

Age:	22
Rank:	Rifleman
Regiment/Service:	Border Regiment
Unit:	1/5th Battalion
Service Number:	23043
Died:	30 September 1918
Cemetery/Memorial:	Vis-en-Artois Memorial
Reference:	Panel 6

Born in Carshalton, Alfred lived at 8 Shorts Road. The youngest of seven children, he worked as a chemist's shop boy. During the war he also served with the East Surrey Regiment. By any standard Alfred had not had an easy war. He had previously been wounded several times in action, receiving gunshot wounds to his face and shoulder in 1916, being gassed in 1917 and wounded in action again in March 1918, when he was shot in his right arm. However, it appears that none of these wounds was serious enough to keep him out of the war and he was killed in action after his battalion had consolidated a new position; the next day they were counter-attacked with the loss of three men killed and thirty-four wounded.

WYATT, Thomas George

Age:	26
Rank:	Lance Corporal
Regiment/Service:	East Surrey Regiment
Unit:	1st Battalion

Service Number:	G/9240
Died:	1 October 1918
Cemetery/Memorial:	Mont Huon Military Cemetery, Le Treport
Reference:	VIII.G.11A

(Mario Fuller)

CWGC Notes: Son of Polly and William Wyatt, of Carshalton; husband of Mrs Wyatt, of 1 Riverside Villas, Mill Lane, Carshalton. Died of wounds 1 October 1918.

Thomas was a greengrocer and had previously lived on William Street in the Wrythe. He married in 1911 and went to France on 30 November 1915. He was most likely wounded in action on 28–29 September when the battalion was involved in an operation to capture Gouzeaucourt. Although the attack was a success the battalion suffered twenty-five casualties. His medal card states that he was 'presumed dead' on 1 October. His name is also on the Willie Bird cross. He was the uncle of Herbert Bowles and James Nicholls, and brother-in-law of Ernest Baker.

On 3 October the British Fourth Army attacked the last line of German defences, the Beaurevoir Line.

LAUNCHBURY, William Henry

Age:	30
Rank:	Private
Regiment/Service:	King's Own Yorkshire Light Infantry
Unit:	1st Battalion
Service Number:	42928
Died:	3 October 1918
Cemetery/Memorial:	Vis-en-Artois Memorial
Reference:	Panel 8

CWGC Notes: Husband of A.W. Launchbury, of 81 Liddell Gardens, Willesden, London.

William was born in Westminster. When the 1911 census was carried out he was living with his family in Hammersmith and working as an advertising clerk. He enlisted in Chelsea and served initially with the 2/1st London Yeomanry. He was married on 3 September 1918, just one month before his death; on his marriage certificate he stated that his current address was Westmead Road, Sutton. On 3 October the battalion attacked 'Prospect Hill' as part of the Battle of Beaurevoir, the objective being taken by 10 a.m. despite heavy shelling. Casualties were forty-four killed, 150 wounded and three missing. The battalion captured 209 prisoners. William's name also appears on the Sutton and St Barnabas church memorials.

Beaurevoir was not captured on 3 October and managed to hold out until 5 October. On 8 October the British launched their final offensive on Cambrai.

COURTMAN, Frederick Arthur Lawrence

Age:	26
Rank:	Private
Regiment/Service:	The Buffs (East Kent Regiment)
Unit:	1st Battalion
Service Number:	G/25276
Died:	8 October 1918
Cemetery/Memorial:	Montbrehain British Cemetery
Reference:	A.34

Frederick was born in Carshalton; married with two children, he and his family lived at 13 Westcroft Road. He worked as a fishmonger and poulterer before he enlisted in August 1917 and he was wounded by a gas shell in August 1918. On 8 October the battalion was part of a successful operation at Magny-la-Fosse. The attack commenced at 5.20 a.m. and two hours later the first objective had been taken. The second objective was also soon reached and although the line was heavily shelled no counter-attack was forthcoming and the operation was a success. Casualties were seven officers and twenty-six other ranks killed, eighty wounded and two missing.

HAYES, Patrick

Age:	28
Rank:	Private
Regiment/Service:	Royal Fusiliers
Unit:	10th Battalion
Service Number:	25661
Died:	8 October 1918
Cemetery/Memorial:	Marcoing British Cemetery
Reference:	II.B.22

CWGC Notes: Son of Mrs Ellen Hayes, of West St, Carshalton.

Born in Woodmansterne and lived at Regent's Cottage, West Street. A grocer by trade, Patrick was the brother of John Hayes and enlisted in December 1915. On 8 October 1918:

> The orders for the regiment to capture the Masnieres–Beauvrevoir Line and the sunken roads … the attacks to be carried out in a SE direction. A barrage was put down at zero hour approximately 300 yards in front of the assembly position and at zero plus four advanced at the rate of 100 yards in four minutes. Close up to this barrage the companies advanced at zero hour 4.30am. There were two strong systems of wire running in front of the Beauvrevoir Line and

as this had not been sufficiently cut some difficulty was experienced in getting through it and heavy machine gun fire was opened up on the leading troops from concrete machine gun posts inside the wire. Having successfully passed through the wire no more serious opposition was met with and the leading companies quickly reached their objectives ... About 200 casualties were suffered by the battalion all either at the assembly position, which the enemy continuously shelled throughout the night, or in getting through the wire.

The following day the Hindenburg Line was overrun.

BRYANT, William Henry

Age:	26
Rank:	Private
Regiment/Service:	Border Regiment
Unit:	1st Battalion
Service Number:	22913
Died:	24 October 1918
Cemetery/Memorial:	Moorseele Military Cemetery
Reference:	C.2

CWGC Notes: Son of Alfred Bryant, of 1 Palmerston Rd, Mill Lane, Carshalton.

Born in Carshalton, when William enlisted in June 1915 he gave his address as 'The Limes', Lodge Road, Wallington, and his occupation as 'bioscope operator'. He also served with the East Surrey Regiment and was awarded the Military Medal. William died of wounds likely to have been received during battalion operations on 20–22 October, following up the 88th Brigade operations to bridge the River Lys on 19 October. As part of the 87th Brigade they were to follow up the next day to gain the line of the Escaut from Hvelghem to Yyaermaerde. Enemy shelling had caused some casualties by this point. On 22 October they attacked with the 1st King's Own Scottish Borderers. The British barrage opened at 9 a.m.; the advance started and came under heavy machine gun fire from a number of German machine guns entrenched on a crest overlooking fields devoid of cover. By 10 a.m. the advance was held up by the enemy. However, the troops gradually advanced towards Kattestraate and the battalion was able to employ trench mortars and rifle smoke grenades. By midday the situation was unclear to HQ, although it was established that the enemy had tried to counter-attack but had been driven off. Casualties were six killed, ninety-three wounded and five missing. Enemy machine guns had been the main problem due to the large number of them in action.

INCHCOMB, Caleb

Age:	33
Rank:	Private
Regiment/Service:	Royal Fusiliers

Unit: 4th Battalion
Service Number: 42477
Died: 24 October 1918
Cemetery/Memorial: Romeries Communal Cemetery Extension
Reference: I.E.18

CWGC Notes: Son of Charles and Jane Inchcomb, of Clapham; husband of Alice S.A. Inchcomb, of 'Rosecot', 14 Lavender Rd, Wallington.

Caleb was born in Clapham and lived at 1 Alexandra Villas, Croydon Road, Beddington. A clerk, he enlisted in June 1916. He died as a result of an assault near Romeries. The attack was a success and many of the enemy surrendered. However, the 4th Battalion suffered 133 casualties, including twenty-two wounded by gas.

Fighting continued in France and Belgium right up to the Armistice of 11 November. William Bryant and Caleb Inchcomb were the last of Carshalton's casualties on the Western Front, a front that had cost Carshalton nearly 200 of its inhabitants.

8. Gallipoli

Whilst fighting had been raging on the Western Front, in 1915 the Allied powers decided to take another approach to try and make a decisive breakthrough by entering Europe through Turkey. Naval shelling of defensive forts protecting the Dardanelles Straits commenced in February and was successful, but follow-up minesweeping operations failed. It was therefore decided to take the Gallipoli Peninsula through a land operation. On 25 April a force of British, French and ANZAC troops landed successfully, but gains were small and the attackers were held back by Turkish troops commanded by German officers.

Progress was slow, with several battles taking place throughout April and May. On 4 June the British and French again attacked in the Third Battle of Krithia.

RAY, Martin Olave

(Keith Fazzani)

Age:	26
Rank:	Private
Regiment/Service:	King's Own Scottish Borderers
Unit:	1st Battalion
Service Number:	17673
Died:	4 June 1915
Cemetery/Memorial:	Helles Memorial
Reference:	Panels 84 to 92 or 220 to 222

Martin was born in Southwark but in 1901 the family were living in Wallington. In 1911 Martin was working as a waiter in London. He was killed in action south-west of Krithia. The bombardment commenced at 8 a.m. and continued intermittently until 11.20 a.m., when there was a lull during which the men checked and fixed bayonets. The Turkish rifle and machine gun fire became very heavy. The bombardment ceased at 12 noon, and two companies of the battalion assaulted. They suffered very severely, the majority being killed close to the parapet, though some succeeded in reaching a small nullah within 100 yards of the Turkish trench. The losses were caused chiefly by oblique and enfilade fire. The battalion advanced rapidly through a maze of Turkish trenches, meeting with little opposition and capturing some sixty Turks and a Hotchkiss machine gun. A period of consolidation and reorganisation followed. The positions were held until the early evening, but at 7 p.m. the Turks were seen massing in a communication trench and D Company was ordered to drive them out with the bayonet. The charge was completed successfully, around sixty Turks being killed, but the company was unable to progress far owing to the superior numbers of the enemy.

Due to the lack of progress after 4 June it was planned to land troops further north at Suvla Bay. A diversionary attack was made at Cape Helles in an attempt to capture the high ground of Achi Baba. The attack failed and the British suffered 3,500 casualties.

GABB, Richard George

Age:	21
Rank:	Second Lieutenant
Regiment/Service:	Essex Regiment
Unit:	12th Battalion, attached 1st Bn
Died:	6 August 1915
Cemetery/Memorial:	Twelve Tree Copse Cemetery
Reference:	Sp. Mem. C.238

CWGC Notes: Son of George B. and E.M. Gabb, of 1 Carshalton Rd, Carshalton.

(Wallington and Carshalton Advertiser)

Richard's father was the landlord of the Windsor Castle pub in Carshalton. Richard had joined the Officer Training Corps whilst at Emanuel School in Wandsworth, after which he lived in Dalston and worked for an engineering firm. He was commissioned in November 1914 and had landed in the Dardanelles in May 1915, immediately being thrown in to heavy fighting. On 6 August:

> The brigade was ordered to attack the Turkish trenches ... 2.20pm At this hour the artillery bombardment commenced and at the same time the Turkish artillery opened very heavy shrapnel and high explosive fire on the trenches and all approaches. This caused a considerable number of casualties. 3.15pm At this hour the divisional batteries of machine guns opened fire on the Turkish trenches and approaches. 3.20pm The field artillery now commenced to bombard. 3.50pm The attack was launched at this hour. On the left the 1st Essex distributed as follows: two companies advancing from south-west ... and one company advancing from the west ... One company was in reserve. The two companies on the right got forward ... with very few casualties but were met with heavy shrapnel fire as they arrived at the enemy's trench. They appear to have taken the trench and the one beyond but were unable to make further progress owing to machine gun fire and rifle fire. They were driven ... gradually back to the corner by the southern barricade. The left company got into ... the trench to the north ... but were unable to retain their position ... This portion was held all night in spite of constant attacks and was consolidated

and slightly extended. 5.45pm The 1/5th Royal Scots sent one company to reinforce the Essex Regiment. Their other company remained in the centre of the line till 9pm when it was also moved off to the left in support. During the night all regiments sent out patrols to endeavour to find out whether any of their men were holding isolated parts of the hostile trenches. From the reports brought back by these patrols it seemed certain that there were no such parties. 7th- 7am The Brigade was relieved by 86th Brigade.

The war diary also remarked that:

The advance of all battalions appears to have been most gallantly carried out and the failure of the attack can only be attributed to the exceedingly heavy rifle, machine gun and shell fire which the Turks were able to bring on the attacking troops. The casualties among the attacking troops were in all cases well over 50 per cent.

After Richard's death the local paper reported:

He was frequently in the thickest of fights and had several narrow escapes. He was, in fact, once wounded in a fight with a German officer, whom he succeeded in killing, but the injury he got did not keep him out of active work. His letters home were always full of good cheer, though the hardships which he, in common with others, suffered were many.

Richard died of his wounds, and is also commemorated on the memorial at Emanuel School. He was the brother of Stanley Gabb.

KNIGHT, William

Age:	29
Rank:	Private
Regiment/Service:	Worcestershire Regiment
Unit:	4th Battalion
Service Number:	10930
Died:	6 August 1915
Cemetery/Memorial:	Helles Memorial
Reference:	Panels 104 to 113

William was born in Carshalton and had previously served in the army for seven years, six of them in India. He was killed in action, having already been wounded in June. He was the uncle of Frank Knight and Ernest Knight.

Whilst the landings at Suvla Bay were a success, the British failed to exploit their initial gains and the situation degenerated into one of trench warfare stalemate with many similarities to the Western Front. Conditions were terrible due to the extreme heat and impossibility of burying the dead, and disease was rife, causing more casualties on both sides than the actual fighting.

HOUSLEY, Harry John

Age:	17
Rank:	Private
Regiment/Service:	The Queen's (Royal West Surrey Regiment)
Unit:	16 Platoon, D Company, 2/4th Battalion
Service Number:	T/3249
Died:	9 August 1915
Cemetery/Memorial:	Helles Memorial
Reference:	Addenda Panel

CWGC Notes: Son of Alice Jane Housley, of 15 Carshalton Rd, Carshalton, and the late H. Housley.

Harry was born in 1898 and educated at Carshalton Council School. He enlisted in the Territorial Force on 11 November 1914 aged just 16, no doubt lying about his age. The minimum age for enlistment in the Territorial Force was 17, and soldiers in the force could not be sent overseas until they were 19, although this caveat was often overlooked. After training in Croydon, Windsor and Bedford, Harry left for the Dardanelles in July 1915, shortly after his 17th birthday. The battalion landed at Suvla Bay on 9 August and the war diary reports:

> 2.30am to 5.30am Disembarked on C Beach. Battalion ordered to proceed to a line southwest of Chocolate Hill (Hill 53) and entrench. 6.40am Urgent message received for battalion to move forward to north-west slope of Hill 53 in order to reinforce 31st Brigade which was then in action. Battalion advanced across open ground south-south-east of Salt Lake during which it came under shell and rifle fire and had several casualties. 7.30am to 8am Arrived at Chocolate Hill and reported to Brigadier General – ordered by him to join 33rd Brigade to advance round north spur of hill and thence east to support the brigade which was hard pressed … Battalion advanced and occupied old Turkish trench running north and south … three companies advanced 600 yards to front on to Hill 70, but were driven back by shell fire from our own guns in rear. Advanced to Hill 70 a second time but had to fall back owing to heavy fire from our guns in rear and the fact that all scrub on hill was ablaze. 12 noon At this point we had many casualties (eight officers and about 250 men). The battalion fell back to Turkish trench and in absence of orders it was decided to strengthen this position and to hold on. 9th–10th Night: much firing from one front and from snipers all around.

Harry was reported missing following this action, but not officially pronounced dead until December 1915.

ROGERS, Albert Thomas

Age:	39
Rank:	Private
Regiment/Service:	Australian Infantry (AIF)
Unit:	A Company, 11th Battalion
Service Number:	1627
Died:	20 August 1915
Cemetery/Memorial:	Beach Cemetery, Anzac
Reference:	II.H.23

CWGC Notes: Son of Thomas and Charlotte Rogers, of 107 Avenue Villas, Carshalton Hill. Native of Caldicot, Mon., England.

Albert was a labourer by trade although he had previously served with The Queen's for twelve years and had seen active service in the Boer War. He joined the AIF in January 1915 in Perth, Western Australia. His attestation papers state that he was born near Cardiff on 21 September 1882, which would make him 32 when he enlisted. However, other sources show his birth date was 21 September 1875, meaning that he was actually 39. It appears he lied about his age to enlist, as the AIF's upper age limit at the time was 35. He joined A Company of the 11th Battalion of the 3rd Infantry Brigade in May 1915. The battalion had landed on the Gallipoli Peninsula towards the end of April 1915 and had been in action since then, and Albert would have been thrown straight into the thick of it. His service record states that he died of wounds received on 20 August. The battalion war diary does not record any action that day, so it appears he was a victim of the steady flow of casualties incurred during day-to-day trench life on the peninsula. He was the brother of other Carshalton casualties Percival and Frederick Rogers.

HARROLD, Ernest James

Age:	20
Rank:	Private
Regiment/Service:	London Regiment (Royal Fusiliers)
Unit:	2nd Battalion
Service Number:	3079
Died:	22 December 1915
Cemetery/Memorial:	Redoubt Cemetery, Helles
Reference:	I.D.13

The brother of Herbert Harrold, Ernest lived at 105 Westmead Road and went overseas at the end of August 1915. His battalion was in the front line for the period 11–29 December in the 'Esplanade' sector; it was noted that the Turks were more daring in this area, with snipers and bomb attacks prevalent. Ernest was probably killed during this time. His name is also on the Sutton and St Barnabas church memorials.

The offensives at Gallipoli had proved ineffective, and the Allied commanders were accused of failing to seize the initiative and instead being content to dig in and wage trench warfare. As winter closed in, conditions changed from one extreme to another, causing further deaths amongst the troops. The commanding officer at Gallipoli, General Sir Ian Hamilton, was replaced and evacuation was recommended. This evacuation took place in December 1915 and January 1916 and was the most successful part of the whole Gallipoli venture, an exercise that had cost the Allies over 200,000 casualties, 46,000 of whom had been killed.

9. Mesopotamia, Egypt, Palestine and Salonika

British troops were also fighting a campaign against Turkish forces in Mesopotamia, primarily to defend Britain's oil interests. In Egypt, the Suez Canal provided a vital supply route and needed to be protected. In Salonika, British troops fought against the Bulgarians in the defence of Greece. The weather and conditions faced on these fronts meant that illness and disease were as much of a danger as enemy soldiers.

STRACEY, Thomas Henry

(Jim Stracey)

Age:	18
Rank:	Private
Regiment/Service:	The Queen's (Royal West Surrey Regiment)
Unit:	B Company, 1/5th Battalion
Service Number:	T/4787
Died:	26 June 1916
Cemetery/Memorial:	Basra Memorial
Reference:	Panel 6

CWGC Notes: Son of Mrs Frances Ellen Field, of 1 Rochester Rd, Carshalton.

The 1/5th Battalion was stationed in Nasiriyeh in what is now Iraq. In one of the many cruel ironies of the war Thomas was not killed in action, but drowned whilst washing in a river. He was the brother of John Stracey.

HOSKINS, Harry

Age:	31
Rank:	Private
Regiment/Service:	The Queen's (Royal West Surrey Regiment)
Unit:	B Company, 1/5th Battalion
Service Number:	4875
Died:	6 July 1916
Cemetery/Memorial:	Basra War Cemetery
Reference:	V.O.16

Harry's family lived at 33 St John's Road. He died in Basra of heatstroke and is also commemorated on Sutton war memorial.

SHEPHARD, Robert Albert

Age:	35
Rank:	Corporal
Regiment/Service:	Army Service Corps
Unit:	493rd M.T. Company
Service Number:	M2/101639
Died:	30 December 1916
Cemetery/Memorial:	Ismailia War Memorial Cemetery
Reference:	A.26

Robert was born in Notting Hill but later lived at 64 Mill Lane, Carshalton. He was married with three children and worked as a fitter. He enlisted in May 1915 and had been overseas, in Ismaila, with his company since February 1916. He died from enteric fever and a perforated ulcer; he had spent much of August and September in hospital and was again admitted on 26 December 1916. He had an operation on 29 December and appeared to be recovering but then died the next day.

KNIGHT, Ernest John

Age:	22
Rank:	Private
Regiment/Service:	East Surrey Regiment
Unit:	1/5th Battalion
Service Number:	200114
Died:	31 December 1916
Cemetery/Memorial:	Basra Memorial
Reference:	Panels 20 & 63

Ernest's mother lived at 38 Mill Lane. Better known as 'Jock', he worked as a gardener before joining the army in 1912 and had served in the Persian Gulf and India. In 1915 he was treated for malaria then in November of the same year he was wounded in action. He was reported as a presumed prisoner of war on 29 April 1916. A number of men from his battalion had been drafted to the 2nd Battalion Norfolk Regiment in 1915. These men took part in the siege of Kut from December 1915 to April 1916. Kut is about 100 miles south-east of Baghdad; British and Indian forces retreating from the Turkish Army fell back there and were besieged. Attempts to relieve them in January and April 1916 failed. The British surrendered on 29 April 1916 and a large proportion of the 10,000 who were captured died from disease whilst in captivity. The War Office later declared that Ernest had died between 29 April 1916 and 31 December 1916. He was nephew of another Carshalton casualty, William Knight, and cousin of Frank Knight.

MORRIS, John

Age:	22
Rank:	Lance Corporal
Regiment/Service:	Duke of Cornwall's Light Infantry
Unit:	1/4th Battalion
Service Number:	3/5362
Died:	6 November 1917
Cemetery/Memorial:	Gaza War Cemetery
Reference:	VII.C.1

Born in Carshalton, John lived in Wrythe Lane with his father and brother and worked as an errand boy. During the period 3–6 November the battalion was heavily shelled, killing three men and wounding sixteen. John's name is also on the Willie Bird cross. He was the cousin of Harty Ayling.

KNIGHT, George Gordon

Age:	26
Rank:	Lieutenant
Regiment/Service:	Dorset Yeomanry (Queen's Own)
Unit:	1st Battalion
Died:	17 June 1918
Cemetery/Memorial:	Jerusalem War Cemetery
Reference:	N.92

CWGC Notes: Son of the late Theodore and Madeleine Knight.

(Churcher's College)

George was born in Clapham but the Knight family later moved to 'The Beeches', Beechnut Tree Road, Carshalton. George was educated at Churcher's College, Petersfield from 1905 to 1908, where he was a member of the Officer Training Corps. His father was a paper merchant and after leaving school George became a clerk in a wholesale stationer's. He joined the City of London Yeomanry (Rough Riders) on 5 September 1914. He landed at Suvla Bay and served in Gallipoli, but was invalided out with heart disease. However, he applied for and received a commission as a second lieutenant in the 3/1st Dorset Yeomanry in August 1916. He was promoted to lieutenant in February 1918 and left for Egypt in April that year. He suffered gunshot wounds to the abdomen in action in Palestine on 17 June during an early morning operation probing the enemy's line, and died later that day at the 104th Indian Combined Field Ambulance.

SPARRICK, Hubert Frank

Age:	30
Rank:	Sergeant
Regiment/Service:	Army Service Corps

Unit: 28th Div Train
Service Number: T4/211496
Died: 30 September 1918
Cemetery/Memorial: Kirechkoi-Hortakoi Military Cemetery
Reference: 175

CWGC Notes: Son of Mr and Mrs Sparrick, of 'Selsey', Stanley Park Rd, Wallington. Native of Hornsey, London.

The Sparrick family had lived at a number of addresses in the local area. Hubert worked as a wages clerk for the Croydon Corporation Tramways. He enlisted in November 1915 and went to Salonika the following August. He served with various units including the 22nd Divisional Train.[61] By May 1918 he had been promoted to acting sergeant, however in August he was admitted to the 42nd General Hospital in Salonika and died the following month of pneumonia and dysentery. During this time a constant stream of men were admitted to hospital with illness, often influenza. His name is also on the Croydon Corporation Tramways memorial plaque located at Thornton Heath bus depot and the Croydon Corporation memorial plaque at Croydon town hall.

JENKS, Arthur Leslie

Age: 22
Rank: Lieutenant
Regiment/Service: Dorset Regiment
Unit: 3rd Battalion, attached 2nd Battalion
Died: 7 October 1918 (wounded 19 September 1918)
Cemetery/Memorial: Kantara War Memorial Cemetery
Reference: F.3

CWGC Notes: Son of Henry and Anne Jenks, of Dunairds, Birnam, Perthshire.

Born in Denbigh, Wales, Arthur and his family later moved to 'Barrow Hedges', Beeches Avenue, Carshalton. Arthur was educated at Temple Grove and Charterhouse (alongside the poet and author Robert Graves) where he was a member of the Rifle Corps. He joined the Public Schools Battalion of the Middlesex Regiment in September 1914 and was commissioned as a temporary second lieutenant two months later, and as a lieutenant in the Dorset Regiment in 1915. It appears that he spent most of the war in England with the 3rd Battalion, who were a training/depot battalion based in Weymouth and Wyke Regis. Sent overseas in 1918, he went to Egypt where he is recorded as battalion 'Orderly Officer' in the list of officers. The battalion was in action during the period 19–21 September and captured considerable ground and prisoners. Arthur was wounded on 19 September, suffering a gunshot wound to the back, and died on 7 October at 44 Stationary Hospital, Kantara. He is also commemorated on Dunkeld war memorial in Perthshire and in the Charterhouse School memorial chapel.

10. The War at Sea

Despite the predominance of the Western Front and the other land campaigns, Britain was also engaged in the war at sea. Before the war Britain had the strongest navy in the world in order to protect the Empire, and felt that any future conflict would be decided by the might of the victor's sea power. Germany was particularly envious of this position, and also sought to increase the size of its navy, ushering in the age of the dreadnought. However, the deterrent role of a navy meant that both sides were unwilling to commit their ships to battle for fear of losing them. Despite initial naval engagements, the war at sea was not as decisive as expected and really petered out after the famous Battle of Jutland in 1916. Nevertheless, throughout the war Britain's ships were under constant threat from German mines and U-Boats.

The merchant navy also played a key role in transporting supplies across the ocean, journeys fraught with danger from the prowling U-Boats. The German tactic of targeting merchant and civilian vessels was one of the reasons America joined the war in 1917, a key contributing factor to Germany's eventual defeat.

1914

GOODRIGHT, George Henry James

Age:	18
Rank:	Ordinary Seaman
Regiment/Service:	Royal Navy
Unit:	HMS *Bulwark*
Service Number:	J/22931
Died:	26 November 1914
Cemetery/Memorial:	Portsmouth Naval Memorial
Reference:	3

George was born in Kingston and lived at 3 Percy Villas, Waterloo Road, Sutton. He worked as an errand boy before he joined the navy in February 1913 and had been posted to two ships before joining HMS *Bulwark* in October 1913. The ship was moored off Sheerness when there was a huge internal explosion, probably caused by cordite overheating, which destroyed it. Only twelve of the crew survived.

1916

Despite some early naval skirmishes, both sides had failed to commit to a decisive naval engagement. Britain's attempts to draw the German fleet into a decisive engagement in the North Sea had proved fruitless, whilst the Germans were content with launching raids on the east coast of England. However, the German Admiral Scheer planned to lure the British fleet towards the German fleet by using a few of his ships as bait. On 31 May, both fleets unwittingly closed in on each other and the Battle of Jutland commenced in mid-afternoon with over 270 ships involved.

WHITE, Albert Edward

Age:	18
Rank:	Private
Regiment/Service:	Royal Marine Light Infantry
Unit:	HMS *Indefatigable*
Service Number:	PLY/17741
Died:	31 May 1916
Cemetery/Memorial:	Plymouth Naval Memorial
Reference:	18

CWGC Notes: Son of William and Emily White, of 2 Palmerston Rd, Mill Lane, Carshalton.

Before joining the navy on 29 July 1914 Albert had worked as a gardener. He had seen action at Dunkirk and the defence of Antwerp in 1914. He is mentioned in the local paper on 30 October 1914, which states that he enlisted only a few days before war broke out and was one of the lucky ones to escape unscathed from the defence of Antwerp. It reads 'White is a smart young soldier, and his parents have great hopes that he will do well in the marines.' HMS *Indefatigable* was sunk by the German ship *Von der Tann* during the Battle of Jutland. Hit five times, she was the first British ship to be sunk.

The battle raged on throughout the afternoon until the German fleet started to withdraw at 6.30 p.m. due to its exposed position. The British gave chase and both fleets attempted a series of moves to outmanoeuvre the other. This brought them into contact several more times during the night.

KILTY, Leonard J.

Age:	19
Rank:	Able Seaman
Regiment/Service:	Royal Navy
Unit:	HMS *Black Prince*
Service Number:	22356
Died:	31 May 1916

Cemetery/Memorial: Portsmouth Naval Memorial
Reference: 13

CWGC Notes: Son of Harriet Kilty, of 7 St James Rd,
Carshalton.

A brickmaker's labourer, Leonard joined the navy in
1913. HMS *Black Prince* was sunk during the last stages
of Jutland after the ship lost contact with the rest of
the fleet and sailed towards the German fleet. Up to
six German ships bombarded the *Black Prince* from
within 1,000 yards and she was sunk in fifteen minutes.   (Bryan Stokes)
Leonard was the brother of William Kilty, and his name
is also inscribed on the Willie Bird cross.

Despite the loss of lives and ships on both sides the battle is considered a tactical victory for
the Germans, although the British Grand Fleet was still strong and was able to return to
the seas quicker than the crippled German High Seas Fleet.

GARRETT, Richard

Age: 49
Rank: Master
Regiment/Service: Mercantile Marine
Unit: RMS *Rappahannock*
Died: 17 October 1916
Cemetery/Memorial: Tower Hill Memorial

CWGC Notes: Son of Richard Eydon Garrett; husband of Ida McDonough
Garrett, of 54 Ashleigh Avenue, Bridgwater, Somerset.

Richard lived at 38 Alma Road. A plaque in All Saints church reads 'Remember
before God Richard Garrett of this Parish. Captain of the RMS *Rappahannock*
torpedoed and sunk with all hands 27th October 1916. RIP.' The *Rappahannock*
was sunk by *U-69* 70 miles off the Scilly Isles, with the loss of thirty-seven men.

1917

COOPER, Angelo James

Age: 24
Rank: Stoker 1st Class
Regiment/Service: Royal Navy
Unit: HMS *Derwent*
Service Number: K/18712
Died: 2 May 1917

Cemetery/Memorial: Portsmouth Naval Memorial
Reference: 26

Angelo was born in Ashford, Middlesex. He lived at 4 Rose Cottages, Pound Street, and had previously worked as a grocer's assistant before joining the navy in April 1913. HMS *Derwent* was a destroyer engaged in anti-submarine patrols and later convoy escorts. She was sunk by a mine laid by a U-Boat off the coast of Le Havre, with the loss of fifty-eight of the seventy-strong crew.

HARROLD, Herbert Frank

Age: 20
Rank: Stoker 1st Class
Regiment/Service: Royal Navy
Unit: HMS *Vanguard*
Died: 9 July 1917
Cemetery/Memorial: Chatham Naval Memorial
Reference: 23

Herbert lived at 44 Sutton Grove and had been a gardener before he enlisted in April 1915. HMS *Vanguard* was at anchor in Scapa Flow when she suffered a massive internal explosion, sinking almost immediately and killing an estimated 843 men. Ernest is commemorated on Sutton war memorial and St Barnabas church memorial, and was the brother of Ernest Harrold.

BOWLES, Herbert

Age: 20
Rank: Able Seaman
Regiment/Service: Royal Navy
Unit: HMS *Recruit*
Service Number: J/27333
Died: 9 August 1917
Cemetery/Memorial: Chatham Naval Memorial
Reference: 21

CWGC Notes: Son of George H. Bowles, of 1 Mason Cottages, St James Rd, Carshalton.

A carpenter's boy, Herbert joined the navy in September 1913. The 'R' Class destroyer *Recruit* was torpedoed on 9 August 1917 by *UB-16* in the North Sea, with the loss of fifty-four men. Herbert's name is also on the Willie Bird cross. He was the nephew of Thomas George Wyatt.

1918

BROOKS, Reginald Cyril

Age:	15
Rank:	Deck Boy
Regiment/Service:	Mercantile Marine
Unit:	SS *Pomerian* (Glasgow)
Died:	15 April 1918
Cemetery/Memorial:	Tower Hill Memorial

CWGC Notes: Son of James Charles and Emma Brooks, of 52 Stanley Rd, Carshalton, Surrey. Born at Sevenoaks, Kent.

Reginald was the brother of Caleb and William Brooks. The *Pomerian* was a Canadian merchant navy vessel torpedoed and sunk by *UC-77* off the coast of Portland Bill, Dorset, with the loss of fifty-five men.

EVERSFIELD, Frederick

Age:	24
Rank:	Able Seaman
Regiment/Service:	Royal Navy
Unit:	HMS *D6*
Service Number:	J/12826
Died:	24 June 1918
Cemetery/Memorial:	Chatham Naval Memorial
Reference:	28

CWGC Notes: Husband of Kathleen Christina Eversfield, of 19 St James Rd, Carshalton.

Frederick was born in Dover and worked as a porter before joining the navy in 1911. HMS *D6* was a British D Class submarine. She was sunk by *UB-73* off the west coast of Ireland on 24 June 1918. Frederick is also commemorated on Stockwell war memorial.

11. The War in the Air

The first powered flight was made in 1903, but as war broke out both sides quickly real-ised the importance of superiority in the skies. Initially this centred on reconnaissance and observation, but as the technology improved planes were able to carry bombs and machine guns. The fledgling Royal Flying Corp (RFC) attracted a number of recruits but the basic technology, coupled with the inexperience of the pilots, meant that many deaths were caused by accidents and pilot error rather than by the enemy.

PEARMAN, Humphrey

Age:	28
Rank:	Lieutenant (Pilot)
Regiment/Service:	Royal Flying Corps, Leinster Regiment
Unit:	2nd Battalion
Died:	13 August 1916
Cemetery/Memorial:	Carshalton (All Saints) Churchyard
Reference:	Old.67

CWGC Notes: Son of Mr D. Pearman, of Elm Cottage, Purley.

Born in Middlesex, Humphrey initially joined the Honourable Artillery Company in August 1914. He proceeded to France in September and became a second lieutenant in the Leinster Regiment in March 1915. He was wounded at Hooge in August 1915, suffering two gunshot and shell wounds, and was invalided home. On his recovery he joined the RFC in March 1916 and received his wings in June, joining the 40th Squadron. He died in Aldershot hospital from burns received when his plane crashed after suffering engine trouble at Farnborough. A tree branch penetrated the petrol tank and the plane burst into flames. His commanding officer wrote, 'He was a most excellent and keen officer and a splendid fellow. He was loved and respected by all who came into contact with him. I had hoped he would have come overseas with me this week. He would have done splendid work, for a gallanter fellow never lived.'

The war had come to England itself with coastal bombardments by German ships in the early days of the war, and the advent of a new threat – air raids. German long-range bombers and Zeppelin airships were both utilised to target towns and cities across England. In July 1917 the local paper reported that Carshalton Council had decided against the use of air raid warnings as there were concerns that 'women are temperamentally unable to stand sudden alarms.' In contrast Sutton did use warnings, which were sounded on several occasions.

ZEPPELIN BROUGHT DOWN IN FLAMES
AT CUFFLEY, NEAR ENFIELD, AT 2.30 A.M., SUNDAY SEPT 3RD 1916.

A postcard showing German Zeppelin SL11 being shot down over London on 3 September 1916. The pilot who shot it down, Captain William Leefe Robinson, was awarded the Victoria Cross. On the back of the postcard is written 'Drawn by Miss Yates, Cotswold, Park Lane, Wallington. As seen at Carshalton'. (Stephen Glanville)

In addition to its planes, the RAF (formed on 1 April 1918) was also responsible for observation balloons, crucial for observing enemy troop movements and directing artillery fire.

WILGOSS, George

Age:	31
Rank:	Air Mechanic 1st Class
Regiment/Service:	Royal Air Force
Unit:	48th Balloon Section
Service Number:	27535
Died:	11 October 1918
Cemetery/Memorial:	Lapugnoy Military Cemetery
Reference:	X.E.12

CWGC Notes: Son of G.T. and Margaret Wilgoss, of Marylebone, London; husband of Daisy Wilgoss, of 29 Tregarvon Rd, Clapham Common.

Born in Marylebone, George was married in 1910 and had two children, and the family lived at 32 Cranfield Road East. George was a chief clerk and buyer for motor accessories prior to enlisting in May 1916. He went to France in February 1917, and died from pneumonia having been admitted to hospital on 3 October 1918.

12. Other Deaths

A number of men listed on the memorial do not fit into the previous sections of the book. They include those who did not die in combat, those who died at home either during the war (where it has not been ascertained exactly when they sustained their injuries) or after it (possibly due to their wartime injuries), and those for whom no records can be found.

SLAYMAKER, George

Age:	45
Rank:	Seaman
Regiment/Service:	Royal Naval Reserve
Died:	8 September 1914

The second child of William and Martha Slaymaker, George joined the navy in 1884 having previously worked as a labourer. He served for twenty-two years on many ships, ending up as leading seaman and petty officer. Leaving the navy in 1906, he had two children and worked as a general labourer. He died at Guy's Hospital in London. He is not recorded on the CWGC database. He was the brother of David Slaymaker.

(Ann Dowsing)

EVANS, Hugh Arthur

Age:	27
Rank:	Lieutenant
Regiment/Service:	Royal Army Medical Corps
Died:	3 June 1915
Cemetery/Memorial:	Nunhead (All Saints) Cemetery
Reference:	Screen Wall 61.24407

Born in Camberwell, Hugh worked as a doctor at Queen Mary's Hospital in Carshalton. He enlisted in September 1914, initially joining the 7th Royal Fusiliers before being commissioned to the RAMC in June 1915. He did not serve overseas.

FULLER, Herbert Charles

Age:	40
Rank:	Private
Regiment/Service:	Army Service Corps
Unit:	28th Labour Company
Service Number:	21066
Died:	8 November 1915
Cemetery/Memorial:	Carshalton (All Saints) Churchyard
Reference:	Old.238

CWGC Notes: Husband of E. Fuller of 4 Orchard Hill, Carshalton.

Born in Haverstock Hill, Middlesex, and worked as a window cleaner. Herbert died in England less than a week before his unit left to go overseas.

LANGRIDGE, Charles Amos

Age:	18
Rank:	Private
Regiment/Service:	Royal Marine Light Infantry
Service Number:	PO/18982
Died:	19 July 1916
Cemetery/Memorial:	Deal Cemetery
Reference:	2.1307

Charles was born in Lambeth and lived at 1 Linton Cottages, St James Road, Carshalton, and worked as a gardener. He enlisted in July 1915 and died of tuberculosis and meningitis at the Royal Marine depot, Deal, less than two weeks after his 18th birthday.

HELLYER, Albert George Neele

Age:	17
Rank:	Boy 1st Class
Regiment/Service:	Royal Navy
Unit:	HMS *Pembroke*
Service Number:	J/30537
Died:	4 October 1916
Cemetery/Memorial:	Carshalton (All Saints) Churchyard
Reference:	Corner of New Ground 219

CWGC Notes: Son of Mr C.E. Hellyer, of 33 Station Rd, Carshalton.

Previously a baker's boy, Albert joined the navy in 1915. HMS *Pembroke* was not a ship, rather it was the name given to the naval barracks at Chatham. He died in Greenwich of pleurisy and meningitis less than a month before his 18th birthday.

DAVIESS, John

Rank:	Private
Regiment/Service:	Tank Corps
Died:	27 December 1916

There is no John Daviess (note the spelling) listed in the Commonwealth War Graves Commission database and no trace of him in birth or census records. However, the written record of local men who served indicates that he lived at 21 Station Road and died on 27 December 1916. The local paper also lists his name in the account of the unveiling of the memorial, stating that he was a private in the Tank Corps. The CWGC database does not record anyone with even a similar name as a casualty on this day, and John Daviess therefore remains an enigma.

TILLMAN, William

Age:	26
Rank:	Private
Regiment/Service:	The Queen's (Royal West Surrey Regiment)
Unit:	1st Battalion
Service Number:	13402
Died:	29 January 1917
Cemetery/Memorial:	City of London Cemetery and Crematorium, Manor Park
Reference:	Screen Wall 235. 49A

CWGC Notes: Husband of M.E. Tillman, of 2 Newcomen Terrace, Newcomen Rd, Lake, Sandown, Isle of Wight.

William was born in Wandsworth and lived at 14 Belmont Cottages, Belmont Road, Wallington. He definitely served overseas, evidenced by his medal entitlement. In January 1917 William's battalion had been training, mainly in the Clery sector, with no casualties until the end of the month. Given that he is buried in England it is possible he had been wounded in action in November or December, or possibly even earlier, and had later succumbed to these wounds after being brought home. He was the nephew of Edward Tillman.

DUNKLEY, Ellis
'Dear old Jack'

Age:	40
Rank:	Private
Regiment/Service:	Royal Fusiliers
Unit:	13th Battalion
Service Number:	9000
Died:	10 March 1917
Cemetery/Memorial:	Hove Old Cemetery
Reference:	E.129

CWGC Notes: Husband of Mary Catlin (formerly Dunkley).

Born in Lillingstone Dayrell, Buckinghamshire, Ellis was married with three children and lived at 4 Badon Villas, Waterloo Road. He worked as a tramway motor-man before going to France at the end of July 1915. He is also commemorated on Sutton war memorial, St Barnabas memorial and a memorial inside Lillingstone Dayrell church.

COLEMAN, Edward James

Age:	53
Rank:	Private
Regiment/Service:	Hampshire Regiment
Service Number:	20820
Died:	22 April 1917
Cemetery/Memorial:	Netley Military Cemetery
Reference:	C.E.1906

CWGC Notes: Son of Edward and Mary Woods Coleman; husband of Alice Maud Coleman of 12 Park Rd, Tunbridge Wells.

Born in Haverstock Hill, Edward lived at 9 Westcroft Road and was an insurance clerk. Netley Military Cemetery is at the site of the former Royal Victoria Military Hospital and was used extensively during the war to treat injured and sick troops. It appears that Edward did not serve overseas and so is likely to have died from some kind of illness or disease.

TILLMAN, Edward

Age:	58
Rank:	Private
Regiment/Service:	Royal Defence Corps
Unit:	13th Battalion
Service Number:	6930
Died:	19 May 1918
Cemetery/Memorial:	Carshalton (All Saints) Churchyard
Reference:	New.10.6

Edward lived in Carshalton Park Road and was married with one daughter. He enlisted in 1914 having previously served with the East Surrey Regiment and at home until September 1917, when he was discharged due to chronic rheumatism. He was the uncle of William Tillman.

JACKSON, Malcolm

Age:	48
Rank:	Lieutenant (Quartermaster)
Regiment/Service:	Royal Engineers

Unit:	3rd Army Special Company
Service Number:	27788
Died:	23 May 1918
Cemetery/Memorial:	Easebourne (St Mary) Churchyard

CWGC Notes: Son of William Gray Jackson and Eleanora Jackson; husband of Edith Rose Jackson, of Sunnyside, Fairview Rd, Sutton. Twice mentioned in despatches.

A draughtsman born in Greenwich, Malcolm joined the army in 1893 aged 23 and spent time in China. He served in France from November 1914 and left the army in November 1915, but was made temporary quartermaster with the honorary rank of lieutenant in February 1916. He was mentioned in John French's despatch of 1 May 1915.[62] He apparently died from the effects of mustard gas, leaving behind a widow and three children. Malcolm's name is also on Sutton war memorial.

EMBERY, George William

Age:	37
Rank:	Driver
Regiment/Service:	Royal Army Service Corps
Unit:	MT 621 Company
Service Number:	177212
Died:	29 May 1918
Cemetery/Memorial:	West Norwood Cemetery

George is another man whose details do not appear in the CWGC database. He was born in Reading in 1881 and died in Epsom in May 1918. A motor driver, he was married and lived in Stockwell prior to enlisting. He served in Egypt in 1916 before being discharged as medically unfit in October of that year. At the time of his death he was living at 37 Stanley Park Road.

BROWN, Bert Daniel

Age:	26
Rank:	Private
Regiment/Service:	Machine Gun Corps (Infantry)
Service Number:	59555
Died:	26 June 1918
Cemetery/Memorial:	Carshalton (All Saints) Churchyard
Reference:	New.10.5

CWGC Notes: Son of Edward Brown; husband of Jane Brown, of 91 Carshalton Grove, Sutton.

Born in Carshalton, Bert gave his occupation as laundry hand when he joined the East Surrey Regiment in June 1916. He died in England and is also commemorated on the Sutton and St Barnabas church memorials.

TYLER, Harry William

Age:	74
Rank:	Major
Regiment/Service:	Army Service Corps
Died:	7 August 1918

Born in Thetford in Norfolk in 1842, Harry was married with three children and lived at Edgecombe House, Grosvenor Avenue. Harry had a long career in the army, serving with the Royal Engineers, Army Commissariat and Army Service Corps. He was first commissioned on 12 February 1879 and retired from the Army Service Corps on 8 December 1892. Well known in the district as a prominent Conservative worker, the local paper reported in October 1914 that he was serving with the home forces. In January 1915 he was an honorary major temporarily employed by the Army Service Corps, although it looks like he had retired by January 1916. He is the oldest casualty named on Carshalton war memorial, but it does not appear that he died of anything related to his service during the war, and given his age he did not serve overseas.

BARBER, Sydney Herbert

Age:	25
Rank:	Lance Corporal
Regiment/Service:	East Surrey Regiment
Unit:	Depot
Service Number:	21581
Died:	17 August 1918
Cemetery/Memorial:	Carshalton (All Saints) Churchyard
Reference:	New.14.2

Born in Carshalton and lived at 13 St Andrew's Road and then 21 St John's Road. Sydney was married with two children and worked as a shoemaker prior to enlisting in September 1915, having previously served with the Royal Garrison Artillery for ten months. He was discharged in August 1917 due to diabetes. He was the cousin of William Buckenham.

GROOMBRIDGE, Herbert Arthur

'I have fought a good fight; I have finished my course'

Age:	25
Rank:	Rifleman
Regiment/Service:	London Regiment (Post Office Rifles)
Unit:	Posted to 8th Battalion
Service Number:	S/7958

Died:	4 September 1918
Cemetery/Memorial:	Carshalton (All Saints) Churchyard
Reference:	New. 14.1

CWGC Notes: Son of James and Susan Groombridge, of 27 Harold Rd, Sutton.

Born in Carshalton, Herbert lived at 27 Harold Road and was a gardener, and was the brother of John Groombridge. Herbert joined the London Rifle Brigade in January 1915 and had previously been wounded in March 1918 when he was shot in the hand. He died in hospital of chest wounds one day after the second anniversary of his brother's death. It is likely he was wounded during a series of battles on 26–28 August south-east of Albert, when the battalion attacked Billon Wood and Fargny Wood. Casualties over the three days amounted to just under 200. The battalion again attacked on 31 August, when they suffered casualties caused by their own barrage falling short. This attack cost another 200 casualties, although it is not clear how many of these were caused by the British artillery. Herbert was buried in Carshalton with full military honours on 10 September 1918 and is also commemorated on Sutton war memorial and the St Barnabas church memorial.

TOWNEND, Bertram Shaw

Age:	32
Rank:	Private
Regiment/Service:	Manchester Regiment
Unit:	12th Battalion
Service Number:	46631
Died:	7 November 1918
Cemetery/Memorial:	Bandon Hill Cemetery
Reference:	M.63

(Sutton Grammar School)

CWGC Notes: Son of Charles Hamilton and Lettice Sarah Townend, of 'Marple', 69 Park Lane, Wallington.

Bernard attended Sutton County School from 1900 to 1902. He later moved to Manchester and worked as a coffee agent. He joined the 12th Manchesters in March 1916 and was in France by December that year. He was wounded by a German aeroplane in October 1917, so badly that his leg had to be removed. He spent time in hospitals in Oxford and Morden and later Denmark Hill hospital. Whilst awaiting discharge he contracted influenza during the epidemic that swept the country and died just four days before the end of the war. His name is also on the memorial at Sutton Grammar School.

JEPSON, Arthur Henry

Age:	27
Rank:	Sapper
Regiment/Service:	Royal Engineers
Unit:	4th Field Survey Company
Service Number:	362618
Died:	15 November 1918
Cemetery/Memorial:	Terlincthun British Cemetery, Wimille
Reference:	XI.A.22

CWGC Notes: Son of Major and Mrs C.W. Jepson, of 23 The Square, Carshalton.

Arthur came from an army family and was born in Curragh Army camp, Kildare. Before the war he worked as a clerk and lived in East Dulwich. He served as a corporal in the Rifle Brigade before joining the Royal Engineers. The Field Survey company was formed of five sections: headquarters, the trigonometry and topography section, mapping and printing section, map issue section and observation section. From June 1916 to the end of the war they suffered 153 casualties, not a great deal compared to a fighting battalion but proof all the same that soldiers did not have to be in the front line to be at risk. It is unclear when or how Arthur was wounded but Terlincthun cemetery is located on the northern outskirts of Boulogne and was used for base camp hospital burials. His father, Major C.W. Jepson, was a career soldier and during the war served at home as a quartermaster with the 3rd Battalion, King's Own Royal Lancaster Regiment.

TUCKER, Charles Herbert Augustus

Age:	50
Rank:	Private
Regiment/Service:	East Surrey Regiment
Unit:	5th Battalion (Reserve)
Service Number:	316088
Died:	October-December 1918

Charles was born in Uxbridge in 1867. A general labourer with eight children, he lived at 29 Wandle Mount and later 49 St Andrew's Road, Carshalton. He had previous service in the army and left in 1891. He re-enlisted in 1914 but did not see service overseas, working instead for the Labour Corps. However, he was discharged in June 1918 suffering from a hardening of the arteries. He was described in his discharge documents as 'honest, sober, and hardworking'. Charles died between October and December 1918 in Epsom.

BRIGHT, Alfred

Age:	49
Rank:	Pioneer
Regiment/Service:	Royal Engineers
Unit:	Construction Company
Service Number:	220538 / WR20018
Died:	1919

Alfred's service record shows that he was he was born in Chesterfield and lived at 32 Mill Lane, Carshalton. A labourer, he was 47 years old when he signed up in December 1916. After serving abroad he was discharged as no longer medically fit for service in January 1919 due to having a tumour in his mouth.

FOWKES, John James

Age:	34
Rank:	Lance Corporal
Regiment/Service:	Machine Gun Corps (Infantry)
Unit:	No. 1 Company
Service Number:	19018
Died:	18 March 1919
Cemetery/Memorial:	Carshalton (All Saints) Churchyard
Reference:	New.20.5

CWGC Notes: Son of Francis and Ellen Fowkes, of 3 St John's Rd, Carshalton.

John was a house painter and played football for Carshalton Athletic. He initially served with The Queen's and went overseas on 1 June 1915. His Machine Gun Corps company was in the field from the beginning of August 1918 right up until the end of October. On the opening day of the allied offensive on 8 August they were in action near Morlancourt. Although the attack was a success they suffered seventy-six wounded, including sixty-six who were gassed. They then saw action throughout the final stages of the war, suffering a steady stream of casualties until the end of October. John was wounded and gassed sometime during this period and died of his wounds the following year in hospital in Nottingham. The local paper reported:

> Military Funeral – The funeral of Cpl John Fowkes, of St John's Rd Carshalton took place in the Parish Churchyard on Monday. Cpl Fowkes who was well known in his immediate locality, and had a brother a postman at Wallington, who has also been through the war, had seen considerable service in France, where he was wounded and gassed. Two or three weeks ago he contracted pneumonia from which he died in a hospital in Nottingham. A firing squad from the Bedfordshire Regiment stationed in Croydon attended. The service was conducted by the Rev. H. Everest.

John's name did not originally appear on the war memorial. Soon after it was unveiled, his mother wrote to the local paper asking how she could get his name added:

> We should like to know why it is that no names are included on the Cenotaph of men who died after 1918.[63] Was not their sacrifice as great as those who went before? They gave their lives as well, and it is up to the Committee or Council, whoever had the handling affairs, to see that one and all should be included on the Roll of Honour. They are all heroes of Carshalton. My son (Lance Corporal J.J. Fowkes MGC) left his work to do his bit with the rest in August 1914, and served all through the war until wounded and gassed in the later days of 1918. He died in hospital in Nottingham in March 1919. His name is not included as a hero of Carshalton. This is only one case of many. Why is it so? What do the Committee intend doing in honour of those men? Their name is entitled to be with the rest of them, and I am sure there are many in Carshalton who think the same.

Evidently her plea was answered, as John's name is now inscribed on the memorial. John served in the same Machine Gun Corps company as George Coppard, who wrote the war memoir *With a Machine Gun to Cambrai*.

ADAMS, Robert Leonard Powys

Age:	24
Rank:	Lieutenant
Regiment/Service:	Indian Army
Unit:	1st Battalion, 35th Sikhs
Died:	17 May 1919
Cemetery/Memorial:	Delhi Memorial (India Gate)
Reference:	Face 3

CWGC Notes: Buried Landi Kotal Cemetery B.18.

Robert was born in St Margaret's Twickenham, but the 1901 census shows that he was living at The Old Rectory in Carshalton with his family. He was educated at Aldenham School, Elstree, from 1908 to 1913, during which time he was in the Officer Training Corps. He initially enlisted with the 1st Battalion Honourable Artillery Company in June 1914 and served with them in France for the duration of the war, at one point attached to the American Army as part of a 'demonstration platoon'. He was commissioned in December 1916. He decided to pursue his military career further and in September 1918 was accepted into the Indian Army as a lieutenant. He was killed in action at Fort Landi Kotal, Loe Dakka, during the Third Afghan War; a conflict now largely forgotten due to the war that preceded it. The *Epsom Advertiser* reported that he 'was a keen athlete and possessed a most genial disposition which made him very popular with his brother officers and men'.

BARBER, Frank Douglas

Age:	24
Rank:	2nd Corporal
Regiment/Service:	Royal Engineers
Unit:	Railway Acc. Department
Service Number:	WR/207102
Died:	22 November 1919
Cemetery/Memorial:	Bandon Hill Cemetery
Reference:	J.50

Born in Lambeth, Frank worked as a railway clerk. In 1911 he was a patient at the Wandle Valley Isolation Hospital, but either he or his family lived at 55 Park Lane. He had previously served with the Worcester Regiment.

ST CLAIR, William Lockhart

Age:	38
Rank:	Major
Regiment/Service:	Royal Field Artillery
Died:	23 February 1920

William was born in India but educated at Sandroyd House in Cobham and St Paul's, London. He applied to the Royal Military Academy in 1900. He served throughout the war and was awarded the DSO in the 1918 New Year Honours list. He was married on 4 October 1919 but died whilst on leave in France. His father was the Honourable L.M. St. Clair of 'Derriana', Mayfield Road, Sutton.

MONK, Benjamin E.

Age:	26
Rank:	Private
Regiment/Service:	East Surrey Regiment
Unit:	3rd Battalion
Service Number:	18352
Died:	23 April 1920

A labourer, Benjamin was born in Clavering and lived at 106 Avenue Villas, Wallington. He joined up in February 1916. The 3rd Battalion East Surrey Regiment was a training battalion, based in Dover for most of the war.

13. Afterword

On Monday 11 November 1918 the church bells at All Saints church were rung to signal the Armistice. The *Wallington and Carshalton Times* reported that:

> When the news arrived, nearly all the local factories closed. Very little business was done in the shops and many put up their shutters quite early. The afternoon was more or less a holiday. Flags – of wartime dimensions – quickly appeared from many windows, the church towers, and all public buildings … A stroll round the district during the evening showed how eager the residents were to avail themselves of easier lighting restrictions … Music and gramophone, sounds, laughter, and dancing … reminded one of Christmas eve or Boxing night celebrations … By Tuesday evening the mourning bands of black that have so long smothered the light of street lamps had been removed. The result was almost magical: 'outer darkness' had vanished from the main thoroughfares. Instead of shuffling doubtfully along, pedestrians paraded with confident tread, and blinked up now and again, with evident satisfaction, at cheerfully radiant gas mantles. The flag decorations remain undisturbed as though their owners had resolved not to strike the Union Jack until the day arrives when one may fondly hope for peace in perpetuity.

The First World War undoubtedly had a lasting effect on Carshalton. It is hard to imagine the anguish relatives felt when receiving the clinical War Office telegram informing them of the death of their husband, son or brother. This could only have been magnified in the local community after large offensives such as the Somme, when multiple casualties were incurred. It has come as a surprise to me during my research to learn how many of these men were connected. However, when you think about Carshalton in 1914, it was a much closer-knit community. Travel was more difficult and many of the men would never have left the area prior to the war. It is therefore not surprising that neighbours and friends ended up being interlinked through marriage. One local resident, Mary Wyatt, lost her son (Thomas George Wyatt), two grandsons (Herbert Bowles and James Nicholls), two nephews (Thomas and Ernest Wyatt) and a son-in-law (Ernest Baker).

A recurring theme from descendants and relatives of the men I have spoken to is how their families were affected by their loss. Analysis of census records and service records shows that the war left at least seventy wives without husbands, and ninety-five children without fathers; the true numbers are likely to be higher.

Many of these families were left with only a meagre service pension to live off and raise their children.

There has been a great deal of debate about whether the First World War led to a 'lost generation'. Carshalton's population was 14,021 in 1921, so it seems that, although the rate of population growth had slowed down, it had not been affected too greatly by the war.[64] However, the war does seem to have had an impact on the birth rate. Statistics show that it fell from 25.9 per thousand in the period 1906–10, to 20.2 in 1911–15, and 17.6 in 1916–20. Even by 1920 it was still lagging behind the national average, but this could have been affected by the flu epidemic that swept across the world in 1918.

It must be remembered, though, that far more men returned home from the war than were killed. Whilst many of these men would have been unscathed by the war (at least physically), over 1.5 million men were wounded, nearly one-third of all those who enlisted. Based on these figures, Carshalton would have been home to several hundred men who had been wounded. Many returned to normal life, but others bore permanent and disfiguring scars of their service and would have found it difficult to gain employment and lead a normal life.

The global implications of the war were huge, setting the scene for many of the key events of the twentieth century and shaping the modern world as we know it. Yet the war also had a profound effect on a smaller scale, each family's grief at the loss of a loved one contributing to the collective grief of one small village, a scene replicated up and down the country as the loss of so many of its boys and men were mourned. The war lasted just over four years, but it effects continued to be felt long after it had ended. As the centenary of the war passes by, now more than ever we must ensure that the memory of the men who laid down their lives is not forgotten.

A huge crowd surrounds the war memorial on Armistice Day 1928, the tenth anniversary of the end of the war. (*The Wallington & Carshalton Advertiser*)

Sources

Carrying out the research for this book has been much like completing a jigsaw, but one where many of the pieces are missing and will never be found. The surge in interest in genealogy in recent years has seen a number of books published that provide a huge amount of advice on tracking down military ancestors. The internet too provides innumerable sources that mean much of the research can be done without even having to leave your own home. A brief guide to the sources used in my research is given below.

The starting point for finding out information about soldiers who died in the First World War is the Commonwealth War Graves Commission (CWGC) database. This holds a record of every British soldier who was killed in the two world wars.[65] Finding the correct entry is sometimes very easy, for example where the surname is uncommon, more than one initial is given or the regiment the man served in is already known. Extra information such as the family's address or locality can also verify the correct entry. However, where the surname is common or only one initial is given, it can be more difficult to identify the correct entry in the database. The problem can be confounded by the fact that soldiers did not necessarily serve in the 'local' regiment (such as the Surrey regiments), but could instead be assigned to a regiment that was short of men. Some regiments also recruited nationally rather than locally (for example the King's Royal Rifle Corps), and many men had a preference for the regiment they wanted to join based on reputation or recommendation

Once the correct CWGC entry has been located, further information may be gleaned from medal index cards (MIC) and service records. Previously, the National Archives held these but most of them have now been digitised by genealogy websites such as Ancestry and are available online. Medal index cards may contain additional information such as other regiments the man served with, a family address, medals awarded and theatres of war served in. They often also confirm the date a soldier went overseas, or even when he was killed.

Service records are far more valuable as a source, but only some 30–40 per cent of these survive as German bombing during the Second World War destroyed the rest. These records usually contain the soldier's personal details, next of kin, previous profession and details of army service – when he signed up, any promotions, offences committed, when he went overseas and information about any wounds. Pension records are also useful if the soldier was discharged or wounded. Further resources such as the 'Soldiers Died in the Great War' database and 'The National Roll of the Great War' can provide additional details and obituaries.

Whilst the number of men named on the memorial who served in other branches of the Armed Forces is comparatively small, there are a number of sources that were used to track down their details, and the National Archives holds several collections that contain details of those men who served in the Royal Navy or the Royal Flying Corps.[66]

One source in particular was extremely useful for establishing links between many of the men and the local area. *Carshalton Men Who Served in His Majesty's Forces in the Great War with a Roll of Honour and a List of Distinctions* is held at the Imperial War Museum, and a copy is now also held at Sutton Local Studies and Archives Centre. Compiled and published by prominent local resident Hugh Peirs after the war, it contains the names and addresses of over 1,900 men from Carshalton who served as well as details of the men who were killed and of gallantry medals awarded to local men.

The local newspapers are a valuable resource for tracing the Carshalton men who served. The *Wallington and Carshalton Advertiser* and *Wallington and Carshalton Times* gave details about many of those who joined up, reproduced some of their letters home, and often reported their deaths alongside brief obituaries and sometimes photos. They contain some details of the memorial fund as well as reporting the unveiling of the memorial with a list of the men and their units. The papers also give a fascinating insight into the progress and perception of the war on the home front and the effect it had on everyday life, although it is interesting to note that 'war news' dwindles in content if not frequency as the war progresses. The papers are held on microfilm at Sutton Local Studies and Archives Centre at Sutton Central Library.

War diaries can be used to trace the movements of a particular battalion and often establish where and how a soldier died. Officers in particular are often mentioned by name, but it is less common to see 'other ranks' mentioned unless in casualty lists or for particular acts of bravery. The war diaries are a record of a unit's movements, orders and actions, and as such usually provide a very clinical account of the actions fought; they can make quite chilling reading given the large number of casualties that often occurred during the battles they fought in. Conversely, the diaries also provide an insight into the daily lives and routines of soldiers both in and out of the line; it has to be remembered that the men did not spend all their time in action in the front line trenches, and the war diaries often record the minutiae of the soldiers' lives whilst posted away from the front, at rest or training. The National Archives hold the original copies but many have now been digitised or transcribed online by organisations or individuals. The East Surrey Regiment and The Queen's (Royal West Surrey Regiment) diaries in particular have been made available online by The Queens Royal Surrey Regiment Association and can be searched by year, month and day, providing an excellent and accessible resource. Regimental histories provide overviews of a regiment's movements and actions, similar to war diaries but written in a more narrative style; brigade and divisional histories are akin to these but contain details of all their composite battalions.

The *London Gazette* was used for notification of promotions and awards for gallantry and its archives are searchable online. Often little information is given other than the soldier's name, rank and regiment, but the paper can be useful for tracking a soldier's progression through the ranks. In the case of acts of bravery that led to gallantry awards, sometimes the citation shows why the award was made.

Many schools, universities, companies and even local authorities published rolls of honour to commemorate their own members or employees who served or were casualties. They are extremely useful as they not only provide biographical details, but are sometimes also accompanied by photos. *Croydon in the Great War* and the *Whitgift School Book of Remembrance* are two such publications that contain the details of some of the men commemorated on the Carshalton memorial.

There are many websites that can assist with carrying out research. Of particular note is The Long Long Trail website, which contains a huge amount of information about the organisation and movements of the various units of the British Army throughout the war. The Roll of Honour website is an impressive resource listing the transcripts of many war memorials across the country. For general First World War research and queries the Great War Forum is a fantastic community of people with a wide range of interests and expertise who can clarify anything from troop movements to tunic types and are always willing to help. There are also many other amateur websites dedicated to particular memorials, battalions, regiments and battles.

This book could not have been accomplished without one final source – the descendants and relatives of the men. Without their input and contributions, the stories of many of the men would have remained untold.

Full details of many of the printed sources used can be found in the bibliography.

Glossary

ADS	Advanced Dressing Station
AIF	Australian Imperial Force
ANZAC	Australian and New Zealand Army Corps
BEF	British Expeditionary Force
CCS	Casualty Clearing Station
CEF	Canadian Expeditionary Force
CWGC	Commonwealth War Graves Commission
DCM	Distinguished Conduct Medal
DOW	Died of Wounds
DSO	Distinguished Service Order
GHQ	General Headquarters
HE	High Explosive
KIA	Killed in Action
MG	Machine Gun
MIC	Medal Index Card
MID	Mentioned in Despatches
MM	Military Medal
MO	Medical Officer
NCO	Non Commissioned Officer
OC	Officer Commanding
OR	Other Rank
OTC	Officer Training Corps
POW	Prisoner of War
RAP	Regimental Aid Post
TF	Territorial Force

Common unit abbreviations

ASC	Army Service Corps (it was given the 'Royal' prefix in 1918)
HAC	Honourable Artillery Company
HMS	His Majesty's Ship
KOSB	King's Own Scottish Borderers
KOYLI	King's Own Yorkshire Light Infantry
KRRC	King's Royal Rifle Corps
LRB	London Rifle Brigade
MGC	Machine Gun Corps
RA	Royal Artillery
RAF	Royal Air Force
RAMC	Royal Army Medical Corps
RE	Royal Engineers
RFA	Royal Field Artillery
RFC	Royal Flying Corps
RGA	Royal Garrison Artillery
RHA	Royal Horse Artillery
RMLI	Royal Marine Light Infantry
RNR	Royal Naval Reserve
RNVR	Royal Navy Volunteer Reserve
SS	Steam Ship

Notes

Introduction

1 There are four names from the Second World War and two from subsequent conflicts (Aden and Northern Ireland).
2 Thiepval memorial to the missing has over 72,000 names inscribed on it.
3 Gilbert, Martin, *Somme: The Heroism and Horror of War* (John Murray, 2007), p. 266. Copyright © Martin Gilbert 2006. Reproduced by permission of the publisher John Murray.

Carshalton before the War

4 5,221 males and 6,413 females.
5 Now the Charles Cryer Studio Theatre.

Carshalton War Memorial

6 Taken from Ecclesiasticus 44:14. The phrase was selected by Rudyard Kipling (who lost his only son in the war) to adorn the 'Stone of Remembrance' that can be found in many of the Commonwealth War Graves Commission cemeteries.
7 Burslem stonemasons still carry out memorial work; unfortunately all their historical records were lost in a fire in 1998. The company also produced the name panels that are on the Menin Gate in Ypres.
8 This should actually read *Ellen* and Ernest as Private Baker had one daughter and one son. Ernest Baker junior, known as 'Sonny', often played 'The Last Post' on his bugle at the Remembrance Sunday services at the memorial.
9 Father of James Jasper, who was killed in August 1918.
10 The River Wandle runs through south-west London and is fed by the ponds.

Other Memorials

11 See, for example, the *Wallington and Carshalton Advertiser*, 31 January 1919.
12 Reported in the *Wallington and Carshalton Advertiser*, 13 August 1915, p. 7.
13 A temperance organisation.

14 Twelve of the thirteen have been identified as William Buckenham, Robert Collins, James Cooper, James Elcock, John Fowkes, Bertie Gough, John Groombridge, David Kirby, Thomas Kirby, James Nash, David Slaymaker, and Bernard Tate.

The Men

15 After the war a list of men who served was compiled by local resident Hugh Peirs. Copies of this invaluable source, entitled *Carshalton Men Who Served in His Majesty's Forces in the Great War with a Roll of Honour and a List of Distinctions*, can be viewed at Sutton Local Studies and Archives Centre and the Imperial War Museum.

16 The location of Sutton war memorial.

17 The first victim of the Red Baron was Morris's observer Lieutenant Tom Rees, who was shot whilst the plane was still in the air. Morris, although wounded, managed to land the plane but died shortly after.

The Roll of Honour

18 This initially had to be paid for at a cost of 3½d per letter, with a maximum of sixty-six characters.

19 Their report, published in May 1921, set out the official names and dates for the battles and campaigns of the war. It split the war into phases, operations, groups of battles, individual battles, actions and miscellaneous incidents.

The Western Front

1914

20 Someone who drove a vehicle used to transport goods.

21 Often referred to by British soldiers as 'Plugstreet' Wood.

22 Where the enemy can fire from the flanks, for example along the length of a trench.

23 Wylly, Harold, *History of The Queen's Royal (West Surrey) Regiment in The Great War* (Gale & Polden Ltd., undated) p. 90.

24 A type of machine gun used by the German Army, technically called the MG08.

25 Traverses gave trenches their well-known 'zig zag' appearance - they were used to prevent enfilade fire along the length of a trench and minimise casualties in the event of a direct hit from a shell.

26 Willcocks, James, *With the Indians in France* (Constable & Company Ltd., 1920), p. 150.

1915

27 Tunnelling has been utilised in wars throughout the ages and the First World War was no different. The static nature of trench warfare gave both sides the opportunity to try and achieve a breakthrough by undermining the enemy's positions. The Germans exploded their first mines in December 1914;

in response, tunnelling companies were set up within the Royal Engineers and were in operation by March 1915. The vast craters that can still be seen at places like Hawthorn Ridge and La Boisselle on the Somme, and the Messines Ridge in Belgium, are testament to the destructive power of these mines.

28 Australian and New Zealand Army Corps.

29 The battalion war diary confirms that on 30 November four men were wounded in the line near Chapigny.

30 The highest decoration a soldier from the ranks could receive other than the Victoria Cross.

31 *The War Illustrated*, vol. 6, p. 2094. *The War Illustrated* was a weekly propaganda publication.

32 A militia force comprised of former soldiers.

33 Literal translation is 'mine launcher' – essentially a mortar. British troops nicknamed them 'minnies'.

34 After the war the building was sold and became an ex-servicemen's club. It is now the United Services Club.

1916

35 Field ambulances were static positions rather than vehicles.

36 The term 'gunshot wounds' was also used during the war to refer to wounds caused by shrapnel or shells.

37 Wheeler-Holohan, A.V., and Wyatt, G.M.G. (eds), *The Rangers' Historical Records: From 1859 to the Conclusion of The Great War* (Harrison & Sons, undated), p. 52.

38 Middlebrook, Martin, *The First Day on the Somme* (Penguin Books, 2001), p. 268.

39 One of the recovered footballs can be seen at the Surrey Infantry Museum at Clandon Park, another at the Queen's Regiment Museum at Dover Castle.

40 Sir Douglas Haig's Somme despatch, published in *The London Gazette*, 29 December 1916.

41 Wheeler-Holohan and Wyatt, *The Rangers' Historical Records*, p. 63.

42 A type of British mortar.

43 The name given to a fortified observation post in the German front line; its remains can be seen today close to the Ulster Tower near Thiepval memorial.

44 *History of the Post Office Rifles 8th Battalion City of London Regiment 1914–1918* (Gale & Polden, 1919), p. 13.

45 Maude, Alan (ed.), *The History of the 47th (London) Division 1914–1919* (Amalgamated Press Ltd, 1922), p. 71.

1917

46 At first glance this seems like a strange objective. However, it has been suggested that analysing the rations could help ascertain the morale of the German troops, the calorific content of their food and the effectiveness of the British naval blockade on Germany.

47 A type of tear gas.

48 Parsons, Stanley, 'The Final Days of Frederick Charles Parsons' (unpublished), p. 1.

49 Flamethrowers.

50 O'Neill, Herbert, *The Royal Fusiliers in The Great War* (William Heinemann, 1922), p. 190.

51 Empty petrol tins and rum jars were commonly used to transport water.

52 *Artists Rifles 1914–1919 Roll of Honour* (Howlett & Sons, 1922), p. xxiv.

53 Gibbs, Philip, *From Bapaume to Passchendaele* (William Briggs, 1918), p. 373.

54 The journal of the Ypres League, an association open to those that served in the salient, and their relatives.

55 Quoted in MacDonald, Lyn, *1914–1918 Voices and Images of the Great War* (Penguin Books, 1991), p. 336.

56 My great-great-uncle William MacDuff was killed on 2 December 1917 in an operation designed to drive the Germans off the ridge once and for all. The attack did not succeed.

57 Pearse, H.W. and Sloman, H.S., *History of the East Surrey Regiment 1917–1919* (The Medici Society Limited, 1924), p. 104.

1918

58 O'Neill, *The Royal Fusiliers in The Great War*, p. 258.

59 Grimwade, Frederick, *The War History of the 4th Battalion The London Regiment (Royal Fusiliers) 1914–1919* (Headquarters of the 4th London Regiment, 1922), pp. 388–91.

60 Ernest is referring to the Battle of Aubers.

Mesopotamia, Egypt, Palestine and Salonika

61 A baggage and supply transport unit.

Other Deaths

62 Soldiers were 'mentioned in despatches' in the *London Gazette* but it is difficult to ascertain the reason for this in most cases.

63 Whilst the name of at least one post-1918 death was on the memorial at the time it was unveiled, it does appear that the names of most of those who died after the war were added later to the smaller additional panels on the memorial. Given that John is buried in Carshalton, it raises interesting questions about the original criteria for inclusion on the memorial.

Afterword

64 The number of males in 1921 was 6,158 compared with 5,221 in 1911.

Sources

65 There are exceptions to this. Many soldiers who died at home or after the First World War are not included; it has to be proven that their death was a direct consequence of the war.

66 The RFC became the Royal Air Force (RAF) on 1 April 1918.

Bibliography

Books

Artists' Rifles 1914–1919 Roll of Honour (Howlett & Sons, 1922)

Banks, Arthur, *A Military Atlas of the First World War* (Leo Cooper, 1989)

De Ruvigny's Roll of Honour (The Standard Art Book Company Ltd., undated)

Dulwich College War Record 1914–1919

Exeter College Register 1891–1921

Fear, Roger, *Carshalton Athletic Football Club: The First One Hundred Years 1905–2005* (Carshalton Athletic FC, undated)

Gilbert, Martin, *Somme: The Heroism and Horror of War* (John Murray, 2007)

Gibbs, Philip, *From Bapaume to Passchendaele* (William Briggs, 1918)

Grimwade, Frederick, *The War History of the 4th Battalion The London Regiment (Royal Fusiliers) 1914–1919* (Headquarters of the 4th London Regiment, 1922)

The History and Register of Aldenham School, 8th edn

History of the Post Office Rifles 8th Battalion City of London Regiment 1914–1918 (Gale & Polden, 1919)

Holloway, W.H., *Northamptonshire and the Great War 1914–1918* (The Northampton Independent, 1920)

James, E.A., *A Record of the Battles and Engagements of the British Armies in France and Flanders, 1914–1918* (Gale & Polden, 1924)

Jones, Arthur, *A Small School in the Great War: The Story of Sutton County School and its Old Boys in World War One* (published by author, 1975)

Jones, Jane, *Images of England: Sutton* (Tempus Publishing Limited, 1998)

MacDonald, Lyn, *1914–1918: Voices and Images of the Great War* (Penguin Books, 1991)

MacIntyre, Colin, *Monuments of War: How to Read a War Memorial* (Robert Hale, 1990)

MacLeod, M.N., *History of the 4th Field Survey Battalion RE* (The National Archives WO 181/388, undated)

Malden, Henry (ed.), *A History of the County of Surrey, Volume 4* (Constable & Company Ltd, 1912)

Mason, M.H.H., *Whitgift Grammar School Book of Remembrance 1914–1919* (Pettitt, Cox & Bowers Ltd, undated)

Maude, Alan (ed.), *The History of the 47th (London) Division 1914–1919* (Amalgamated Press Ltd, 1922)

Middlebrook, Martin, *The First Day on the Somme* (Penguin Books, 2001)

Moore, H.K. (ed.), *Croydon in the Great War* (Corporation of Croydon, 1920)

O'Neill, Herbert, *The Royal Fusiliers in The Great War* (William Heinemann, 1922)

Pearse, H.W. and Sloman, H.S., *History of the East Surrey Regiment 1914–1917* (The Medici Society Limited, 1923)

Pearse, H.W. and Sloman, H.S., *History of the East Surrey Regiment 1917–1919* (The Medici Society Limited, 1924)

Peirs, Hugh, *Carshalton Men Who Served in His Majesty's Forces in the Great War with a Roll of Honour and a List of Distinctions* (published by author, undated)

Phillips, John, *Old Carshalton* (London Borough of Sutton, 2008)

Phillips, John, Shawcross, Kathleen and Harris, Nick, *The Archive Photographs Series: Carshalton, Wallington and Beddington* (Tempus Publishing Limited, 1995)

Short History of the London Rifle Brigade (Gale & Polden, 1916)

Symonds, John, *The Men Who Marched Away: Old Churcherians in Two World Wars* (Churcher's College, undated)

Walker, G.G. (ed.), *The Honourable Artillery Company in the Great War* (Seeley, Service & Co. Ltd., 1930)

Weetman, William, *History of the 1/8th Battalion Sherwood Foresters 1914–1919* (Thomas Forman & Sons, 1920)

Wheeler-Holohan, A.V. and Wyatt, G.M.G. (eds), *The Rangers' Historical Records: From 1859 to the Conclusion of The Great War* (Harrison & Sons, undated)

Wilks, Stella and Rookledge, Gordon, *The Book of Carshalton* (Halsgrove, 2002)

Willcocks, James, *With the Indians in France* (Constable & Company Ltd., 1920)

Williamson, J., *Carshalton Urban District Annual Report of the Medical Officer of Health 1920*

Wylly, Harold, *History of The Queen's Royal (West Surrey Regiment) in The Great War* (Gale & Polden Ltd., undated)

Newspapers

Cheltenham and Gloucester Graphic
Epsom Advertiser
Newcastle Journal
Sutton Advertiser and Surrey County Reporter
The Croydon Advertiser
The Illustrated Sutton and Epsom Mail
The Times
Wallington and Carshalton Advertiser
Wallington and Carshalton Times

Miscellaneous Sources

Australian Red Cross Society Wounded and Missing Enquiry Bureau Files

Census of England and Wales 1911: Areas, Families or Separate Occupiers, and Population, Volume 1 (HMSO, 1912)

Census of England and Wales 1921: County of Surrey (HMSO, 1923)

Ibis Magazine

Parsons, Stanley, 'The Final Days of Frederick Charles Parsons' (unpublished)

Pile's Sutton and District Directory (William Pile Ltd, 1914–1921)

Roll of Honour of the Institution of Electrical Engineers
Scout Association Roll of Honour
St Barnabas, Sutton, *Parish Magazine*
St Olave's Fallen
Surrey Recruitment Registers
Territorial Service Gazette
The London Gazette
The Sphere
The Suttonian
The War Illustrated

Index of Names

If you enjoyed this book, you may also be interested in…

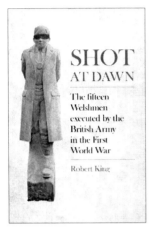

Shot at Dawn: The fifteen Welshmen executed by the British Army in the First World War
Robert King

Amid the carnage of the battles of the First World War a handful of men serving in Welsh regiments absconded from their regiments. Despite mitigating circumstances and with derisory field trials, they were found guilty and sentenced to death by firing squad. This book documents those cases. In 2006, a motion was put forward to pardon those men, except in cases of murder. This was successful and 305 men, albeit nearly a hundred years later, were exonerated.

978 0 7509 5642 0

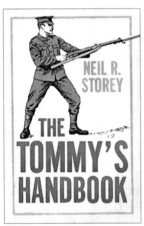

The Tommy's Handbook
Neil R. Storey

In the years immediately before the First World War, the British Army was comprehensively reformed, and new training manuals were issued. Covering topics such as uniform, trench construction, reconnaissance work, modern military techniques and strategy and how casualties and POWs should be dealt with, these guides were issued in response to the latest developments in warfare. Packed with excerpts, this volume provides an authentic overview of how a typical Tommy was trained during the First World War.

978 0 7509 5568 3

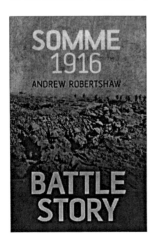

Battle Story: Somme 1916
Andrew Robertshaw

The Battle of the Somme raged from 1 July to 18 November 1916 and has come to signify for many the waste and bloodshed of the First World War, as hundreds of thousands of men lost their lives. Yet this battle was also to witness new methods of warfare, with infantry units and the new Tank Corps fighting alongside each other.

Complete with detailed maps and photographs, as well as fascinating facts and profiles of the leaders, this is the best introduction to this legendary battle.

978 0 7509 5565 2

GREAT WAR BRITAIN

Great War Britain is a unique new local series to mark the centenary of the Great War. In partnership with archives and museums across Great Britain, the series provides an evocative portrayal of life during this 'war to end all wars'. In a scrapbook style, and beautifully illustrated, it includes features such as personal memoirs, letters home, diary extracts, newspaper reports, photographs, postcards and other local First World War ephemera.

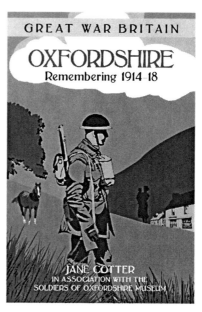

Lightning Source UK Ltd.
Milton Keynes UK
UKOW05f0824160914

9 780752 489919